Measure for Measure,
the Law, and the Convent

Measure for Measure, the Law, and the Convent

Darryl J. Gless

Princeton University Press
Princeton, New Jersey

For Ruth

Contents

Preface

The focus of this book, as its title suggests, is Shakespeare's *Measure for Measure*; but I should make my readers aware from the outset that my method (explained in the Introduction) precludes an undeviating exercise in *explication de texte*. By this I do not mean that one should expect the kinds of extrinsic materials usually offered by studies that concern themselves with a single Shakespearean play. I present and grapple with few previous interpretations, and I spend little time reexamining the play's sources. These things have already been done, sometimes with great skill. My method demands, instead, careful attention to elements of intellectual history that relate directly to the thematic concerns of Shakespeare's play.

My first two chapters are predominantly concerned, therefore, with materials that belong to the play's immediate intellectual background. Prominent among the topics considered are the full implications of the biblical measure-for-measure text; the complex interrelationships among Renaissance conceptions of civil law, theological law, charity, and providence; the ethical import of Protestant salvific doctrine; and the currency, complexity, and potential literary uses of antimonastic satire.[1] Chapters 3-6 mingle cultural history and literary interpretation, but they lean sharply in the direction of the latter. In these chapters especially, I address the major interpretive issues that bedevil students of *Measure for Measure*, and I show how the materials explored in the first two chapters provide solu-

[1] Renaissance specialists may find my treatment of law and providence somewhat too lengthy. But the current state of scholarship and criticism devoted to *Measure for Measure* suggests that the knowledge of many readers familiar with these conceptions may be too general to be of value for interpretation. In a book intended not only for experts but for students and hardy nonspecialists as well, I have chosen to err on the side of generosity.

tions to such vexing questions as the following: To what extent can characters in the play be considered "allegorical"? Does Isabella's defense of her chastity mark her as aspiring saint or as an unfeeling prude? Why are the Duke's attitudes toward honor, ceremony, and the administration of law consistently inconsistent? Why does the subplot focus repeatedly on Lucio's comic slanders of the Duke? How are we to assess the often-remarked discordance between the play's early scenes and its conclusion? How does the Duke's famous death speech function? And why does Isabella agree to marry?

These interpretive cruxes cannot, I am convinced, be satisfactorily explained in isolation from the backgrounds discussed in chapters 1 and 2, and they require supplemental incursions into further historical contexts. Hence my final four chapters include sections on a variety of topics not covered earlier. These include an often overlooked ambivalence in contemporary attitudes toward honor (especially the honor of monarchs); the normative structure of treatises on the art of dying; Protestant doctrines that should discourage the search for literary "Christ-figures"; and commonplaces of civil *and* religious law that explain the Duke's judgments in act 5.

As this selective overview suggests, readers concerned primarily with Shakespeare's text should be prepared to come to terms with the kind of knowledge that makes a complicated play understandable. I hope gradually (beginning most directly in chapter 3) to justify the reader's patience by demonstrating that my earlier chapters do in fact establish contexts necessary for accurate comprehension of Shakespeare's text. But my background sections have a further, independent rationale. They are meant to contribute to our understanding of Shakespeare's intellectual milieu by illuminating materials often ignored, neglected, or imperfectly understood by scholars of the period. This study aspires, therefore, to fill some gaps in cultural history as well as to offer a coherent and thorough interpretation of the play.

The historical portions of this effort require some explanation, for while I often draw on works (especially *The Basilicon Doron* and the Sermon on the Mount) that left identifiable traces in Shakespeare's play, I am seldom concerned with precise influences. I am interested primarily in ideas that represent common intellectual currency of the Jacobean age—conceptions Shakespeare could adopt, subvert, extend, or explore while seeking to vivify and render significant the gripping but sensational old tale he inherited from Cinthio and Whetstone. Consequently, my argument often draws on works that probably had no direct influence on the genesis of Shakespeare's play. They illustrate, instead, ideas and ideals that audiences at the Globe or at court could be counted on to know—with varying degrees of accuracy and perfection, of course, but certainly with greater familiarity than that of their modern descendants in academia. By quoting extensively, say, from Calvin's commentary on the Sermon on the Mount, I do not imply that Shakespeare necessarily drew particular ideas from that work, but rather acknowledge that the great Reformer provides an influential statement of ideas that were current in Shakespeare's England and, often, had been conventional in Christian exegesis since patristic times.

As this example suggests and as the nature of the play requires, much of the historical material that bears on *Measure for Measure* is religious. And since religion during Shakespeare's age was chronically and violently controversial, I draw the doctrinal points that are important for my argument from writings by leaders of each of the major divisions of Reformation Christianity—from the critical but loyal Catholic Erasmus; from the Anglican homilists, the magisterial Hooker, and his influential fellow Anglican, Perkins; from Luther and Melanchthon; and from Bullinger, Zwingli's successor at Zurich, as well as from Calvin himself. This catholicity of reference is valid both because it reflects the eclecticism and comprehensiveness of the Elizabethan Settlement—which, as we shall see, is itself reflected and extended in the deep tolerance of *Measure for*

Measure—and because it serves to emphasize that *Measure for Measure* explores ideas with which most members of Shakespeare's audience, despite the combativeness of the times, could readily agree. With a few salient exceptions to be noted below, these theological and ethical doctrines (unlike conceptions of ecclesiastical governance and discipline) were common, not controversial, and to indicate their currency I usually quote the Continental Reformers from contemporary English translations.

The document that appears most often in the historical portions of my argument is the one Protestants sought assiduously to place in the hands of every Christian—the vernacular Bible. Here my interpretation differs from earlier ones that deal with scriptural influences, for I assume that the meanings of scriptural texts themselves are not at all self-evident. It is not enough for Christianizing interpreters to quote often cryptic statements from the Gospels, to juxtapose them with lines from *Measure for Measure* that somehow correspond, and to assert an identity of meaning. My tacit assumption throughout is that authors who allude to the Bible have also troubled themselves to learn the meaning of the text to which they allude. We must do the same, and sixteenth-century interpretations very often may help us discover the meaning of the Gospels themselves. These meanings are equally discoverable today, but only by that rare breed of Christian, or still rarer breed of scholar, who takes the study of Scripture as seriously as did his Jacobean predecessors. If these predecessors did not study the Word freely, as many did, then they did so perforce in the schools and at Sunday and holiday services.

My insistence on thoroughly understanding the biblical passages to which Shakespeare alludes extends also to my treatment of all the play's major sources and generic prototypes. When an author refers systematically and repeatedly to earlier works or to established kinds of works, I believe we must press beyond the usual mechanical noting of parallel phrases. Like my attention to intellectual history, this conviction also lends the subsequent pages a scope somewhat broader than is normal in a book that focuses on a single literary work. But my analysis of the text will, I hope, demonstrate that *Measure for Measure* urges us to cast our nets very wide indeed.

Here I should add two supremely important points. It is difficult, perhaps impossible, to discuss a play that calls importantly on Christian doctrine without seeming to imply that the playwright was himself a religious zealot, delivering a homiletic rendition of convictions peculiarly his own. I *never* mean to endow Shakespeare with cope and surplice. I am convinced, however, that he was nearly as learned as he was ingenious, that he was sufficiently au courant to know in considerable detail the fundamental religious debates current in his age, and that he chose—pervasively in *Measure for Measure*, less centrally in other plays, not at all in still others—to turn commonplace religious themes to aesthetic ends. Whatever his now inaccessible private convictions, Shakespeare often employs received doctrine, religious and secular, to impose artful form and impressive thematic unity on the somewhat intractable narrative materials on which *Measure for Measure* is based. My undeviating conviction is that Shakespeare is *using* conventions of language and meaning; he is not necessarily voicing personal beliefs.

My final point concerns the nature of the conventions Shakespeare chose to use in *Measure for Measure*. All intellectual systems and their attendant literary modes, even those we call realism or naturalism, are discovered to be blunt instruments when tested, as they usually are in drama, by direct confrontation with the complexity of an illusion that closely parallels actual human experience. Today we tend to expect that religious systems are likely to be the bluntest instruments of all. But this expectation is somewhat anachronistic. Reformation theology harbored rigidities aplenty, but it also directed the energetic attention of intelligent men toward human anxieties, frustrations, and all the mental and spiritual torments that we suffer, mutatis mutandis, in the modern world. This persistent preoccupation issued in a flood of published works concerned above all else with the application of religious doctrine to the daily business of living. The concerns of Reformation and subsequently of Counter-Reformation Christianity are not, therefore, as remote from human realities as we may at first suppose. Contemporary works concerned with pastoral care normally contain careful observations, keen insights, and tolerant judgments based securely on what we ought to recognize as realities of human experience.

Because of the pervasive practical impulse in contemporary religious thought, one can hope to evade a pitfall that persistently entraps literary scholars who find themselves dealing with religious doctrines. That is, of course, a disposition to be overly doctrinaire and therefore to violate the reader's sense of the human realities reflected in the dramatic situation by imposing standards of judgment that seem rigid and remote from the immediate experience. Although I may on occasion fall into this error, Shakespeare, I think, did not. He appears consistently to have selected and dramatized doctrines that are especially flexible and tolerant of adjustment to particular circumstances. His process of selection was relatively easy because a good deal of Christian theology *does* tolerate such adjustments. There is no greater fallacy than the notion that doctrine is by definition doctrinaire. The very volume of doctrinal output is evidence of a pressing need—indigenous to Christian thought and especially marked during the Reformation—for extrapolation from the general to the particular. For any writer who uses the Christian tradition, the way is ever open to explore and not simply to illustrate the possibilities of moral choice that arise when inherited principles confront specific human circumstances. It is the very fact that Christian thought is itself in a constant process of renewal and evolution that makes possible both the volume of religious publications and the creative flexibility of writers, like Shakespeare, who exploit for aesthetic ends the complexities and indeterminacies of the doctrinal system.

As my interpretation shows, Shakespeare adopts the most benign implications of his play's scriptural source (the measure-for-measure text), and at times he employs these implications in ways that closely parallel the published ideas of contemporary religious authorities. At other times he is quite willing to imply that Christian ethical doctrines might, in extreme situations, encourage behavior that the theologians rarely discuss. The playwright is never enslaved by the pronouncements of the theologians. In *Measure for Measure*, he often adopts conceptions similar to theirs, but he is not at all averse to adapting and elaborating them. As often happens in great art, Shakespeare's use of linguistic and theological conventions engenders meanings that refuse to be altogether circumscribed by the conventional. In revealing how far Shakespeare's play reflects the best thoughts of the best religious minds of his era, I never mean to deny him a mind of his own.

NOTE: All references to *Measure for Measure* are from the edition by J. W. Lever, the Arden Shakespeare (London: Methuen, 1965). Quotations from early prose works have been modernized; titles and poetry, however, are given in original spelling. Unless noted otherwise, all biblical quotations are taken, for the reader's convenience, from the King James version.

Acknowledgments

This book has benefited from the kindness of many. Thanks must go, first, to a large number of my predecessors in Shakespeare studies whose work, which cannot be directly acknowledged, has adumbrated, inspired, or provoked the interpretations presented here. I owe still deeper gratitude to my early mentors at the University of Nebraska, especially T. Edmund Beck and Paul A. Olson, who first taught me to value medieval and Renaissance literature and whose influence continues to shape my professional life. Tutors at Oxford—Nick and Cicely Havely, Alastair Fowler, and John Wilders—labored benignly and at times heroically to refine my critical skills and to extend my learning. More recently, my teachers at Princeton, Thomas P. Roche, Jr., and D. W. Robertson, Jr., shared their immense learning and offered penetrating criticism while helping me bring to birth the earliest version of this book. Then as now, Earl Miner provided timely encouragement and sage advice.

Colleagues at the University of Virginia have improved the final version by giving generously of their time, erudition, and critical acumen. Martin C. Battestin, Edward I. Berry, Leopold Damrosch, James Nohrnberg, Arthur Kirsch, and Richard Waswo read and criticized—acutely, sometimes combatively, always constructively—the entire work at various stages of its development. Austin Quigley has helped me bring to its early sections a trace of the lucidity that distinguishes his own studies of modern drama and literary theory. Lester Beaurline and William Kerrigan offered incisive and salutary counsel.

Barbara Lewalski, who read the manuscript for Princeton University Press, merits special thanks for rescuing me from a particularly threatening dragon of error and urging me on in the difficult task of relating doctrine to literature. My thanks also to John Rumrich, research assistant *ex-traordinaire*; to John Robertson and Anne Quigley for typing more expert than one has any right to expect; to Alice M. Swayne, for wonderfully acute editing; and to the University of Virginia's research committees for needed economic aid.

A final note of gratitude is recorded in my dedication.

Measure for Measure,
the Law, and the Convent

A Note on Method

If a "problem play" is one that has proved especially destructive of scholarly harmony, then *Measure for Measure* stands preeminent in its class. Perhaps more than any other Shakespearean play, it has elicited and continues to elicit interpretations that violently conflict. Despite an almost infinite variety in treatment of individual passages, the critical commentary that has engulfed *Measure for Measure* divides, roughly speaking, into two hostile camps. On the one hand, a significant number of critics—Knight, R. W. Chambers, Battenhouse, Siegal, and others—would have us believe the play is a parable whose characters embody and whose plot illustrates central concepts of Christian doctrine. A larger, more heterogeneous division refuses to perceive in *Measure for Measure* any specifically Christian meanings whatsoever, and some argue that its implications are positively anti-Christian. Along with these divergent interpretations, inevitably, come opposing judgments of value, and again the field divides into warring factions: some (notably Leavis) rank *Measure for Measure* among Shakespeare's greatest plays; others judge it a magnificent failure; still others, especially the Romantics and their intellectual heirs, condemn it roundly or find its sole saving graces in seemingly gratuitous jewels of characterization—like Barnardine. In general, Christian interpretations encourage favorable assessments of the play's aesthetic integrity. Anti-Christian interpretations do not.

One measure of failure common to Christian and anti-Christian interpreters of *Measure for Measure* is a chronic reluctance to read the entire play with uniform care. Neither faction has so far attempted to approximate the ideal rightly to be sought in literary interpretation—a reading that determines the play's thematic structure, "the most general principle of organization which binds together and makes sense of all the detail of a text in combination."[1] My primary justification for offering yet another study of *Measure for Measure* is my belief that I can meet this need by providing a general statement of the meaning of the text that accounts as comprehensively as possible for the major overt elements of structure, plot, and characterization; the dominant tone; the statable and reiterated local themes; and the characteristics of syntax, diction, and visual and verbal imagery that sustain tone and give themes dramatic life.

Previous interpretations of Christian bias have most clearly violated this ideal. Besides adopting sentimentalized and uninformed ideas of Elizabethan Christianity, they have in the main adhered to the notion that all allegory is necessarily personification allegory. Their interpretations therefore readily run afoul of the play's and its characters' recalcitrant variety. Even the better interpretations of this kind betray a certain willfulness that becomes most apparent in heavy dependence on very loose analogies with scriptural figures and narratives and, above all, in the undisciplined use of scriptural allusion as an interpretive key. Too often, what critics call an allusion is in all probability the coincidental appearance in Shakespeare and in the Bible of a few identical words. The allusion in such cases often exists *only* because the reader is an avid student of the Bible—or of Richmond Noble—and is therefore predisposed to see an allusion. Allegorizing interpreters have

---

[1] A lucid theoretical statement of this commonsense principle appears in John Ellis, *The Theory of Literary Criticism: A Logical Analysis* (Berkeley: University of California Press, 1974), p. 206.

A Note on Method   5

therefore tended to impose a unity on the play that exists mainly within the subjectivity of the beholder.

For most of the play's hostile critics—and these tend in general to discount the relevance of Christianity—such bogus unity has not posed significant difficulty. To them, my desire for a comprehensive statement of the text's most general principle of organization may appear to beg a fundamental question. A reigning orthodoxy of recent criticism holds, in fact, that the play is essentially incoherent. This view, promoted especially by E.M.W. Tillyard, argues that *Measure for Measure* divides into two incompatible parts.[2] The evidence for this assertion is varied. The play's style, we are told, suddenly (at 3.1.151) loses its vitality and lapses predominantly into prose. Where poetry appears thereafter, the author's "tension" seems to have relaxed, as is evident, oddly enough, in his increased use of rhyme. This stylistic degeneration coincides with inexplicable and illogical mutations in the nature of principal characters. Although he plays an insignificant role at the outset, for example, the Duke suddenly becomes dominant. Isabella, formerly undeviating in her pursuit of virtue, joins blindly and without resistance in the Duke's incomprehensible and morally dubious plot, and despite her once fervent commitment to virginity and to her impending vows, she tacitly but clearly agrees to marry him. Angelo, once "invulnerable to temptation," was in love with Mariana, as we eventually discover, even before he becomes obsessed with Isabella.[3] All these inconsistencies arise, the argument

[2] E.M.W. Tillyard, *Shakespeare's Problem Plays* (Toronto: University of Toronto Press, 1949), pp. 129-43; A. P. Rossiter, *Angel with Horns and Other Shakespeare Lectures*, ed. Graham Storey (London: Longmans, 1961), p. 164; Marco Mincoff, "*Measure for Measure*: A Question of Approach," *ShakS* 2 (1966): 145-56; Harriet Hawkins, *Likenesses of Truth in Elizabethan and Restoration Drama* (Oxford: Clarendon Press, 1972), pp. 51-52, 76; Rosalind Miles, *The Problem of "Measure for Measure"* (New York: Barnes and Noble, 1976), pp. 254-55, 261-62.

[3] For these criticisms, see especially Tillyard, *Problem Plays*, pp. 132-34; Hawkins, *Likenesses of Truth*, pp. 60-62; and Mary Lascelles, *Shakespeare's "Measure for Measure"* (London: Athlone Press, 1953), pp. 152-53.

runs, because Shakespeare allows his narrative and its
storybook resolution to eclipse the play's earlier concern
for dialectic and for dramatic confrontations between fully
realized characters.

These hostile views reach a climactic extreme in the
comprehensive indictment brought by Harriett Hawkins,
one of Tillyard's most cogent recent followers. According
to Hawkins, the point of view, the tone, and the very mode
of the play alter drastically and for the worse in act 3. Since
she forcefully articulates attitudes implicit or explicit in all
the disintegrators' interpretations of *Measure for Measure*,
Hawkins's statement warrants detailed consideration:

> The detached point of view predominant in the second
> half of the play does not extend back to encompass the
> first half, and the intense personal involvement aroused
> by the first half is not sustained or even permitted in the
> second half. . . . In their great confrontation scenes
> Shakespeare moves this triumvirate [Angelo, Claudio,
> and Isabella] in what seems to be an inexorably tragic di-
> rection. Surely an audience which has watched these
> confrontations is left not with a vague impression but
> with the absolute conviction that, given their situation,
> each of these characters would choose to bring tragic suf-
> fering upon another. Indeed, Angelo, Isabella, and
> Claudio themselves (in turn) convince us that Angelo
> would, without doubt, take Isabella and dishonour her in
> spite of his own horrified conscience; that Isabella would
> never yield to Angelo, even to save her brother's life;
> that Claudio could not willingly choose death even to
> save his sister's honour. In the first half of the play
> Shakespeare makes these tragic decisions seem both
> probable and necessary. Thus, just before he alters the
> course of action in the direction of comedy, he passes a
> dramatic point of no return. For he creates in his audi-
> ence a very simple and passionate appetite to watch these
> characters enact their tragic choices.[4]

[4] Hawkins, *Likenesses of Truth*, pp. 52-55.

This energetic onslaught focuses eventually on what is, in literary interpretation, a problematic notion—audience expectations. Although Hawkins raises the issue only intermittently, she is right to draw our attention to this key point in arguments over the coherence of this (or any other) play. Whatever the diverse elements that enter into the composition of the play, can it be regarded as making the kind of consistent and integrative use of audience expectations that would enable a comprehensive interpretation to emerge? Hawkins would say that *Measure for Measure* does not, but there may be grounds for revising this opinion. In any consideration of the function of expectations in literary interpretation, recent developments in literary theory—and in cognitive theory generally—offer assistance. Advances in our understanding of the nature of language and its reception have demonstrated that meaning expectations play an immense role in all interpretation of language, spoken or written. The relevant point of this relatively new learning is that neither the bare text of a literary work nor the sound pattern of spoken language in itself absolutely determines the meaning an interpreter finds in it.

It is not enough to say, with Hawkins, that some elements of the play seem at first glance incompatible and that the play is therefore internally inconsistent. We must ask, instead, whether there is some set of expectations, including a notion of the whole, which we can bring to the play and which will change our judgment of the diverse parts from one of apparent incompatibility to one of functional contrast. To approach the play in this way is to align oneself with the well-established view that an understanding of a text is always in part a construction of the receiving mind itself. E. D. Hirsch, expressing a consensus among hermeneutic and cognitive theorists, explains that the meaning expectations that guide these constructions are determined by the interpreter's hypothesis concerning the type of meaning, or "genre," being expressed. This notion of generic type controls the meaning that is derived from the

text: "the details of meaning that an interpreter under-
stands are powerfully determined and constituted by his
meaning expectations." Some details that appear in the
text before him cause the interpreter to guess, on the basis
of previous linguistic experience, that " 'this is a certain
type of meaning,' and his notion of the meaning as a whole
grounds and helps determine his understanding of details."[5] This is not a one-time movement but a recurrent al-
ternation, moving from detail to notion of type, back again
to detail, and so on, with each movement in the cycle helping to define more accurately both the notion of type and
the meaning of individual details.

"Genre" understood as "types of meaning" can include,
in addition to the restatable message or theme—which will
nevertheless be my primary focus in considering *Measure
for Measure*—"a number of elements that may not even be
explicitly given in the utterance or its context, such as the
relationship assumed to exist between the speaker and interpreter, the type of vocabulary and syntax that is to be
used, the type of attitude adopted by the speaker, and the
type of inexplicit meanings that go with explicit ones."[6]
Defined thus broadly, "type of meaning" can embrace what
we ordinarily call the genre (epic, tragedy, elegy, etc.) of a
literary work of art. But Hirsch extends the idea of "genre"
to include multitudes of other types of meaning that we
constantly meet and use in our literary and nonliterary linguistic activities.[7] At the same time, this theory renders the

[5] E. D. Hirsch, *Validity in Interpretation* (New Haven: Yale University
Press, 1967), p. 72; cf. pp. 76-77. See also his *Aims of Interpretation*
(Chicago: University of Chicago Press, 1976), p. 79.

[6] Hirsch, *Validity*, p. 72.

[7] A similar and equally imperialistic desire to extend the conception of
genre beyond the impoverished list acceptable to Aristotelian critics
found lively champions in the Renaissance. See Rosalie Colie's discussion
of a number of these critics, including Minturno, Sidney, and "Francesco
Patrizi, [who] (like E. D. Hirsch) argued that every poem on any subject
had its poetic kind; and that 'misti poemi' were valuable precisely because
they combined various 'sets' on the world into a larger collective vision"

term more precise by positing the conception of "intrinsic genre," which is "a stable generic conception, constitutive of meaning, which lies somewhere between the vague heuristic genre idea with which an interpreter always starts and the individual, determinate meaning with which he ends."[8]

Often the intrinsic genre of a work is composed of numerous "parent genres," larger categories that contribute in combination to the particular text's individuality. One of the paradoxes of literary interpretation, as of cognition generally, is that to understand the individual work we must accurately recognize the types that constitute it. The particular can be known only by means of the typical.[9] It is not enough, then, for Hawkins and others to show us that parts of the play, seen as isolated components, seem to register an irreconcilable incompatibility. Before such a judgment is made we need a comprehensive study of the parts *in the context of the meaning types to which they belong.*

(*The Resources of Kind: Genre Theory in the Renaissance* [Berkeley: University of California Press, 1973], pp. 20-21).

For a very clever partial list of the variety (nineteen!) of genres relevant to the study of irony, see Wayne C. Booth, *A Rhetoric of Irony* (Chicago: University of Chicago Press, 1974), pp. 209-13.

[8] Hirsch, *Validity*, p. 81. An intrinsic genre in this sense is a novel typological synthesis derived from the creative use of a set of utterance types that frequently exist prior to the text and provide a starting point for original extrapolation.

[9] This implies that our conception of the text's intrinsic genre does not simply fade into the particular meaning. It remains as an essential determining element of that meaning. Our retrospective glance at the work as a whole exists as an amalgam of type and object, intrinsic genre and particular artifact. The type or generic conception grounds our awareness of specific details. See Hirsch, *Validity*, pp. 81-85, 94, 110, 269-74.

Lest it appear at this point that I base my method too readily on narrow theoretical authority, let me point out that the validity and utility of the conception of intrinsic genre has been corroborated by recent research in the diverse but allied fields of developmental psychology, cognitive theory, and art history as well as literary theory. See the evidence in Hirsch, *Aims*, p. 32, and cf. also Booth's excellent use of genre conceived in this way, in *Irony*, esp. pp. 94-101.

Only then can questions of their consistency or inconsistency be appropriately answered. And since the parent genres invoked in *Measure for Measure* are often types of discourse that enjoyed special currency in Shakespeare's age, we can truly know the play only by pursuing the study, and establishing the relevance, of the materials that I have mentioned in the Preface and discuss in detail in subsequent chapters.

There is some risk of confusion about this use of the term "genre." But not only does this conception aid the interpreter to remain sensitive to the way language actually works, it allows him to talk in a more controlled and controllable manner about things that historical scholars have discussed rather loosely in the past. It is thus possible to demonstrate how things we have regarded vaguely as historical backgrounds become part of one's experience of the literary foreground while the play is being heard or read. Although it includes much else, "genre" as "type of meaning" can subsume and provide a controlling structure for the use of historical data that are often misused when placed in such vague frameworks as "tradition" or "historical context." By considering antimonastic satire, for example, not simply as an element of Shakespeare's general intellectual background but as a type of language—a genre—that certain elements of *Measure for Measure* participate in, we can discover how the antimonastic elements of the Elizabethan background contribute directly to our perception of details in the play. It is also possible to discover how the background allows us to perceive clearly implications that are hinted at but never made totally explicit in the text itself.

Furthermore, to conceive of such traditions as genres or as conventions of thought and language is to gain and maintain necessary flexibility. When employing them in literary interpretation, scholars are prone to use traditions or backgrounds or conventional motifs as if they were vehicles that always carry predetermined meanings. When traditions are so conceived, the tacit implication is that an author who makes a traditional sort of remark or adopts a traditional motif must intend a traditional meaning. The term "genre" as employed here includes such phenomena; yet it specifies no determined, unitary meaning. It offers instead a range of potential implications, any or any number of which may be realized, subverted, or extended, depending on their use in the play. Genre as "type of meaning" is where interpretation starts, not where it must end. Thus employed, the term "genre" helps us preserve our power to perceive both conventional meanings *and* original ones.

In dealing with *Measure for Measure* in this way, it is important that we be mindful of the normal pattern of cognition—the movement from vague generic expectation, through progressively narrowing intrinsic genre (or *corrigible schema*, to use Piaget's parallel phrase), and, partly by that genre's power to determine meaning, to the individual meaning itself. This pattern suggests a sound method for literary interpretation. Since normal understanding of language begins with a broad type idea that is simply narrowed and made more explicit in the course of interpretation, it follows that this narrowing process must not be prematurely retarded. The schema must for an appropriate time remain corrigible; the vague early generic conception must be used heuristically. Otherwise the meanings it sponsors will be out of touch with the particular details of the text; the interpretation will be partial and invalid.[10] The reading or listening process should therefore approximate the method characteristic of all cognitive processes. An interpretive hypothesis arrived at in part by intuitive response to details confronted early in the text sponsors further observations of textual detail, and the hypothesis in turn is progressively refined in the light of those detailed observations. By adopting such a method, we can avoid the

[10] Hirsch, *Validity*, pp. 88-89.

failing that is most apparent in symbolic interpretations of
works like *Measure for Measure*—their remoteness from vast
areas of the text.[11]

Less obviously but just as definitely, the position Hawkins presents arises from a premature and rigidly maintained judgment of the type of work Shakespeare wrote.
Her ability simply to perceive the structural and linguistic
detail of the text exhibits limitations fostered, perhaps, by a
personal predilection for tragedy or by an uncritical adop-
tion of Tillyard's poorly substantiated view that *Measure for
Measure* falls apart in the middle. We are told, for example,
of intense personal involvement, of great and potentially
tragic confrontations between Angelo, Isabella, and
Claudio, and of the very simple and passionate appetite for
tragedy created in the first half of the play. This in fact
constitutes a responsible description of important parts of
the first half (to be precise, of 2.2.26-187; 2.4; and 3.1.48-
150). In a spirit of extreme generosity one might add also
those sections that establish preliminary characterizations
of the three main participants in potential tragedy (1.2.
108-84; 1.4; 2.1.1-40). But to ascribe to these sections anything remotely akin to intense personal involvement, as my
subsequent analysis will show, would severely stretch the
point.

In effect, therefore, Hawkins's interpretation discards
most of the play's first three scenes and much of its fifth
(2.1.41-283) and writes off as inconsiderable fairy tale the
entire latter half of the work. Precisely because it ignores
the play's opening scenes—the scenes that do most to establish key themes, introduce important characters, set the
dominant tone, launch patterns of diction, imagery, and so
on—*in short, the scenes that function especially to evoke generic*

[11] This model of critical procedure is promoted by Ellis, *Theory of Literary Criticism*, chap. 6. And I should add that it does not rule out, a priori,
the possibility that the work may be flawed or incoherent. It does encourage a very careful search for alternative explanations of troubling literary
phenomena.

expectations—such an interpretation cannot identify with any precision what type of utterance the play is. When generic considerations appear in Hawkins's interpretation and, still more centrally, in Rosalind Miles's recent study, notions of genre remain fixed at the level of very vague kinds—especially, for example, of other contemporary plays that have disguised dukes in them.[12] These generic categories remain rigid standards of judgment rather than flexible, preliminary devices used to deepen our understanding. Such judicial criticism not only spawns trivializing and inaccurate interpretations of individual texts; it also has the intellectually stifling effect, characteristic of much modern criticism, of isolating literature from the universe of linguistic experience of which it is a special category.

In general, then, with Christian interpretations based on allegorical personifications and on biblical analogues and allusions, the controlling conception of genre is insufficiently active, and as a result parts of the play are interpreted idiosyncratically and erroneously. The movement from part of the play to part of the Bible is an interpretive act that needs the control of generic notions of type of meaning—control that is largely neglected by allegorizing critics. Miles and Hawkins, on the other hand, approach the play with too little conviction that the text might be a whole, and they fail to be open-minded in their ongoing encounter with the detail of the text. What has not yet been provided in criticism of the play is a sustained dialectic between evolving notions of the text as a generic whole and notions of the significance of its complex detail. To create and describe this dialectic in a satisfactory manner is to study the play in ways that resolve most of the problems it has presented to previous critics. In the process, we can recognize that many of those problems are illusory—that

[12] Hawkins, *Likenesses of Truth*, pp. 52-54, bases much adverse comment on an extended comparison with Marston's *Malcontent*. Cf. Miles, *Problem of "Measure for Measure,"* pp. 195-96 and passim.

they are less the product of textual inconsistency than of the procedural inadequacies of critical practice. In chapter 1, therefore, I will let *Measure for Measure* announce its own generic allegiances. What it declares there will guide our endeavors in subsequent chapters.

The Problem of Kind

Since accurate identification of genre in part determines accurate response to linguistic detail, a valid interpretation of *Measure for Measure* ought to deal carefully with its usually neglected early scenes.[1] In those scenes, Shakespeare reveals quickly and forcefully that he is writing neither a tragedy nor a satiric comedy like Marston's *Malcontent*. If we restrict our attention for the moment to large, overt plot elements, we learn in act 1, scene 1 and act 1, scene 3 that *Measure for Measure* concerns a duke who departs mysteriously only to return as a disguised observer of his substitutes. As every student familiar with the play's sources knows, and as ordinary observers can recognize on their own, the motif belongs generally to folklore, more immediately to the broad genre of romance. The central figure in this romance motif is altogether appropriate, since we can readily foresee that the Duke's social and political stature, and his disguise, confer upon him powers beyond those of ordinary men. They grant him an unnatural degree of freedom from his environment, a seeming omniscience and omnipotence. Although he recognizes (in 1.3) certain limits to his political powers, the Duke's disguise promises new autonomy born of the hidden knowl-

[1] For some suggestive remarks on the importance of the reader's primary experience of literary texts, see Hans Robert Jauss, "Literary History as a Challenge to Literary Theory," in *New Directions in Literary History*, ed. Ralph Cohen (Baltimore: Johns Hopkins University Press, 1974), p. 16.

edge to be gained from espionage. At the outset, then, we recognize that the Duke has strong affinities with heroes typical of romance.[2]

Our preliminary generic conception therefore begins to specify a range of possibilities about the category of language to which *Measure for Measure* belongs. That range is broad indeed, for romance embraces anything from the naive tale in which exciting action is alpha and omega to the somewhat weightier popular narratives Shakespeare found in Italian novellas, to the sophisticated hybrid romance epics of the high Renaissance. Our knowledge of Shakespeare's immediate sources supports the belief that his drama belongs broadly to the same eclectic family of romantic story that authors as diverse as Ariosto, Sidney, and Spenser found so malleable and potent in pleasurably communicating heavy intellectual freight. This generic identity raises expectations of further events that have little in common with what we ordinarily call "realism." Our expectations will of course be modified as the play proceeds, but we are led at the outset to expect that other nonrepresentational motifs may join that of the disguised and spying Duke, motifs such as the substituted bed mate and the comprehensive and unnaturally merciful judgment scene of the conclusion. These expectations are present at first only as part of a provisional guess at the kind of meaning we confront.

Along with the initial plot motif that predicts romance, there appear concurrent indications that the play is to be a comedy—at least of some sort. A startling feature of most Christian-symbolic and of hostile-realistic accounts of the play is their common refusal to acknowledge the play's insistently comic mood. As Arthur Kirsch has pointed out, "one would hardly guess in reading the pages of many of its critics that the play is often funny. The most insistent

[2] Cf. Northrop Frye, *Anatomy of Criticism* (1957; rpt. New York: Atheneum, 1965), p. 33. For the Duke's relationship to the comic *eiron*, see p. 174.

comedy, of course, occurs in the subplot. . . . Before the main action develops, we are introduced to a judgment scene (II,i), the play's first, which is dominated by a mélange of Elbow's malapropisms and Pompey's puns, and a similar mood, broad and usually bawdy, is sustained whenever the low-life characters appear."[3] For the purpose of ascertaining generic expectations, we should note that this mood of broad and bawdy humor appears well before act 2. In the play's second scene, Lucio and his dissipated colleagues regale us with a rapid-fire series of jokes—frowned upon by the graver sort of critics—that turn repeatedly on some especially significant themes: the law, sexual license, and its consequence, the pox. From the beginning of the play, therefore, the serious and potentially tragic tone of *Measure for Measure* is modulated by long stretches of boisterous and freewheeling comedy. In short, it is manifest—especially in the theater, where narrow prejudgments undergo insistent assault from the art of living actors and the ingenuity of directors as well as from language alone—that uniformity of tone is to be found in *neither* half of the play. If there is to be tonal consistency in *Measure for Measure*, we expect from the outset to find it neither in an unvarying comic or an unvarying tragic mood, but rather in a purposeful blend of varying local tones generated by a mixture of styles, high and low, poetic and prosaic.[4] This blend, it is true, becomes increasingly

[3] "The Integrity of *Measure for Measure*," *ShS* 28 (1975):101.

[4] This expectation reduces the likelihood that we will perceive the stylistic and tonal chasm the Tillyard school locates at 3.1.151. The possibility of perceiving a clear break is further reduced by the mere fact that the play is intended for production, not for silent reading. Speaking of his recent experience in directing the play, John Barton has conceded that a "change is obvious enough in the study; but in the theatre, I think that the difference disappears. This is because the actors, if they have brought their characters to life in exploring the first half, can carry through that life into the play's more superficial resolution." "Directing Problem Plays: John Barton Talks to Gareth Lloyd Evans," *ShS* 25 (1972): 65; quoted by Kirsch, "Integrity of *Measure for Measure*," p. 103. I believe we can go be-

comic as the play moves toward its conclusion, but there is no uniquely abrupt alteration in act 3, scene 1.[5] To require a uniformly comic mood is to demand farce; to hunger for an unmitigated tragic tone is to demand melodrama.

Taken together, the persistence of comic elements in the earliest scenes and the promise of a typical romantic plot imply that interpretations centering on "a very simple and passionate appetite" to watch the impending tragedy of Angelo, Claudio, and Isabella are less than comprehensive. They also—and this is crucial—misconstrue the single characteristic that most powerfully determines the play's intrinsic genre. This characteristic relates *Measure for Measure* to a literary kind much broader than the tradi-

---

yond this to suggest that even mediocre actors, by providing simple consistencies of voice and appearance, will greatly mitigate any sense of sharp bifurcation.

[5] One fact that makes the transition at 3.1.151 seem unusual is that the Duke's reappearance from the shadows follows immediately on the play's chief emotional climax. Although this represents an abrupt change in tone, it differs from the norms established elsewhere in the play only in degree, not in kind. In effect, this change and the subsequent lowering of tension and poetic complexity correspond to the normal rhythms of drama, whether classical or Shakespearean. To borrow the classical terminology, we can say that it is precisely here that the play's *protasis* and *epitasis*, its exposition and complication, have produced an emotional climax of exceptional intensity. The normal rhythm of dramatic structure demands a reduction of tension, a corresponding muting of poetic intensity, and a simultaneous increase in exposition as the plot moves from climax to *catastasis*. That in turn prepares, as I shall argue below, for a denouement in which the emotional and intellectual engagement of the audience, the suffering of the principal characters, and the energetic complexity of the poetry once again become extremely intense. Informed statements on Shakespearean dramatic structure support this view. A consideration of Bernard Beckerman's analysis of the normative structure illustrated in *King Lear* (*Shakespeare at the Globe* [London: Collier, 1962], p. 43) suggests that the overall shape of *Measure for Measure* is comparable to that of unquestioned Shakespearean masterpieces. The change at 3.1.151, therefore, represents a dramatic rhythm far too common to support the notion that Shakespeare suddenly gave up his struggle to sophisticate a fairy tale. See also Emrys Jones, *Scenic Form in Shakespeare* (Oxford: Clarendon Press, 1971), p. 69.

tional genres, and I incline to call it the mode of the play. By this term I mean the play's rhetorical stance, its peculiar orientation toward the audience—an orientation established by certain characteristic types of syntax, diction, imagery, allusion, and informational lacunae. Properly understood, its rhetorical posture is the trait that chiefly gives *Measure for Measure* an undeniably artful coherence. In brief, the primary quality of the play's distinguishing mode is a deliberate reticence about key issues, a calculated vagueness that combines with imagery, diction, and allusions of cosmic amplitude to generate implications of immense scope. This combination establishes a relationship with the audience that has little to do with "appetite" of any kind, much less an appetite for tragedy.

A look at the play's first lines will help to clarify my meaning and set us on the right path to discover the literary kind of the play—the generic type of meaning that characterizes the text and helps us assign appropriate meaning to its various parts.

Duke.   Escalus.
Esc.   My lord.

This is as simple in its way as is the more famous opening gambit of *Hamlet*, and in both plays simplicity is deceptive. *Measure for Measure* might appropriately begin with line 3 ("Of government the properties to unfold"), which initiates requisite exposition. But the playwright chooses to direct our attention, before all else, to Duke Vincentio's relationship with one of his deputies, and the nature of this relationship is not explained, it is dramatized—defined as much by silence as by statement. In the absence of all prior knowledge of the Duke, of Escalus, and of their present situation (we wait until line 18 to be told, and then obliquely, that the Duke plans an "absence"), Escalus's curt reply invites interpretation. His "My lord," accompanied no doubt by a reverential gesture, implies obedience—the prompt, usually unquestioning readiness to obey his superior that marks Escalus's behavior throughout the play. And the very brevity of his answer suggests, simultaneously, his reluctance to call attention to that prompt obedience.

On stage this is suggested fleetingly, but its purpose becomes apparent moments later, when a new deputy is called to engage in a parallel ritual of deputation. This time the Duke receives a response considerably more copious:

Ang. Always obedient to your Grace's will,
        I come to know your pleasure.
                                    [1.1.25-26]

Unlike Escalus, Angelo is self-dramatizing; he is eager to have his prompt appearance interpreted as evidence of undeviating loyalty. His opening speech, therefore, because of the tacit contrast with Escalus's, suggests the vainglory that will soon be revealed as one of Angelo's ruling passions. In both cases, minute hints highlighted by an unspoken contrast evoke, or at least seem calculated to evoke, expectations that are fulfilled as the play proceeds.

Though it may at first appear trivial, this point is worth dwelling on yet longer because the presentation of Escalus and of Angelo generates precise expectations about the type of language the play continually employs. This can best be identified by analogy, for Escalus's laconic obedience renders him comparable to one of Western literature's most familiar exemplars of self-abnegating obedience: "God . . . said unto him, Abraham: and he said, Behold, here I am" (Gen. 22:1). This analogy is pertinent not because Shakespeare intended an allusion to the biblical story, but because his manner of presenting the relationship between the Duke and Escalus is in significant ways similar to the Elohist's presentation of the relationship of God and Abraham. It will be helpful therefore to recall Eric Auerbach's discussion of the mimetic manner of the Elohist as it contrasts with Homeric mimesis. Unlike Homer's "externalized, uniformly illuminated phenome-

na, at a definite time and in a definite place, connected together without lacunae in a perpetual foreground,"[6] the
Elohist gives us narrative shorn of all but the essential
foreground, and indeed of all temporal and spatial coordi-
nates. Abraham's "here I am" is no indication of space;
"the Hebrew word means only something like 'behold me,'
and in any case is not meant to indicate the actual place
where Abraham is, but a moral position in respect to God,
who has called to him—Here am I awaiting thy command."
The same holds true for temporal details, like the three
days' journey that for Abraham begins "early in the morning," itself a detail intended not to indicate actual time, but
to symbolize "the resolution, the promptness, the punctual
obedience of the sorely tried Abraham." Similarly, of all
the instruments, beasts, and characters in the story, only
Isaac receives any kind of description: God says, "Take
Isaac, thine only son, whom thou lovest." Yet this is no description in the usual sense; it is included only "so that it
may become apparent how terrible Abraham's temptation
is, and that God is fully aware of it." The magnitude of this
terrible temptation is of course the central point of the
story, but it is not developed in explicit detail. It is left to us,
by interpretation of sparse yet significant narrative details,
to discover the gravity of the temptation.

This is also true of direct discourse, for although the
characters speak, "their speech does not serve, as does
speech in Homer . . . to externalize thoughts—on the contrary, it serves to indicate thoughts which remain unexpressed. God gives his command in direct discourse, but he
leaves his motives and his purpose unexpressed; Abraham,
receiving the command, says nothing and does what he has
been told to do." In short, it is the dearth of foreground,
the suppression of all but the most significant mimetic de-

---

[6] *Mimesis: The Representation of Reality in Western Literature*, trans. Willard
Trask (1953; rpt. Garden City, New York: Doubleday, 1957), p. 9. My
subsequent quotations from the discussion of Homer and the Elohist are
from pp. 5-12.

tails, the terse, unexpressive dialogue, that endow the Elo-
histic text, even in its factual and psychological elements,
with an aura of mystery. And this sense of mystery, of hidden depths, positively demands the subtle investigation
and interpretation it has received from untold generations
of scholars, Rabbinic and Christian.

Drama is by nature more prodigal of detail than is the
Elohist's text. But despite our knowledge of the Duke's and
of Escalus's spatial relationships, of their physical stature,
clothing, voice timbre, and so on, the opening of *Measure
for Measure* is comparable to the story of Abraham in its
calculated reticence. Each author deliberately and consistently suppresses linguistic and thematic ligatures and
withholds information for which he nonetheless creates an
appetite. The suppression of ligatures, both linguistic and
thematic, is well illustrated in the contrast between the
opening speeches of Escalus and Angelo. Their contrasting
characters and their relationship to a developing theme of
obedience remain implicit; yet these things are nonetheless
clearly revealed through parallels of action, through subtle
contrasts in language, and, if we have tenacious memories
(or opportunity for a second reading or viewing), through
subsequent events.

Perhaps the most apparent informational lacuna of
scene 1 is that which shrouds Duke Vincentio's departure
in unrelieved mystery. Shakespeare allows only a sidelong
reference to "our absence," twice tantalizes his audience
with the ceremonial conferral of commissions whose contents are given in only the vaguest terms, and concludes
with allusions to an affair that demands extreme haste:

> of so quick condition
> That it prefers itself, and leaves unquestion'd
> Matters of needful value.
>
> [1.1.53-55]

Far more than Abraham's Lord, the Duke gives commands
and engages in direct discourse aplenty, but his motives

and purposes remain altogether unexpressed. And this leaves unquestioned matters we ordinarily think needful at the beginning of a dramatic narrative.

Duke Vincentio's overt behavior is only the most apparent focus for mystery in scene 1. His language itself frequently lapses into an infectious interrogative mood. While they enhance our power to discern the implicit contrast between the deputies, the repeated interrogatives that precede Angelo's entrance help induce an attitude of questioning attentiveness that will soon come to characterize our total response to the play.

Duke.   Call hither,
    I say, bid come before us Angelo.
    What figure of us, think you, he will bear?
    For you must know, we have with special soul
    Elected him our absence to supply;
    Lent him our terror, drest him with our love,
    And given his deputation all the organs
    Of our own power. What think you of it?
                     [1.1.14–21]

The Duke's questions solicit our own and ensure that we watch Angelo's behavior with special care. With this speech, we begin to participate in the play's basic, most pervasive and significant thematic activity. We begin to observe characters narrowly, with an eye to assessment; we begin, in short, to judge.[7]

Shakespeare's effort to engage his audience in direct intellectual participation in the play's thematic and dramatic activities is evident not only in the Duke's repeated interrogatives. It appears more generally in the dark suggestiveness of language "fraught with background." Such language is well suited to a figure who remains markedly mysterious throughout the play and whom critics have

[7] This is not to suggest that we are encouraged to sit emotionally disengaged and smug in self-righteous condemnation of the characters. See below, chap. 6.

long recognized as a prime determinant of our overall response.[8] In his role as initiator of the action and contriver of subsequent plots to rectify his subjects' errors, the Duke in large part determines the play's structure, and from the outset it is his conspicuously enigmatic character that feeds, encourages, and provides a focus for our most insistent questions. In terms of traditional comic types, he therefore appears to combine the structural function of contriving *eiron* and the mood-focusing function of the buffoon.[9]

But the mood he generates is mysterious, not festive, and in the speech quoted above the enigma results largely from diction that gives the character's very opacity a distinctly theological cast. "With special soul," the Duke has "elected" "Angelo," a name heightened in rhetorical force by its odd position at the end of a syntactically distorted sentence. Since the name translates as "angel" and so constitutes a pun that later results in thematically significant wordplay (2.4.16-17), we are encouraged to recognize, at least dimly, the patently theological terminology that accompanies it. The Duke allusively presents himself as an analogue of God, specially electing this Angelo to receive the terrible godlike power and the paternal love proper to absolute monarchy—and to deity.

The imagery of lending and of dressing suggests a sharp disjunction between Angelo's inherent powers and those granted from without. This disjunction is itself introduced by the word "figure" (l.16), which constitutes a metaphor that stresses Angelo's continuing dependence on higher authority and hints that his powers derive altogether from the obedience that is a thematic concern in this scene. The language asks, in short, that we view Angelo from the outset as an image or likeness—a cipher "dressed in a little

---

[8] F. R. Leavis, *The Common Pursuit* (London: Chatto and Windus, 1952), p. 163; Michael Goldman, *Shakespeare and the Energies of the Drama* (Princeton: Princeton University Press, 1972), Appendix C; Kirsch, "Integrity of *Measure for Measure*," p. 103.

[9] Frye, *Anatomy*, pp. 172-75.

brief authority"—of an absent power. This, at first, is an interpretive guess. It soon proves valid, since the idea of dependence is reintroduced whenever the other characters name Angelo, as they persistently do, the "deputy" or "substitute" (1.2.146, 171; 3.1.88, 187, 255; 3.2.33, 34; 4.2.76; 4.3.113; 5.1.136, 142). The notion of dependence is further elaborated in scene 1 itself by means of the sententious expostulation with which the Duke greets Angelo:

> Thyself and thy belongings
> Are not thine own so proper as to waste
> Thyself upon thy virtues, they on thee.
> Heaven doth with us as we with torches do,
> Not light them for themselves; for if our virtues
> Did not go forth of us, 'twere all alike
> As if we had them not. Spirits are not finely touch'd
> But to fine issues; nor nature never lends
> The smallest scruple of her excellence
> But, like a thrifty goddess, she determines
> Herself the glory of a creditor,
> Both thanks and use.
>
> [1.1.29-40]

As this passage demonstrates, the rich sense of thematic depth that characterizes Shakespeare's language in *Measure for Measure* results in part from his persistent and judicious and very delicate use of allusion. Editors customarily find in the words "Heaven doth with us as we with torches do, / Not light them for themselves" a reference to Luke 8:16. But the parallel passage in Matthew, which contains its own gloss, is more revealing.[10] "Ye are the light of the world. . . .

[10] On the other hand, in both Luke 8:16 and its close parallel Mark 4:21, the passage about the candlestick is directly followed by the words "For nothing is secret, that shall not be evident: neither anything hid, that shall not be known, and come to light" (Geneva). Bringing hypocrisy to light is a primary concern not only of these texts but also of *Measure for Measure*, and it could be argued that Lucio at 3.2.170-72 alludes directly to the passages from Luke and Mark (or to 1 Cor. 4:5, a text for which the Geneva [like the Vulgate] version gives cross references to Matt. 7:1 and

Neither do men light a candle, and put it under a bushel, but on a candlestick; and it giveth light unto all that are in the house. Let your light so shine before men, that they may see your good works, and glorify your Father which is in heaven" (5:14-16). Although Luke (and his probable source, Mark 4:21) record the image of the candle and urge that it be displayed, the remark lacks a defining local context. But as is his practice, Matthew provides the needed context—and aids us to see multiple points of comparison between the Duke's speech and the famous passage from the Sermon on the Mount. In both, the light that should not be hidden is made visible in good works (virtues that "go forth of us"). The sermon enjoins that these works appear in men who, like Angelo, will be their lord's substitutes after his departure. Moreover, Christ urges in the sermon that the light of good works lead observers to admire not the actors themselves, but God, source through grace of all human goodness.[11] This follows because Christ's disciples are instruments dependent for their special powers on a Lord who has elected them, his absence to supply. Duke Vincentio gives less explicit yet equal stress to the proper assignment of praise. As the entire deputation makes plain, Angelo receives his powers as gifts not only from "heaven," which works in part through "nature," but also from the Duke himself, a human agent who assists in transmitting divine gifts. For those who recognize it, then, and of course not everyone in a given audience will, the allusion to Matthew—or Mark or Luke—serves primarily to strengthen meanings implicit in Shakespeare's language itself. The overt theme of Vincentio's speech, as of its scriptural prototype(s), concerns a gratui-

---

to Rom. 2:1). These related passages may therefore help illuminate the genesis of significant portions of *Measure for Measure*.

[11] In Shakespeare's dualistic elaboration of this idea ("spirits . . . nature"), "nature" receives the "glory." As in the works of Alain de Lille, Jean de Meun, Chaucer, and Spenser, Shakespeare's Nature acts as God's vice-regent charged with the ordering of material affairs.

tous bestowal of special abilities and a prescription that re-
cipients employ their gifts in the world with answering
generosity and due humility.

While the Duke's words echo a scriptural text made especially familiar by its inclusion in the Sermon on the
Mount, his actions may owe a more general debt to one of
Matthew's and Luke's well-known parables. As Richmond
Noble first noticed,[12] the plots of both *Measure for Measure*
and the parable of the talents (Matt. 25:14-30; Luke
19:12-27) concern a ruler who departs on an unspecified
journey, leaving various numbers of "talents" in the hands
of his servants. He returns in the end to judge their uses of
his gifts. The lord in the parable is of course a transparent
figure for the Lord himself. Because he rewards those who
invested and increased their talents, the Geneva gloss on
the story appears perfectly apt in commenting that powers
delegated by grace ought to issue in charitable action: we
are to "do good with those graces that God hath given us."
Because the evil servant simply hid his talent, a further
Geneva note adds the obvious corollary: "The graces of
God shall be taken away from him that doth not bestow
them to God's glory and his neighbor's profit." Since its essential burden corresponds perfectly with that of the
candlestick allusion, and since its central narrative motif
neatly parallels the outline of events in *Measure for Measure*,
the parable of the talents adds significantly to the Duke's
potential figural depth and helps impart to the play's first
scene an immense range of doctrinal implications.

The immensity of these implications can be felt even by
those in the audience whose defective learning, feeble
memory, or fitful attention compels dependence solely on
the explicit meaning of the Duke's speech. We have already
noticed that the Duke presents Angelo's "election" in a

[12] *Shakespeare's Biblical Knowledge* (London: Society for Promoting
Christian Knowledge, 1935), p. 221. Arthur Kirsch, "Integrity of *Measure
for Measure*," pp. 98-100, argues persuasively that this parable, as glossed
in the Geneva Bible, is a fundamental scriptural source in the play.

quasi-theological light, and I should add that Escalus's response perpetuates this theological suggestiveness:

> If any in Vienna be of worth
> To undergo such ample grace and honour,
> It is Lord Angelo.
>
> [1.1.22-24]

The terms here are precise, for the honor accorded to monarchy results from a prior operation of the grace that elects monarchs. In this context, therefore, Escalus's conditional "if" clause provides the barest hint that no one in Vienna merits such gifts. In cases of "election" by "special soul" to "grace and honour," the probability is strong that all men will be found unworthy. Grace by definition and by universal acknowledgment is undeserved.

Thus, before we reach the Duke's richly allusive statement to Angelo, the grand theme of divine grace and its relationship to human worth is unobtrusively introduced. This theme gains prominence from the conception that we are all heaven's torches, for that metaphor posits a particular relationship between man and God. We have already noticed both that heaven, through nature, receives all the glory accrued by the virtues that go forth and that heaven's right to the glory derives from its absolute proprietorship of those virtues: "thyself and thy belongings / Are not thine own." This point receives subtler expression when the Duke adds that "Spirits are not finely touch'd / But to fine issues; nor nature never lends . . ." (1.1.35-36). We should note in passing that these lines contribute to a radical dualism that here begins to pervade the play and to endow the familiar antinomy between outward appearance and hidden reality with deep philosophical implications. But more significant still, these words continue to develop the theme that all human virtues derive entirely from the immediate action of deity.

Taking "touch'd" in its graphic sense (cf. sonnet 17, l.8), we glimpse the divine artisan creating, as with delicate strokes of brush or pencil, a human soul. That soul's "issues," the Duke's elliptical argument runs, ought to reflect the excellence of the divine craftsmanship. As often in scriptural metaphor, man is implicitly conceived here as God's art, mere clay to the potter, a creature utterly dependent. Beyond this, "touch'd" and "issues," with "fine" (i.e., "refined"), refer, as Lever has shown (1.1.32-36 n), to "the 'touch' placed on gold coins of standard fineness before they were passed into circulation." In the same context, "touch'd" suggests the testing of gold and silver by rubbing it on a touchstone—much as the Duke's plot tests Angelo's virtue and finds it unworthy of the ducal imprint placed on him as on a coin ("what figure of us"). Whether "touch'd" refers to drawing or painting, to marking a coin, or to the testing that precedes such marking, the fundamental implication of this image complex is man's utter dependence for his value, his currency, on God viewed as artist or coiner.

This idea is overtly expressed in Angelo's reply to the Duke:

Ang. Let there be some more test made of my metal,
   Before so noble and so great a figure
   Be stamp'd upon it.

   [1.1.48-50]

Angelo represents himself as receiving current authority, just as a coin would, from the ducal imprint. The metaphor of stamping again conveys a sense of the passivity and emptiness of the recipient on whom powers must be conferred from without (or at best of an inchoate, potential value translated into active virtue by the stamp).[13] And furthermore, Angelo's metaphor adds a new dimension of meaning to his very name. In Elizabethan idiom, "angel" could refer not only to a divine messenger, but also to a ten-shilling coin.[14] In both senses, the deputy's name reminds us, persistently, of his dependence on the Duke—

[13] For stamp imagery used with identical implications and stunning effect, see Dante's *Purgatorio* 10.44-45 and *Paradiso* 2.131-32.

[14] I owe this observation to Professor Martin C. Battestin.

and on the Deity of whom earthly monarchs themselves are mere figures. We should notice, too, that this monetary symbolism reinforces Shakespeare's tacit allusion to the characters and the narrative of the famous parable about "talents."

If, on the one hand, Shakespeare's imagery in scene 1 stresses the relative insignificance of the human microcosm, it simultaneously insists on God's immanent presence in the macrocosm. We catch a fleeting glimpse of this divine immanence in the cosmology suggested by the Duke's entire speech, a view that conceives even the particularities of individual human talents as immediate functions of divine ordinance. The horizons of implication[15] of this speech are coextensive with the typical medieval and Renaissance conception of the cosmos itself, for the idea at issue is the venerable and complex conception of divine providence. Of course, many have argued that the Duke behaves as if he were intended to embody this concept on stage. But to understand how the correspondence works, how truly pervasive it is, what limitations contain it, and above all what it might signify—all topics to be considered later—we need to review more information about Renaissance ideas of providence than scholars usually provide.

While most commentators are content simply to assert the likeness, modern usage offers little help since it fosters a generalized and trivialized conception of providence that denotes especially careful foresight and prudent management of affairs. When we do use the word in its numinous sense, we tend to conceive of a very general divine guidance that imposes dimly perceptible, roughhewn shape on the flux of events. Both of these reduced senses were cur-

---

[15] I use this term as it is employed by Husserl. See Hirsch, *Validity*, p. 221. According to this usage, "horizons of implication" comprise elements not explicitly conscious but which are nonetheless constituent parts of a meaning experience. Although we may be consciously attending only to the bark of a tree, for example, roots, branches, leaves, sap, cambium, etc., are all present as "horizons" of our experience.

rent in Shakespeare's age, but providence could also be an immediate intellectual concern because it was of central importance in the religious life of individual men. A significant article of Elizabethan religion contained the solidly Pauline, Augustinian, and Calvinist assertion that "predestination to life is the everlasting purpose of God, whereby before the foundations of the world were laid, he hath constantly decreed by his counsel, secret to us, to deliver from curse and damnation those whom he hath chosen" (article 17).[16] Predestination to eternal pain receives prominent, though less detailed attention. Since individual salvation or damnation was normally considered a special and direct function of divine providence,[17] we can understand why the topic could command greater attention in Shakespeare's age than it does in our own.

As the logical foundation for his dogmatic assertion of eternal predestination, Calvin advanced and made current an extremely dynamic conception of providential ordinance. He assailed those scholastics who, among others, "confine God's providence to such narrow limits as though he allowed all things by a free course to be borne along according to a universal law of nature." Though it normally works in harmony with natural laws (which are its instruments),[18] providence is, on the contrary, a divine omnipotence that is truly omniscient and omnipresent, immanent

[16] I quote the articles from *The Thirty-nine Articles of the Church of England*, ed. William Wilson (Oxford: Abrams, 1840).

[17] Cf. John Philpot, *The Examinations and Writings of John Philpot*, ed. Rev. Robert Eden, Parker Society (Cambridge: Cambridge University Press, 1842), pp. 402-403. "There is no apter word . . . [than 'providence'] to express that men call predestination; for providence signifieth rather a certain purveyance and administration of those things which be included in destiny."

[18] See *The Institution of Christian Religion* 1.16.2. I quote throughout from the translation by Thomas Norton (London: Richard Harrison, 1562), hereafter cited as *Institutes*. The present reference is to fol. 56^r. Cf. Hooker's identical conception of natural law as "nothing else but God's

in every detail of created life, determining its nature and directing its every motion. It is "waking, effectual, working and busied in continual doing."[19]

This conception of an intensely active immanent deity is not at all original with Calvin. Its immediate and best sources, in themselves poems of great beauty, were recited each month in the Anglican liturgy. In a glorious celebration of natural harmony, "David" describes the complete dependence of all creatures great and small, both on land and in

> this great and wide sea, wherein are things creeping innumerable, both small and great beasts. . . . These wait all upon thee; that thou mayest give them their meat in due season. That thou givest them they gather: thou openest thy hand, they are filled with good. Thou hidest thy face, they are troubled: thou takest away their breath, they die, and return to their dust. Thou sendest forth thy spirit, they are created: and thou renewest the face of the earth.
>
> [Ps. 104:25-30]

This divine attention to detail in the natural world extends also to men, and in his discussion of providence, Bullinger (*Decades* 4.4) quotes Psalm 139, a beautiful expression of God's intimate knowledge of, and virtual presence in, individual men:

> O Lord, thou hast searched me, and known me. . . . Thou hast possessed my reins: thou has covered me in my mother's womb. . . . My substance was not hid from thee, when I was made in secret, and curiously wrought in the lowest parts of the earth. Thine eyes did see my substance, yet being unperfect; and in thy book all my

---

instrument," in *Of the Laws of Ecclesiastical Polity*, introduced by Christopher Morris (New York: Dutton, 1907), 1:60.

[19] *Institutes* 1.16.3; fol. 56^r.

members were written, which in continuance were fashioned, when as yet there was none of them.

[ll.1-16][20]

These striking and, in earlier ages, widely familiar celebrations of the divine immanence find confirmation in New Testament texts that preoccupied Calvin as he wrote about providence—as they do Hamlet after his voyage: "Are not two sparrows sold for a farthing? and one of them shall not fall on the ground without your Father. But the very hairs of your head are all numbered" (Matt. 10:29-30). And of course a celebrated expression of this conception of "special providence" immediately precedes the measure-for-measure text in the Sermon on the Mount, where we are bid to recall the lilies of the field and their colleagues, the birds of the air. Taken together, these quotations suggest that the idea of providence—for a Christian audience reminded of it[21]—could cast a numinous light on every detail of literary, as well as actual, experience.[22]

[20] I quote Bullinger's *Decades* from the edition of the Rev. Thomas Harding, Parker Society, 7-10 (Cambridge: Cambridge University Press, 1849).

[21] Calvin knew that men readily neglect invisible truth, even though they may know it fully and look directly upon its works: For "according to the common sense of the flesh accounting all to be but chance that happeneth, of both sorts[,] we are neither encouraged by the benefits of God to worship him, nor pricked forward with his scourges to repentance" (*Institutes* 1.17.8; fol. 63ᵛ).

[22] A fine literary example of this outlook appears in the Nausikaa episode of Chapman's *Odyssey*, 6.160-68, where Minerva considers

What meanes to wake Ulysses might be wrought
That he might see this lovely-sighted maid,
Whom she intended should become his aid . . .
Her meane was this (though thought a stool-ball chance):
The Queene now (for the upstroke) strooke the ball
Quite wide off th'other maids, and made it fall
Amidst the whirlpooles.

Chapman comments: "The piety and wisdom of the Poet was such that (agreeing with the sacred letter) not the least of things he makes come to

Inherent in this conception of God's dynamic omnipresence, moreover, is the contrasting and ontologically prior idea of divine stasis. Calvin's stress on active presence balances his equal belief in divine immutability. The paradox of the unmoved mover is of course a venerable one that we may discern in the psalmist's assurance that "in thy book all my members were written, which in continuance were fashioned, when as yet there was none of them." This contrast between immutable book and serial enactment of its contents is presented in clear conceptual terms by Hooker. And Hooker, it should be said, is paraphrasing St. Thomas (*ST*, 1, q. 116, art. 2), who depends in turn on Boethius (*De Cons.*, bk. 4):

> the natural generation and process of all things receiveth order of proceeding from the settled stability of divine understanding. This appointeth unto them their kinds of working; the disposition whereof in the purity of God's own knowledge and will is rightly termed by the name of Providence. The same being referred unto the things themselves here disposed by it, was wont by the ancient to be called natural Destiny. That law, the performance whereof we behold in things natural, is as it were an authentical or an original draught written in the bosom of God himself; whose Spirit being to execute the same useth every particular nature, every mere natural agent, only as an instrument created at the beginning and ever since the beginning used, to work his own will and pleasure withal.[23]

In Hooker's judicious restatement of Boethius's distinction between destiny and providence, we perceive the unspoken doctrinal frontiers of the complex idea introduced in

pass, *sine Numinis providentia.*" The idea persisted tenaciously in English literature, see Martin C. Battestin, *The Providence of Wit* (Oxford: Clarendon Press, 1974), esp. pp. 156-63. See also Keith Thomas, *Religion and the Decline of Magic* (New York: Scribner's, 1971), chap. 4.

[23] *Laws*, 1:159-60. Cf. Calvin *Institutes* 1.16.2; fols. 55^{v}-56^{r}.

Duke Vincentio's address to Angelo, the idea of a world instinct in all its details with divine essence and purpose.

While that speech is perhaps our best illustration of the mode of scene 1—its sense of being rich with implicit meaning—it also simultaneously bears on the central theme of the play, and theme is always, of course, a fundamental determinant of the type of language to which any utterance or literary work belongs. Like the motives of the Duke himself, however, this subject, which is central to the scene and to the play at large, remains studiously inexplicit. That central subject, one that should begin forming in our minds as soon as we hear the play's title, is law.

The first point to be made about law in *Measure for Measure* is that it constitutes a startling example of the play's deliberate vagueness. Shakespeare's most daring ellipsis is his refusal to tell us *what* law causes all the stir. In striking contrast to earlier plays—*The Comedy of Errors, A Midsummer Night's Dream*, and especially *The Merchant of Venice*—the law on which this plot turns is never explicitly defined. We are made to divine from Claudio's circumstances and his explanation at act 1, scene 2, lines 155-60 that the "drowsy and neglected act" forbids fornication. We learn no more from Lucio (1.4.64-68); only at act 5, scene 1, line 73 do we hear outright of "the act of fornication"; and even there all other details are withheld. It may be tempting to assign this vagueness to slipshod workmanship, the author's amnesia or despondency, or to the law's simple irrelevance (i.e., "it's merely a premise of the plot"), but I believe that the omission is both purposeful and important.

While the particular law with which *Measure for Measure* deals remains vague, analyses in subsequent chapters will show that "the law" in a larger sense is absolutely ubiquitous in the texture of the play's language. Hooker's pronouncement on providence helps us recognize this, for "that law, the performance whereof we behold in things natural" *is* providence, and vice versa. Elsewhere, Hooker names God's ultimate ordering principle the law eternal, "being that order which God before all ages hath set down with himself, for himself to do all things by." From that first eternal law springs a second: "that which with himself he hath set down as expedient to be kept by all his creatures."[24] In his identification of providence with God's immutable law, Hooker was preceded by Calvin, who quotes with approval his own mentor, Augustine, to the effect that God's "providence is an unchangeable law."[25]

This traditional and exalted conception of law suggests the potential amplitude of the theme as it appears in *Measure for Measure*. The very word evokes horizons of implication that are in part directly available to modern speakers of English, for "law" preserves vestiges of its earlier, transcendent denotation. This is true, for instance, when we use "law" to denote principles of conduct conceived to be of natural origin, or a divinely instituted code of behavior, such as the Law of Moses. These definitions retain a somewhat archaic, realist aura that implies that laws are entities ontologically independent of men, rules subsisting instead in a transcendent will.

This realism appears full blown in Augustine's, Calvin's, and Hooker's conceptions of law and providence. In ages less skeptical than our own, even laws unquestionably instituted by men could be viewed as transcendent wisdom manifesting itself through human agents.[26] Citing Cicero (*De legibus* 1.14-25) as his authority, for example, Bullinger asserts that law "is an especial reason, placed in nature, commanding what is to be done, and forbidding the contrary. And verily the law is nothing but a declaration of God's will, appointing what thou hast to do, and what thou

---

[24] *Laws*, 1:154.   [25] *Institutes* 1.17.2; fol. 61ʳ.

[26] With typical Protestant disparagement of human powers, Hooker stresses that these agents remain mere passive tools: "laws apparently good are (as it were) things copied out of the very tables of that high everlasting law. . . . Not as if men did behold that book and accordingly frame their laws; but because it worketh in them, because it discovereth and (as it were) readeth itself to the world by them, when the laws which they make are righteous" (*Laws*, 1:225).

oughtest to leave undone. . . . All good and just laws come
from God himself, although they be, for the most part,
published and brought to light by men."[27] Hooker both
concurs and specifies the mechanism by which God revealed his laws to the Gentiles: "by the force of the light of
Reason, wherewith God illuminateth every one which
cometh into the world, men being enabled to know truth
from falsehood, and good from evil, do thereby learn in
many things what the will of God is." They therefore "seem
the makers of those Laws which indeed are his, and they
but only the finders of them out."[28]

These discussions demonstrate that both classical tradition and contemporary orthodoxy conceived law not as a
human construction, abstracted from countless judicial
and legislative decisions, but as a transcendent reality
grounded in the ultimate pattern of cosmic ordinance,
God's providence. This immutable and indivisible essence
appears to men in a hierarchy of partial manifestations. It
is named accordingly:

> Now that law which, as it is laid up in the bosom of God,
> they call Eternal, receiveth according unto the different
> kinds of things which are subject unto it different and
> sundry kinds of names. That part of it which ordereth
> natural agents we call usually Nature's law; that which
> Angels do clearly behold and without swerving observe is
> a law Celestial and heavenly; the law of Reason, that
> which bindeth creatures reasonable in this world, and
> with which by reason they may most plainly perceive

[27] *Decades* 2.1; Parker Society, 7:193. Bullinger supports his claim (*Dec-
ades* 2.1, Parker Society, 7:197-203) by adducing analogues of each of the
Ten Commandments gleaned from the works of Seneca, Cicero, Marcus
Aurelius, and other pagan authors. Cf. John Hooper's *Declaration of the
Ten Commandments*, in *Early Writings of John Hooper*, ed. Rev. Samuel Carr,
Parker Society (Cambridge: Cambridge University Press, 1843), p. 273.
See also Sir John Fortescue, *A learned commendation of the politique lawes of
England*, trans. Robert Mulcaster (London: Richard Tottel, 1573), sig.
B1r.

[28] *Laws*, 1:176-77.

themselves bound; that which bindeth them, and is not
known but by special revelation from God, Divine law;
Human law, that which out of the law either of reason or
of God men probably gathering to be expedient, they
make it a law.[29]

Though superior in coherence and grandeur of expression, Hooker's vision of a hierarchy of laws descending
from the "first eternal law" of God is a common presuppo-
sition of the age.[30] Like Hooker, contemporary jurists exhibit belief in a hierarchy in which laws more exalted in
status could nullify deviant human ones. On this principle,
Coke asserts that "a statute which conflicted with the Law
of Nature, that is, the dictates of reason, could not prevail";
he is joined in this view by distinguished figures like St.
Germain.[31] In harmony with these authorities, Henry
Swinburne (1560-1623), a bachelor of civil laws from Oxford and a distinguished proctor and consistory judge in
the ecclesiastical courts at York (*DNB*), illustrates ways this
principle was put into practice. In his elaborately docu-
mented *Treatise of Spousals*, Swinburne repeatedly confirms
the justice of the laws in question by asserting their agreement "to the Law of God and Nature."[32] A significant

[29] *Laws*, 1:154-55.

[30] We do well to recall that Hooker was not only a cleric; he was also
from 1585 to 1591 master of the Temple and learned in common law as
well as theology.

[31] G. W. Keeton, *Shakespeare's Legal and Political Background* (New York:
Barnes and Noble, 1968), pp. 74-75. Keeton adds that Coke is echoing
Bracton, who was himself following Thomas Aquinas. The concept of a
hierarchy grounded in God's law persists even in Blackstone, who derives
all law from God's "law of nature" and asserts that "no Human laws
should be suffered to contradict these." See Sir William Blackstone, *The
Sovereignty of the Law: Selections from Blackstone's "Commentaries on the Laws of
England,"* ed. Gareth Jones (Toronto: University of Toronto Press, 1973),
p. 30. In chapter 1 of his influential legal textbook, St. Germain provides a
complete survey of the systems of laws which derive from God's eternal
plan, "the law eternal." See Christopher St. Germain, *The Doctor and Student*, ed. William Muchall (Cincinnati: Robert Clarke, 1874).

[32] London: S. Roycroft for Robert Clavell, 1686, sig. H1^r.

instance of this concerns the laws governing conditional marriage contracts. Reciting the traditional purposes of marriage, purposes attested by the familiar texts in Genesis 2 and 1 Corinthians 7 and incorporated into the Anglican marriage rite,[33] Swinburne asserts that marriage was established: "First, for the procreation of children to be brought up in the fear of God. . . . Secondly, for the avoidance of fornication. . . . Thirdly, for the mutual cohabitation and comfortable help and society, never to be dissolved."[34] Swinburne's subsequent catalog of specific laws governing conditional spousals is controlled firmly by the principle that any conditions that contradict the divinely established purposes of marriage render the contract to which they belong automatically void in the ecclesiastical courts.

In these courts, which had jurisdiction over crimes that were deemed primarily spiritual in nature, revealed law could be translated directly, if imperfectly, into the law of England.[35] Such translation was in fact the ideal recommended by Bullinger, Hooker, and many others. Still more to the point in a study of *Measure for Measure*, however, this ideal is repeatedly asserted in the king's *Basilicon Doron*, one of the play's probable sources. In the "Argument" to his treatise, James warns that

> If then ye would enioy a happie raigne
> Observe the statutes of your heavenlie King,
> And from his Lawe, make all your Lawes to spring.
> [ll. 5-7][36]

---

[33] *The Book of Common Prayer, 1559*, ed. John E. Booty (Charlottesville: University Press of Virginia, 1976), pp. 290-91.

[34] Swinburne, *Treatise of Spousals*, sigs. S3^v-S4^r.

[35] For a vivid though somewhat partisan assessment of corruption and inefficiency in the ecclesiastical courts, see Christopher Hill, *Society and Puritanism in Pre-Revolutionary England* (London: Secker and Warburg, 1964), chap. 8.

[36] All quotations of *The Basilicon Doron* are taken from the edition edited by James Craigie (Edinburgh: William Blackwood and Sons, 1944) and refer to the text of 1603. Further citations appear in the body of my text.

The first book of the treatise locates all effective and virtuous government in the ruler's obedience to the divine will as it is revealed in Scripture (1.27-29). And when James prescribes a program of study for his successor, he reaffirms the primacy of divine over human law: "First of all, then, study to be well seen in the Scriptures. . . . Next the Scriptures, study well your own laws."[37]

The principle that a nation's laws should spring from God's revealed law was not, as some Shakespearean scholars suggest, a doctrine peculiar to the radical Protestants whom we tend very indiscriminately to name "Puritans." Yet since "the law" in religious contexts (in Jacobean as well as modern English) may denote especially the Mosaic code as distinct from the Gospels, controversy often arose when men sought to institutionalize their ideals. Yet the Reformation had inherited common guidelines that encouraged a selective reading of the Mosaic code, and although disagreements appeared in plenty, no major Protestant writer advocated wholesale reinstitution of the Old Law—that Parliament should enact a statute prohibiting, say, farmers from plowing with an ox and an ass together or commanding that men make three fringes on the four quarters of their vesture (Deut. 22:10, 12). Instead, the Old Law was commonly subsumed under three categories—the moral, the ceremonial, and the judicial. The advent of Christ was thought to have abrogated the latter two categories, leaving only the moral law eternally in force. As Calvin explains in the *Institutes*, the Mosaic moral law was amenable to ready summary: "Moral law . . . is contained in two chief points, of which the one commandeth simply to worship God with pure faith and Godliness, and the other to embrace men with unfained love." This "is the true and eternal rule of righteousness, prescribed to the men of all ages and times

---

[37] Cf. Fortescue, *Politique lawes of England*, sigs. A5^v-A6^v where kings are enjoined, again on the authority of Deuteronomy 17, to study carefully the works of "the chiefest lawmaker Moses."

that will be willing to frame their life to the will of God."[38]
In essence, therefore, Moses' moral law prescribes that
men live according to the dual law of charity—love of God
(the root, as Hooker says, of "all offices of religion towards
God") and love of neighbor (the root of "all laws of duty to
men-ward").[39]

Old Testament ceremonial law, Calvin further explains,
was an external codification—engraved on hard yet perishable tables of stone—of God's required worship. Judicial
law comprised a collection of similarly temporal and temporary precepts enforcing the required love among men.
Each judicial law therefore "tended to no other end, but
how the self-same charity might best be kept which is
commanded by the eternal law of God."[40] It follows therefore that if they are to be truly just, all laws enacted in
post-Mosaic times must conform to the ultimate rule of
charity: "it alone . . . must be both the mark and rule and
end of all laws."[41] King James joins Calvin in basing just
government, ecclesiastical and civil, on "the whole service
of God by man . . . which is nothing else but the exercise of
Religion towards God, and of equity toward your
neighbour" (*BD*, 1:29-31).[42]

In short, the orthodoxy of Shakespeare's period can be
said to agree with an axiom most succinctly put by Bullinger: "the sum of all laws is the love of God and our

[38] *Institutes* 4.20.15; fol. 496ᵛ. Hooker (*Laws*, 1:179-80) explains that this
dual precept, first directly revealed by Christ as the two essential commandments of the law (Matt. 22:36-40), was made available—through the
gift of reason—even to pagans.

[39] Hooker, *Laws*, 1:179-80.   [40] Calvin *Institutes* 4.20.15; fol. 496ᵛ.

[41] Ibid. 4.20.15; fol. 497ʳ. Cf. Bullinger *Decades* 2.1; Parker Society,
7:196.

[42] Probably owing to its Latin root, the somewhat judicial term "equity"
appears to have been commonly used as a synonym for charity. See Calvin, *A Harmonie upon the Three Evangelists*, trans. E[usebius] P[aget] (London: George Bishop, 1584), sig. O4ʳ; William Perkins, *The Whole Treatise of
the Cases of Conscience* (1606; rpt. in facsimile, New York: Da Capo Press,
1972), p. 515.

neighbor."[43] With this epitome, I believe we may safely conclude that, especially for Shakespeare's contemporary audience, the word "law" could carry richly complex horizons of implication. In particular, "law" could refer as readily to invisible or revealed divine laws as to statutory or common ones—and the latter could easily suggest the former as their ideal prototypes.

As contemporary discussions usually reveal, moreover, the fundamental texts that nourished this conflation of civil and sacred conceptions of law were to be found not in the Pentateuch alone but in the Pentateuch as it was glossed by the authors of the New Testament. We may assume provisionally that a Renaissance author intending to use law as the thematic structuring idea of his work would have been aware of key New Testament texts that inform nonliterary discussions of law. In post-Reformation Europe, these texts would include, certainly, Christ's assertion (Matt. 22:36-40) that the two greatest Mosaic laws were the ones commanding love of God (Deut. 6:5) and love of neighbor (Lev. 19:18). It would have been difficult indeed to escape knowledge also of Paul's immensely influential views of law as they are presented throughout the Epistle to the Romans, in Galatians 4-5, and elsewhere. And there is one seminal New Testament statement on law that Shakespeare not only can be assumed to have known, but one that he tells us he both knew and used in *Measure for Measure*—the Sermon on the Mount (Matt. 5-7).

I have already argued that Shakespeare's Duke may allude in scene 1 to an early passage in the illustrious sermon. That allusion raises the possibility that the sermon as a whole may be a continuing source of the play's allusive

---

[43] *Decades* 2.1; Parker Society, 7:193. See also Alexander Nowell, *A Catechism*, ed. George Elwes Corrie, Parker Society (Cambridge: Cambridge University Press, 1853), p. 138: "For all the warnings, commandments, exhortations, promises, and threatenings, which the law itself and the prophets and apostles do everywhere use, are directed to nothing else, but to the end of this law [charity], as it were to a mark."

richness, for, as most will agree, Shakespeare's very title echoes Matt. 7:1-2: "Judge not, that ye be not judged. For with what judgment ye judge, ye shall be judged: and with what measure ye mete, it shall be measured to you again." It is possible, of course, that the title comes instead from Luke 6:37-39 or Mark 4:24, but as with the candlestick allusion, Matthew's version provides a clear context for understanding the passage on judgment and, consequently, the significance of the allusion.

Moreover, the whole of the sermon raises a startling number of issues that reappear prominently in *Measure for Measure*. By using a variety of strategies that will absorb much of our attention later on, Shakespeare in fact establishes the Sermon on the Mount as the primary ethical standard *intrinsic* in *Measure for Measure*. With this in mind, I must ask the reader to work through a brief exposition of key passages of the sermon. I offer in apology for this affliction, first, a promise that patience will be rewarded when we return to the play itself (in this and subsequent chapters) and, second, the observation that both the sermon and the play are statements about law—statements written in similarly suggestive, complex, and hyperbolic styles. Although one is indeed a sermon and one a play, therefore, our understanding of both is conditioned to some extent by their common membership in a vague genre that might be labeled, only half facetiously, "oracular statements about law," a very general class of texts or utterances to which we will unconsciously but inevitably assign them.

Although Matthew's version of the sermon presents the precepts of Christ in an orderly fashion, his ordering principles are unexpressed; and although his Lord speaks at length, therefore, his meaning is veiled in suggestive darkness. As before, we must forge the connections and locate the underlying unity for ourselves. If we consider it carefully in its context, we perceive that the "judge not" pronouncement constitutes a particular application of the sermon's central theme. Taken in isolation, it is, in its apparent prohibition of all judgment, a startling and extravagant statement. But the local context offers necessary qualification: "And why beholdest thou the mote that is in thy brother's eye, but considerest not the beam that is in thine own eye? Or how wilt thou say to thy brother, Let me pull out the mote out of thine eye; and, behold, a beam is in thine own eye? Thou hypocrite, first cast out the beam out of thine own eye; and then shalt thou see clearly to cast out the mote out of thy brother's eye" (Matt. 7:3-5). It would be unsettling indeed to suggest that the Lord here utters a self-consuming artifact. Yet if we can divest ourselves of the sleepy responses with which we habitually greet religious commonplaces, it becomes apparent that the passage does not absolutely forbid judgment of individuals by other individuals.[44] The second line (7:2) assumes that judgments will in fact be made and that an unspecified judge will make an equivalent return.

This interpretation is subsequently confirmed, for the man with the hyperbolic beam in his eye is prohibited from judging only until the obstruction has been removed: "then shalt thou see clearly to cast out the mote out of thy brother's eye." Judgment is not forbidden, therefore, but the manner of proper judgment is specified.[45] One is to judge only after recognizing that he has himself committed greater crimes (probably against the elusive judge of 7:2)—*and* after attempting to purge his own guilt. Matthew appears, furthermore, to suggest the means for this purgation in verses 7-11: "Ask, and it shall be given to you." This procedure of prefacing judgment by self-judgment and petitions for divine aid or forgiveness—forgiveness for carrying logs in our eyes—leads to a summary conclusion that renders explicit the broadest implication of the open-

[44] *Pace* Elizabeth M. Pope, "The Elizabethan Background of *Measure for Measure*," *ShS* 2 (1949):66-82, and the many whom her learned and cogent article has misled on this point.

[45] This specification is elaborated at Matt. 18:15-17.

ing injunction, "Judge not": "Therefore all things what-soever ye would that men should do to you, do ye even so to them: for this is the law and the prophets" (7:12).[46] To recognize one's own frailties before presuming to judge others is to conform to the rule of "equity" engraved in our hearts. We all wish to be judged only by a magistrate or a peer who is aware that our errors result from weaknesses that are or could be as readily his as ours. In short, the "judge not" passage is meant to govern all human judg-ment, private or institutional, and it enjoins that judgments conform to the law of charity, which "is the law and the prophets."

Although this reading of Matt. 7:1-2 is no independent amateur effort[47] (and although dissent is always possible, even likely), it is available to all who read carefully with a clear sense of local context and faith in the integrity of Matthew's text. The interpretation can be tested, fur-thermore, by reference to the wider context of the sermon. Thinking in terms of the structure of the Bible, we can see that Matthew 5-7 presents the first sustained revelation of Christian doctrine or, more precisely, of the New Law. At the beginning of the sermon, this point is made with the quiet artfulness characteristic of Scripture. Christ, "seeing the multitudes," "went up into a mountain." The mountain remains unnamed, its very presence being previously un-mentioned. Yet since Christ has earlier been identified as the antitype of Moses (see especially Matt. 2:20), the moun-

[46] Cf. the Geneva note to Matt. 7:12: "The whole Law and the Scrip-tures set forth unto us, and commend charity." See also Luther's discus-sion of Matt. 7:12 in *The Sermon on the Mount*, in *Luther's Works*, ed. Jaroslav Pelikan and Helmut T. Lehmann, 55 vols. (Philadelphia: Fortress Press, 1955-73), 21:235-40. (Hereafter cited as *Works*.) For a scholarly modern statement of the same argument, see Gerhard Barth, "Matthew's Under-standing of the Law," in *Tradition and Interpretation in Matthew*, ed. Günther Bornkamm, pp. 76-80 (Philadelphia: Westminster Press, 1963).

[47] See, inter alia, J. C. Fenton, *Saint Matthew* (Harmondsworth: Pen-guin, 1963), and David Hill, ed., *The Gospel of St. Matthew*, New Century Bible (London: Oliphants, 1972).

tain is intended to recall that on which the Old Law was given. The point made with artful economy is that the Sermon on that Mount presents the Christian equivalent of the Old Law.[48] These hints become more explicit as Christ delivers his startling series of beatitudes and proceeds to assert that his subsequent statements will lay down the law for Christians, a new law that is mysteriously related to the old: "Think not that I am come to destroy the law, or the prophets: I am not come to destroy, but to fulfil. . . . Till heaven and earth pass, one jot or one tittle shall in no wise pass from the law, till all be fulfilled" (Matt. 5:17-18).

This cryptic introduction (what precisely does "fulfillment" mean?) leads directly to the Savior's reinterpretation, sometimes expressed in hyperbolic metaphor, of salient laws of Moses (Matt. 5:21-48). In each case, Christ internalizes what had been, or had been misinterpreted to be, an ordinance governing external acts. The new ordinances, all of which become important issues in *Measure for Measure*, deal, in order, with murder, lust or adultery, oaths, revenge, and love. They each assert that intents are as serious as acts. Anger, a prime motive of murder, is therefore equivalent to murder. Lustful intent is equivalent to adultery. The old seeming permission to exact an "eye for an eye" becomes an injunction, expressed in audacious hyperbole ("turn the other cheek"), that one be willing to receive a double wrong rather than to desire revenge. The series climaxes in a comprehensive interpretation that is also the first explicit announcement of the New Law's essence:

[48] Fenton, *Saint Matthew*, p. 77. Cf. David Hill, *Gospel of St. Matthew*, p. 109. Early commentators who were trained in the exegetical methods of Renaissance humanism provide exemplary interpretations—and theirs are often the more interesting for being less tentative than modern ones. It may be worth noting here, too, that in his introductory statement on Matthew 5-7 (*Harmonie*, sig. K7ʳ), Calvin maintains that "it was the purpose of . . . [the Evangelist] to gather together into one place the principal points of the doctrine of Christ, which did belong to the rule of godly and holy life."

Ye have heard that it hath been said, Thou shalt love thy neighbour, and hate thine enemy. But I say unto you, Love your enemies, bless them that curse you, do good to them that hate you, and pray for them which despitefully use you, and persecute you; That ye may be the children of your Father which is in heaven: for he maketh his sun to rise on the evil and on the good, and sendeth rain on the just and on the unjust. . . . Be ye therefore perfect, even as your Father which is in heaven is perfect.

[Matt. 5:43-48]

A modern reader attuned to the unobtrusive artfulness of Matthew may find here an explanation of the mysterious idea that "the law and the prophets" are to be "fulfilled" by Christ. This fulfillment is to occur, that is, by means of a perfect, indiscriminate love, patterned on that of the Father who daily benefits both friend and enemy.[49] Christ's new covenant is therefore simpler than the old, for it is reducible, as Matt. 7:12 confirms, to the single law of charitable love. And yet, like the measure-for-measure passage itself, this ethical ideal contains a manifest self-contradiction. For in both Hebrew and Christian traditions, the perfection of the Father is utterly unattainable by men (cf. 7:11 "If ye then, being evil"). As human experience indicates, to avoid all anger, all secret lust, all hatred of enemies is beyond the power of man. While it is characterized on the one hand by sublime simplicity, therefore, the New Law is also simply impossible to obey.[50]

---

[49] "Indiscriminate love" does not imply the destruction of institutions necessary for social order. It ensures instead that those institutions have the good of the subject as their true end, and it recognizes that that good sometimes includes punishment. This implication of the New Law is as available to readers today as it was to commentators from patristic times through the Reformation. It resides in the wider context of the Gospels, a context that unerringly gives Caesar his due.

[50] Protestant doctrine provided a way out of this unsettling apparent contradiction by arguing that men may participate, by grace, in Christ's

This implication becomes a prime consideration as
Matthew moves from Christ's revaluation of Old Law ethical precepts to rules governing the worship of God, which
are also, as we shall see, an issue in *Measure for Measure*.
This section manifests a rigorous dualism as it locates the
essence of worship in inner piety and warns against allowing external acts of devotion to encourage vainglory:
"Take heed that ye do not your alms before men, to be
seen of them: otherwise ye have no reward of your Father
which is in heaven" (Matt. 6:1). They are hypocrites who
give alms or pray "standing in the synagogues and in the
corners of the streets, that they may be seen of men" (Matt.
6:5). To pray rightly, by contrast, is to pray "in secret" and
according to the pattern set down in the Lord's Prayer, a
statement whose central drift corresponds to the implications of the candlestick reference—that is, it concerns the
dual concept of total submission to the glory and will of
God and concomitant abasement of self. We implicitly confess our imperfection and unsuitability for glory in the petition "And forgive us our debts, as we forgive our debtors"
(Matt. 6:12). The centrality of the petition for forgiveness
is reaffirmed by the footnote Matthew adds to the prayer:
"For if ye forgive men their trespasses, your heavenly
Father will also forgive you: But if ye forgive not men
their trespasses, neither will your Father forgive your trespasses" (Matt. 6:14-15).

Like the "judge not" passage, Christ's admonition to love
one's enemies (5:43-48) and this gloss on the petition for
forgiveness are particular instances of the sermon's essential burden. Charity based on the simultaneous recognition
of divine perfection and of one's own *inevitable* offenses
(the beams in one's eye) *is* the New Law to be observed
toward all men at all times, "for this is the law and the
prophets." Matt. 6:14-15, furthermore, along with the sub-

---

perfection, but it also insisted that men recognize the Law's disconcertingly extreme demands. See chap. 2, below.

sequent passage concerning man's dependence on providence (6:24-34), allows us to determine that God is the
judge who will return measure for measure. If we wish him
to judge us mercifully, we will grant merciful judgment to
other men.[51] For according to the vengeance that is solely
his, God will return an absolute and a just measure for
measure.[52] In sum, therefore, the measure-for-measure
text enjoins (and threatens divine enforcement of) judgment in harmony with the New Law's newly promulgated
essence.

Having placed his play's titular source in its scriptural
context, we may return to Shakespeare's text. As I suggested earlier, interpreters unaware of the scriptural background will begin to form ideas about law merely from the
play's title, which entirely on its own suggests retribution.
But whether we recognize it or not, a central idea of the
scriptural measure-for-measure text is enacted in the play's
first speech:

Of government the properties to unfold
Would seem in me t'affect speech and discourse,
Since I am put to know that your own science
Exceeds, in that, the lists of all advice
My strength can give you.

[1.1.3-7]

[51] In the Geneva version, Luke provides the alternative reading that
"men" will return the measure we give them. Commentators now, as in
earlier ages, regard the readings as complementary, not contradictory—
and therefore can save us from the puzzlement that troubled Elizabeth
Pope ("Elizabethan Background," passim) and, she thought, troubled
Shakespeare. See David Hill, *Gospel of St. Matthew*, p. 146; Calvin, *Harmonie*, O1[v]; and Erasmus, *The First [second] tome or volume of the Paraphrase
of Erasmus upon the Newe Testamente*, 2 vols. (London: E. Whitchurche,
1548-49), 1, fol. G2[r] and F6[v].

[52] Fenton, *Saint Matthew*, suggests a useful gloss from Ps. 18:25-26:
"With the merciful thou wilt shew thyself merciful; with an upright man
thou wilt shew thyself upright; / With the pure thou wilt shew thyself
pure; and with the froward thou wilt shew thyself froward."

"Government" introduces the theme of law in its social and political aspects—and adds an overtone of self-government, the control one exercises over one's own actions. More significantly still, the passage also originates the theme of humility that is promoted with greater clarity by the imagery of stamps, figures, and torches: the Duke is "put [i.e., compelled] to know" that Escalus's administrative expertise exceeds his own. The first judgment in a play filled with judgments, then, is a self-judgment in which the Duke exhibits a becoming deference toward one of his subjects. This apparently objective self-assessment is Shakespeare's first covert dramatization of a central implication of his play's scriptural source: the Duke shows himself suited to judge others by his willingness first to judge and therefore accurately to "know himself" (cf. 3.2.226-27 and see chap. 4, below). Similar allusions to and dramatizations of fundamental ideas of the Sermon on the Mount recur throughout *Measure for Measure*. They ensure that that central statement of Christian law, especially its insistence on humane judgment, becomes an intrinsic standard by which we judge Shakespeare's characters and their actions.

Returning to the speech at hand, we should note that "lists" initiates a pattern of diction and imagery closely related to the themes of dependence and of law. The word suggests limits on the Duke's powers. It functions loosely as a synonym for "law," which in its most general sense is a rule or system of rules that governs action, a limit within whose scope one may exercise his powers. "Lists" belongs, therefore, to the category of words represented also by "nature" (considered as determinant and standard of human behavior), "scope," "restraint," "contract," "order," "bond," "circummur'd," "vow," and their numerous synonyms and variants. "Scope" and "restraint" will later become especially prominent, for they express economically the paradoxical idea of freedom within limitation, a restricted sphere within which one must exercise his talents.[53] To Escalus, uncommon scope is allowed because his talents are uncommonly great:

> Then no more remains
> But that, to your sufficiency, as your worth is able,
> And let them work.

[1.1.7-9]

There is textual corruption here, but we may be sure nevertheless that emphasis is given to the deputy's sufficiency, his worth or ability to work effectively. He is to work within limits set not only by

> the nature of our people,
> Our city's institutions, and the terms
> For common justice

[1.1.9-11]

but also by another kind of law, this one embodied in a stage property and waved tantalizingly before our eyes here and later (1.47)—"There is our commission" (1.13).

These documents visibly contribute to this scene's oblique fixation on law, the play's central subject. As a further example of this fixation, we may point to the moral of the "Heaven does with us" speech: it is heaven's self-imposed rule of proceeding to grant powers for particular purposes, and we are obliged, by a law paraphrased from the Sermon on the Mount, to use those powers in the world. Similarly, the theme of human powers and their scope closes the scene, keeping it firmly in the interrogative mood—and keeping us in a corresponding attitude of curiosity. Although Angelo's scope, we are told, is equivalent to the Duke's, it is nonetheless hedged about by the

---

[53] Michael Goldman (*Energies of the Drama*, p. 166) puts this well: " 'Scope' suggests not only liberty but license—an opportunity for 'too much liberty' (I, ii, 129)—but it also suggests limitation, a prescribed arena in which one is free to move. 'Restraint' implies a loss of liberty, but (to a lesser degree) suggests control and balance as well."

terms of the commission. We are left at the conclusion of
scene 1 asking the question that preoccupies Escalus:

> A power I have, but of what strength and nature
> I am not yet instructed.
>
> [1.1.79-80]

While he thus elicits our questions about a key theme in
the scene, Shakespeare further excites our frustrated desire for information and aggravates our sense of the Duke's
enigmatic nature. For although the Duke offers to comment at last on one of his motives, he contrives to do so in
an obscure and self-contradictory way:

> I'll privily away. I love the people,
> But do not like to stage me to their eyes:
> Though it do well, I do not relish well
> Their loud applause and *Aves* vehement.
>
> [1.1.67-70]

As we shall see, this ambivalence is not inexplicable, but it
is, deliberately, obscurely put. What does "it" "do well"?

One further point to be made about the Duke is that, at
the end as at the beginning of the scene, he absolutely dominates. The most suggestive poetry is his. He has monopo-
lized our attention and engaged our curiosity so firmly that
we await eagerly, even in the scenes before he reassumes
direct control of the plot, further information about him.
If we should be inclined to forget him, he returns (in 1.3
and 2.3) to remind us that the real power in Shakespeare's
Vienna is present and watching unobserved.[54] Even in the
Duke's absence from the stage other figures stir our curiosity by speculating repeatedly on his activities, and this
speculation begins the very moment he departs (1.2.1-3,
163-64; 1.4.50-55). It is evident, then, that from the beginning of the play Shakespeare labors to make his Duke the
focus of our most pressing questions. His dominance in the

---

[54] Kirsch, "Integrity of *Measure for Measure*," p. 103.

second half is not new; it is simply more overt and comprehensive. Duke Vincentio there begins to control the actions of his fellow characters as he increasingly dominates
the spectators' attention.

It follows that the master key to understanding the play's
meaning and form is, as many have asserted, Duke Vincentio. Our responses to him provide one of the work's essential sources of coherence. That coherence is not diffused by
the mysteries and discontinuities and self-contradictions of
his character, for this problematic characterization fits the
Duke to the peculiar nature both of scene 1 and of the plot
he later initiates and governs. As we have seen, enigma
pervades *Measure for Measure* as fully as it does narratives of
the Old Testament and oracles of the New. It is this persistently enigmatic quality that leads to a final observation
necessary to accurate recognition of the play's generic
identity. The enigmatic tone, evident in the play's opening
lines and early scenes, hints from the outset that *Measure
for Measure* may be related to the fertile Renaissance tradition of allegorical literature.

The term asks cautious definition. Allegory is no genre
in the traditional sense. Considered broadly, it is nearly
identical with the conventional Elizabethan theory of
poetry, a theory maintaining that real poetry by its very nature communicates truth—theological, moral, political, or
scientific—through enigmatic veils. Viewed more narrowly, allegory is, as the rhetoricians maintained, a continued metaphor in which the narrative or dramatic fiction
is persistently shadowed by "a second narrative, or a pattern of ideas—an argument, or any program of alternate
significances with some topological similarity to the original
literary pattern."[55] This penumbra of second meanings is
introduced, as in *Measure for Measure*, "by allusion, or by

[55] For fine short introductions to Renaissance allegory, see Thomas P.
Roche, Jr., *The Kindly Flame: A Study of the Third and Fourth Books of
Spenser's "Faerie Queene"* (Princeton: Princeton University Press, 1964),
chap. 1, and James Nohrnberg, *The Analogy of "The Faerie Queene"* (Prince-

some reference extrinsic to the ostensible fictional frame-
work. The pattern of such allusions forms the allegory."[56]

Thus defined, allegory is a very common literary phe-
nomenon, nearly coextensive with literature itself, all
commentary being in a sense allegorization, all intentional
meaning that transcends the letter of the text being allegory. It is more common than many critics realize, therefore, because we are still captive in part to the formulation
of Goethe and other Romantic authors who were concerned to elevate, at the expense of allegory, a mystical
conception of symbolism.[57] Allegory should not be limited
to the mere personification of abstractions, a reduction apparent in English criticism as early as Johnson's "Life of
Milton," nor should it be restricted to the psychomachia
form, in which faculties of one mind struggle for suprem-
acy in the continuing internecine wars of the spirit. Allegory can take many forms and enrich portions of any narrative in which the author chooses to stress intellectual or
instructional content.

It can also be present, and this is always important in
dealing with Shakespeare, in varying degrees of intensity.
Northrop Frye uses this fact to classify allegories according
to their levels of explicitness. The relatively pure allegorist,
Tasso or Spenser or Bunyan, attempts clearly "to indicate
how a commentary on him should proceed." Shakespeare
occupies the exact center of Frye's "sliding scale," which
ranges "from the most explicitly allegorical . . . at one extreme, to the most elusive, anti-explicit and anti-allegorical
at the other." Shakespeare's middle-of-the road ranking

---

ton: Princeton University Press, 1976), pp. 89-102. The present quotation
is from Nohrnberg, p. 94.

[56] Nohrnberg, *Analogy*, pp. 93-94.

[57] See Paul de Man, "The Rhetoric of Temporality," in *Interpretation:
Theory and Practice*, ed. Charles S. Singleton (Baltimore: Johns Hopkins
University Press, 1969), pp. 173-210; Angus Fletcher, *Allegory: Theory of a
Symbolic Mode* (Ithaca: Cornell University Press, 1964), p. 13, esp. n. 24.

stems from the tactful obliquity that determines that his "structure of imagery," though suggestive, is related only implicitly to thematic content.[58] Another criterion for measuring the allegorical intensity of a given work is the importance of the allegory in shaping the fiction.[59] This criterion assumes sovereign importance for an accurate understanding of the latter half of *Measure for Measure* (see below, chap. 5).

Throughout the play, however, typical features of the allegorical mode solicit our attention. Prominent among these is the portentous, oracular tone—allegory's distinguishing music (*melos*)[60]—generated, as we have noticed at length, by powerfully evocative imagery, mysterious ellipses, surprising juxtapositions, and concurrent obscurity. While qualities like these destroy mimetic naturalness, they enhance the power of allegorical texts to challenge us to active interpretation. They thus account for the peculiarly active state of mind provoked by successful allegory. Ellipsis in speech, which fragments the utterance and gives it, as Angus Fletcher says, "the appearance of a coded message needing to be deciphered"[61] induces a similar kind of mental activity.

Because of this typically riddling elusiveness, sophisticated allegory communicates a great part of its meaning through silence. "The silences in allegory mean as much as the filled-in spaces, because by bridging the silent gaps be-

[58] Frye, *Anatomy*, pp. 90-91.

[59] Nohrnberg, *Analogy*, p. 94.

[60] I have appropriated Professor Nohrnberg's helpfully systematic description of allegory in terms of Aristotle's six parts of poetry. See *Analogy*, pp. 95-101.

[61] Fletcher, *Allegory*, p. 107. See also pp. 101-107 and cf. Michael Murrin, *The Veil of Allegory: Some Notes toward a Theory of Allegorical Rhetoric in the English Renaissance* (Chicago: University of Chicago Press, 1969), pp. 55-58. Murrin is himself covering ground traversed earlier by Rosemond Tuve, *Allegorical Imagery: Some Mediaeval Books and Their Posterity* (Princeton: Princeton University Press, 1966), pp. 246-47.

tween oddly unrelated images, we reach the sunken under-structure of thought (the biblical exegetes' 'underthought,' *hyponoia*, the Russian schoolboy's 'undertext')."[62] To revert to the Aristotelian terminology, we might say that by sup-plying omissions in an elliptical text, we reconstruct its hid-den and supervisory intellectual theme (*dianoia*). This is the point of the allusive and alluring obscurity I earlier iden-tified as the rhetorical mode of *Measure for Measure*. It si-multaneously demands interpretation and supplies a struc-ture of allusions that guide our interpretive efforts.

The obscurity of style and characterization we observe in the play serves well to provoke active analysis and interpre-tation—and it leads us to expect that subsequent portions of the play will demand continued effort to decipher mean-ingful silences.[63] In addition, the obscurity of scene 1 foreshadows difficulties we are soon to have with the Duke's plot, especially with the problematic and improba-ble substitution of Mariana for Isabella. Having recognized that early scenes declare the play's allegorical proclivities, we are prepared for surprising turns of event and may therefore recognize the notorious "bed trick" and the climactic universal forgiveness as instances of the deliber-ately startling action characteristic of romance in general but especially of allegorical plots (allegory's typical *mythos*). Murrin, who prefers to call this the "absurdity principle" in allegory, aptly cites Chapman's prefatory letter to the *Odys-sey*: "If the Body (being the letter, or history) seems fictive,

[62] Fletcher, *Allegory*, p. 107.

[63] On the importance of meaningful silence in one of Western litera-ture's greatest allegories, *The Romance of the Rose*, see Tuve, *Allegorical Imagery*, pp. 243-46. For the seminal medieval rationale for obscurity in allegorical poetry, see Augustine's *De doctrina Christiana* and the commen-tary in D. W. Robertson, Jr., *A Preface to Chaucer* (Princeton: Princeton University Press, 1962), chap. 2. Cf. Fletcher, *Allegory*, pp. 234-35. The Augustinian doctrine on obscurity in poetry was summarized for Elizabethan schoolchildren in Erasmus's textbook, *De copia rerum ac ver-bum*. See the translation by D. B. King and H. D. Rix (Milwaukee: Univer-sity of Wisconsin Press, 1963), p. 70.

and beyond possibility to bring into Act: the scene then and Allegory (which is the soul) is to be sought."[64]

To understand the silences that help us to discover the "soul" of *Measure for Measure*, we must, as I have said, concentrate on the Duke. It has become an accepted critical orthodoxy to assert that the Duke exists in *Measure for Measure* as an alien type altogether unlike the other characters, and therefore that we cannot analyze him "as if he were a 'mere character, an actor among the others' . . . because he will not stand up under the kind of analysis which we can give with no effort at all to, say, Lucio or Barnardine."[65] This errs in two directions: It assumes both that the Duke is more alien than he is and that the other characters, including Isabella, Angelo, and Claudio, are much more complex, three-dimensional, and "realistic" than they in fact are. I suggest and expect to demonstrate that the Duke and the rest in fact share a very limited range of characteristics. They all have in common a narrowness sometimes dimly recognized even by critics who at other times praise their realistic variety.[66] This is not to suggest, of course, that they altogether lack idiosyncrasy. One notable idiosyncratic characteristic of the Duke is his marked fondness for aphorism, a partiality of which numerous examples leap to mind (e.g., 3.2.254-75; 4.2.110-11). This linguistic trait be-

[64] Murrin, *Veil of Allegory*, pp. 146-47; cf. Tuve, *Allegorical Imagery*, p. 222, n. 1, and Nohrnberg, *Analogy*, pp. 99-101.

[65] Hawkins, *Likenesses of Truth*, p. 62, quoting Leavis.

[66] Hawkins, *Likenesses of Truth*, p. 54: "The three are all absolutists. Angelo is absolute for the letter of the law, then for Isabella. Isabella is absolute for chastity. Claudio soon becomes absolute for life." It may be helpful to consider that all mimesis, being itself a selection from material filtered through the categorizing web of language, which is itself controlled in part by subjective expectations and preoccupations, tends toward the constriction that marks allegorical figures. Shakespeare most likely meant to hold the mirror up to nature in his imitation of Claudio, Isabella, and Angelo, but his glass was more selective than were those of Dickens, George Eliot, and James—and of the Shakespeare who wrote *Hamlet* and *King Lear*.

comes most prominent as the action approaches its final
climax:

> Haste still pays haste, and leisure answers leisure;
> Like doth quit like, and Measure still for Measure.
>
> [5.1.408-9]

Clearly, the Duke's taste for gnomic utterance not only is
part of his individuality, it is also important in furthering
the play's themes. I shall discuss the thematic significance
of this speech later. Here, however, we should note that
proverbial utterance is an element of the characteristic diction (*lexis*) of allegory.[67] The Duke's habit of speech
deepens our conscious or unconscious sense that *Measure
for Measure* belongs to the eclectic class of allegorical texts
that declare, sometimes quite explicitly, their didactic designs.

Despite considerable verisimilitude, however, each of the
major characters in *Measure for Measure* exhibits the con-
stricted meaning typical of allegorical figures who are limited "in an almost psychological way. . . . What is felt as a
narrowed iconographic meaning is known to us readers
through the hero's characteristic way of acting, which is severely limited in variety."[68] Although all the major characters exhibit this restricted, typically allegorical *ethos*, the
Duke does differ from the others, and his difference results
primarily from the obscurity of his motives. We know what

[67] Nohrnberg, *Analogy*, p. 96.

[68] Fletcher, *Allegory*, p. 38. Fletcher also argues (p. 40) that we sometimes meet living allegories as we go about our day-to-day affairs: "if we
were to meet an allegorical character in real life, we would say of him that
he was obsessed with only one idea, or that he had an absolutely one-track
mind, or that his life was patterned according to absolutely rigid habits
from which he never allowed himself to vary." This suggests that "life" as
we perceive it can sometimes be less various than allegory. Since the rule
in Renaissance allegories, as Roche (*Kindly Flame*, chap. 1) and Tuve (*Allegorical Imagery*, passim, esp. p. 222, n. 1) point out, is flexibility of signification, obsessive and compulsive people can be less flexible than Redcrosse Knight.

Angelo, and Isabella, and Claudio, and Mariana want to achieve. The vagueness of the Duke's motives, as well as his dominance, joins with the evocative nature of his language to demand that we extrapolate from what we do know. And what the allusions in scene 1 repeatedly tell us, especially in lines 16-45, is that Duke Vincentio acts in a way analogous to God himself. We are compelled to view him as a human link, with human limitations (ll.5-7), in a great chain, delegating to Angelo gifts that heaven first delegated to him.[69] Although we recognize this analogy at the outset, later scenes may fulfill, modify, or subvert the expectations raised here. As a provisional hypothesis, however, I suggest that Shakespeare makes the analogy apparent, first, to provide certain standards by which the Duke's subsequent behavior is to be judged—we now expect godlike actions and are often invited to "come to judge"; and, second, to render the Duke an apt vehicle for the cosmic implications his language introduces in scene 1. That is, the Duke's mysterious characterization is designed in part to further meanings appropriate to what Tuve considers allegory proper—to matters, that is, not merely of ethical but of spiritual import.[70]

This kind of allegorical implication is tactfully present in *Measure for Measure*, and to see this most clearly we had best begin by returning to the theme of law and its power to determine our perceptions of the play's major characters. This emphasis on character as it is conditioned by theme is appropriate, because the structure of the play can best be described as a series of rigorously logical interactions among carefully defined figures. The necessary precondition for these interactions is established by the Duke's mysterious departure, and, after the characters have been

---

[69] Pope, "Elizabethan Background," pp. 70-71, demonstrates that the analogy was a contemporary commonplace. The commonplace is activated and made apparent by details worked repeatedly into the texture of the language.

[70] *Allegorical Imagery*, pp. 13-15.

given scope to act toward one another as their particular natures decree, the Duke begins (in 2.3) to treat his fellows in ways designed to provoke our questions. We are repeatedly forced into an analytic frame of mind by the very opacity of his motives for treating others as he does. Not only the chief character of the play, therefore, but also the entire plot, a sequence of actions increasingly of the Duke's own contriving, exhibit one of the central features of allegory. They persistently compel us to fill in silences that themselves contain essential elements of the play's meaning.

As we move past the play's first scenes, then, we anticipate that the type of language we are to deal with is likely to contain a statement centered on the theme of law, more precisely on man's relationship to common as well as eternal law in its varying manifestations. That statement, we further expect, will be channeled within the conventions of romantic comedy (or tragicomedy), and its language, characterization, and plot will show strong affinities with the allegorical mode. Having gained this provisional, broad yet narrowing generic conception, we will be less than ordinarily prone to make inappropriate or prematurely reductive critical judgments.

Chapter 2

The Law and the Convent

Law and the attendant ideas of scope and restraint, powers and their limits, receive varied expression in the scenes that precede the great dramatic and problematic confrontations of *Measure for Measure*. From the beginning of scene 2, however, that variousness tends increasingly to focus first on divine law, then, more narrowly, on a specific human elaboration of divine law. The play gradually focuses our attention, that is, on monastic rules, and in doing so it announces generic affinities with a specialized and, in Shakespeare's age, widely current type of literary statement,[1] a rich and vigorous tradition of antimonastic polemic and satire. As I demonstrate in the next few paragraphs, *Measure for Measure* demands unusually careful and detailed thought about monasticism and its doctrinal and human implications. Because this subject bulks very large in the play and because it constituted an important element of Shakespeare's intellectual environment, a comprehensive survey of contemporary statements about monasticism is both historically significant and necessary for interpreting *Measure for Measure*. In chapter 3, we can turn at last directly to the play and examine Shakespeare's use of conventional attitudes toward the devoted life. He employs these conventions, above all, to characterize the play's most conspicuous protagonist, Isabella, a figure

---

[1] I do not mean "literary" in the usual, exclusively belles-lettristic sense. I refer instead to the world of "letters" of which the consciously artful is a small and specialized part.

whose nature is related in significant ways to the contemporary genre of antimonastic satire.

Our readiness to respond to prominent features of this
rather specialized genre is carefully prepared well before
we meet Isabella herself. We have noticed clear theological
overtones in scene 1. In scene 2, theological references become bold and persistent as Shakespeare begins to develop
the specifically religious implications potentially present in
the theme of law. These references have gone unnoticed in
published criticism partly, I suspect, because the author's
spokesmen here are Lucio and his dissipated colleagues.
Their tone cannot be described as religious, nor does their
humor transcend the mediocre; yet, as often happens in
Shakespeare, comedy conceals thematic utility. The law
Lucio urges on our attention is quite centrally the law of
God:

1 Gent.   Heaven grant us its peace, but not the King of
              Hungary's!
2 Gent.   Amen.
Lucio.   Thou conclud'st like the sanctimonious pirate,
              that went to sea with the Ten Commandments, but
              scrap'd one out of the table.

                                                    [1.2.4-9]

The opening echo of the Litany ("Heaven grant . . .") and
the reference to the commandments initiate this bawdy
scene's obsession with liturgical allusion, religious law, and
self-interested reinterpretation of that law:

     There's not a soldier of us all that, in the thanksgiving
     before meat, do relish the petition well that prays for
     peace.

                                                    [1.2.14-16]

Even more directly than the sanctimonious pirate, this sol-
dier would allow personal inclinations to subvert divine law
and the peace its observance should bring.

Although law is the focus of religious references in this scene, grace receives due attention:

Lucio.   . . . I think thou never wast where grace was said.
2 Gent.   No? A dozen times at least.
1 Gent.   What, in metre?
Lucio.   In any proportion, or in any language.
1 Gent.   I think, or in any religion.
Lucio.   Ay, why not? Grace is grace, despite of all controversy;

[1.2.18-25]

For us, Lucio's remark[2] serves to evoke the larger historical context of an age in which religious controversy was rife. His jocular point, as acceptable to orthodox Anglicans as to a libertine like himself, is that human disagreements do not affect the essentials of belief—grace transcends the partial understandings and the puny struggles of men. From grace we turn again to law:

Lucio.   I have purchased as many diseases under her roof as come to—
2 Gent.   To what I pray?
Lucio.   Judge.

[1.2.42-45]

Lucio's pun alludes to the familiar formula in the creed, recalling specifically its prophecy of apocalyptic judgment: "From thence shall he come to judge the quick and the dead."[3] In its literal sense, the remark suggests that Lucio's diseases have "Come to judge," that he has received justice

[2] In which, unhappily, I fail to see the allusion, often asserted to be there, to Rom. 11:6—though that allusion would suit my interpretation admirably.

[3] The statement appears, of course, in the Apostles' Creed that was recited by priest and congregation at morning prayer; it recurs slightly modified in the Nicene Creed, recited at Holy Communion. See *The Book of Common Prayer, 1559*, pp. 58, 251.

in painful measure. The allusion, however, reminds us of
the promised end, and therefore of the origin, ultimate val-
idation, and goal of all justice.

Although they are comic and quite random, Lucio's repeated references to divine law prepare for preoccupations
that soon begin visibly to dominate the play. If we remain
conscious that dramatic meaning arises from visual as well
as verbal elements, we begin to understand why *Measure for
Measure* continues to mystify so many of its critics, for no
reading so far published has accounted for its single most
striking visual effect.[4] This effect, one that Shakespeare
chose—without any hint from his sources—to keep directly
before our eyes throughout most of the play, results from
his decision to dress two major characters as well as several
minor ones in the robes of the regular clergy.

Although monks, nuns, and friars appear with some frequency in plays of Shakespeare's period,[5] in *Measure for
Measure* their prominence is unique. This fixation on
monastic imagery originates in scene 3, when Duke Vincentio appears with Friar Thomas in his monastery, praises
the "life removed," and arranges to acquire the habit that
he continues to wear, with one short interval, until the
climactic peripeteia of act 5. While reading the play we are
prone to forget this costuming. We forget likewise that
after she departs from her convent, Isabella's very appearance continues to announce her intended profession (cf.
2.4.18), and that she constantly carries with her, in full view
of a theater audience, whatever implications the playwright
has given to the convent. Many critics also overlook the related fact that Isabella first appears inside the convent of·
St. Clare, where a nun (named Francisca in the stage directions) relates for her novice and for us an excerpt of the

[4] This judgment applies also to the recent treatment by Rosalind Miles
(*Problem of "Measure for Measure,"* pp. 167-75; 216-17), who discusses at
some length the monastic elements in the play but fails to recognize their
significance.

[5] Ibid., pp. 169-72.

rule under which St. Clare's votarists live (1.4.7-14). As a result of understandable scholarly inattention to such matters, Shakespeare's chosen visual effects fail to color our interpretation of the play's language and our sense of relative emphasis in ways he clearly intended. The obvious monastic materials I have mentioned are supported, furthermore, by numerous less obtrusive ones. But even taken by themselves, they indicate that monasticism receives insistent emphasis in *Measure for Measure*. Shakespeare's aim in giving his play its ostentatiously religious and specifically Roman Catholic aura therefore demands careful attention.

We have, as it happens, some unusual and telling evidence that the self-consciously Catholic elements of *Measure for Measure* were apparent to one careful, nearly contemporary reader. Sometime in the mid-seventeenth century, Father William Sankey, S.J., an official censor for the Holy Office, expurgated a copy of Shakespeare's Second Folio in preparation for its use by students of the English College at Valladolid. Of the entire Shakespeare canon, Father Sankey judged only *Measure for Measure* totally unfit for the chaste eyes of the students; the play was "neatly cut out with a sharp instrument."[6] Since the play has proved so difficult for its interpreters, any information about contemporary response may be helpful. Sankey's action consequently affords intriguing matter for scholarly speculation. Accordingly, Roland Frye has inferred "that *Measure for Measure* obviously did not seem so very Christian to this Jesuit censor. . . . That much appears quite indisputable."[7] But to assume that the Jesuit censor was necessarily reacting to broadly anti-Christian implications in Shakespeare seems disputable in the highest degree. Inquisitors often seek more limited ends, and in an age of vitriolic religious controversy, Sankey probably reacted as

---

[6] For a thorough account of this early exercise in Shakespearean bowdlerism, see Roland Mushat Frye, *Shakespeare and Christian Doctrine* (Princeton: Princeton University Press, 1963), appendix.

[7] Ibid., p. 291.

sensitively to anti-Catholic as he did to anti-Christian ideas. (For him, most likely, the two did not greatly differ.) And since the play exhibits a patently Roman Catholic coloration, Sankey's action should increase our determination to attend with special care to Shakespeare's treatment of the Old Faith.

This undertaking must itself begin with a brief account of the attitudes that Elizabethan and Jacobean Englishmen might have entertained concerning the regular clergy. Although we have monks and nuns among us today, their role in society and in the life of the church is seldom a burning issue in the minds of thoughtful men. In Shakespeare's period, the situation was somewhat different; for though the religious houses in England had been dissolved in 1539, treatments of monasticism continued to appear with considerable frequency in influential English books throughout the century. As we shall see, the question of monastic devotion retained this vitality because it brought into focus a fundamental doctrinal conflict between Catholics and Protestants, a disparity that bulked large in the religious controversies of Shakespeare's lifetime. The issue of the devoted life was so commonplace, in fact, that Shakespeare and his contemporaries could hardly have avoided hearing or reading detailed considerations of the life of monks and of their relationships to God and to their fellowmen. We therefore may infer that Shakespeare's contemporaries brought to the theater preconceived ideas— ideas held with individual and therefore varying degrees of conviction and with equally varying degrees of clarity and complexity—about friars, monks, and nuns. These orthodoxies constituted shared ideas or types that the playwright could exploit to communicate meaning. These typical ideas were shaped by two major intellectual currents: (1) the tradition of medieval antifraternal satire descending from Guillaume de Saint-Amour and (2) the advent of Reformation theology. The latter in its antimonastic aspect represents both a renascence and an extension of the former.

Although it may at first appear anachronistic to link the names of Shakespeare and Guillaume de Saint-Amour, it is useful to recollect that during the English Renaissance Geoffrey Chaucer was considered the unparalleled patriarch of English letters. His prestige is confirmed not only by adulatory comments of poets like Spenser, but by the more tangible fact that his works appeared in no fewer than fourteen editions between 1532 and 1604. As is well known, Chaucer's work also provided Shakespeare with source material for elements of *A Midsummer Night's Dream*, *Troilus and Cressida*, and *Two Nobel Kinsmen*. Therefore, unless we assume that Renaissance readers like Shakespeare overlooked Chaucer's portraits of the Friar in the "General Prologue," in the *Summoner's Tale*, and in the partial (and as we have since learned, at least partially spurious) translation of the *Roman de la Rose*, we must recognize that one of the most prestigious of Shakespeare's literary ancestors helped guarantee Guillaume's antifraternal satire a certain currency even when the King's Men first produced *Measure for Measure*.[8]

Remarkably, the failings that Chaucer's antifraternal writings attribute bluntly to friars and nuns include a number of characteristics that Shakespeare, as we shall see, tactfully ascribes to Isabella. The bluntest Chaucerian or pseudo-Chaucerian attack on the regulars appears in Fragment C of the *Romaunt*, where Guillaume de Saint-Amour's manifold criticisms of mendicancy are personified in Jean de Meun's Fals-Semblant. In his elaborate sermon on the text "abit ne maketh neither monk ne frere" (l.6192).[9] Fals-Semblant reveals that he inhabits, indeed possesses like an evil demon, men and women of all walks

---

[8] On Chaucer's own debt to the tradition of antifraternal polemic inaugurated by Guillaume de Saint-Amour and extended by Jean de Meun, see Arnold Williams, "Chaucer and the Friars," *Speculum* 28 (1953): 499-513.

[9] I quote Chaucer throughout from *The Works of Geoffrey Chaucer*, ed. F. N. Robinson, 2d ed. (Boston: Houghton Mifflin, 1957). Further references appear in my text.

of life. But because hypocrisy finds its "sikerest hidyng . . . undirnethe humblest clothing" (ll.6147-48), he favors the aspect of an "hooly heremyte" (l.6481). In the *Romaunt*, this disguise includes "the cope of a frer" (l.7408). Fals-Semblant employs his religious costume simply to camouflage his besetting sins of pride and avarice, sins manifested in his cupidity for "worship of this world" and for "gret pitaunces" not to mention "gode morcels delicious" and "good wyn precious" (ll.6173-80).

Fals-Semblant's spiritual kin and literary offspring, the Friar of the *Summoner's Tale*, betrays his avarice and luxury more obliquely but no less clearly. He is still more direct concerning the pride that Fals-Semblant appears to consider an occupational malady of friars. Membership in a fraternity, the Summoner's Friar implies, confers spiritual value superior to that of ordinary men. Wasn't the Lord thinking especially of friars when he remarked "Blessed be they that povere in spirit been" (l.1923)? Don't the ascetic efforts of the friars confer special value on their prayers (ll.1883-89, 1906-14, 1936-41)? By claiming special access to the ear of the heavenly King—and bolstering his claim with contempt for the laity and the secular clergy—Chaucer's Friar exhibits remarkable "poverte of spirit."

Since the proud and avaricious are as a rule ill-disposed to love their enemies, the friars show a marked inclination to avenge insults to their inflated self-esteem and encroachments on their equally inflated ecclesiastical revenues. Vindictiveness therefore characterizes Jean de Meun's lupine Frere Wolf (ll.6429-32). It is equally characteristic of the Summoner's Friar, who preaches a delightfully ill-applied homily demonstrating that "ire is, in sooth, executour of pryde" (l.2010).[10] Shortly thereafter, the Friar unwittingly becomes his own exemplum, waxing "wood for ire" (l.2121) at Thomas's flatulent assault on his

---

[10] Cf. Chaucer's Parson, who adduces the relevant commonplaces of moral theology: (1) "He that is proud . . . is lightly wroth" and (2) "Ire, after the discryvyng of Seint Augustyn, is wikked wil to been avenged by word or by dede" (*Parson's Tale* ll.534-35).

dignity and vowing revenge by deed or by word ("I shal disclaundre hym," l.2212). Slander, according to antifraternal polemic, was a weapon much favored by the garrulous and articulate friars.

Vindictiveness is an appropriate trait for friars as they are depicted by antifraternal satirists. In religion, Fals-Semblant confides, he takes the "strawe" and leaves the "corn" (l.6354). This renders explicit Fals-Semblant's deepest thematic significance in the *Roman de la Rose*, and it helps to explain the symbolic vitality he communicates even today, centuries after the skirmish in academic politics that ultimately gave him birth. One who takes the chaff and leaves the fruit is a literalist who adheres to the letter in religion just as he pursues carnal loves in the world. He reads as he lives, fastening on the ephemeral husk of religion and of life. The hypocritical friars reincarnate a timeless breed. They represent a new race of Pharisees, and Fals-Semblant tells us so with momentarily disarming forthrightness (ll.6889-95). The Pharisees and their colleagues the scribes are, of course, notorious as the "whited sepulchres" of Scripture. They adhere to the external requirements of Moses' law—paying the "tithe of mint and anise and cummin," while omitting "the weightier matters of the law, judgment, mercy, and faith" (Matt. 23:23). It is precisely because the Pharisees and their medieval antitypes are literalists for whom the Old Law represents a system of barren external forms that they reduce it so readily to a pretext for revenge, "eye for eye, tooth for tooth." They have no ears to hear the Law's true burden.

Before concluding our review of Chaucer's contribution to English antifraternalism, we should note that Jean de Meun personifies the Pharisaic legalism of the regulars in yet another figure, Dame Abstinence-Streyned. This personage, who is Fals-Semblant's "lemman" and ironical *socius*,[11] suggests legalistic formalism by means of her very

---

[11] John Fleming, *The "Roman de la Rose": A Study in Allegory and Iconography* (Princeton: Princeton University Press, 1969), p. 163.

name. Her abstinence, what little there is of it, results from external compulsion only. She repents ever having taken vows (ll.7399-400).

> And if of good wyl she began,
> That wyl was fayled her than.
>   [ll.7441-42]

Dame Abstinence is in bondage to the law of her vows, and the result is hypocrisy: she and her confessor become so intimate that often one can see "two heedes in oon hood at ones" (l.7386).

Reformation theologians both revived and broadened these medieval attacks on the regular clergy. Jean de Meun's special emphasis on mendicants disappears, and religious vows themselves become the new focus of attack. Monks, nuns, and friars are therefore criticized without distinction in the Reformers' works. All do remain firmly in Fals-Semblant's tribe as the traditional charge of hypocrisy echoes through the writings of influential Lutheran, Calvinist, and Anglican churchmen. In his sermons Hugh Latimer, for example, hammers home the conventional view that "pure religion . . . standeth not in wearing of a monk's cowl" but in acts of charity. "The other which was used [i.e., religion under vows] was an unreligious life, yea, rather an hypocrisy."[12] Orders noted for strictness—like the Order of St. Clare—escaped none of the Reformers' fury. Bullinger insists that "those that seem to be governed by more severe discipline are defiled with hypocrisy."[13] In his popular handbook *Enchiridion militis christiani*, Erasmus reiterates the charge: "amongst these religious men no

---

[12] *Sermons*, ed. George Elwes Corrie, Parker Society (Cambridge: Cambridge University Press, 1844), 1:392.

[13] *Decades* 5:10; Parker Society, 10:514. It may be useful to recall that Bullinger exerted considerable influence on the early development of the Anglican church. See Owen Chadwick, *The Reformation* (Harmondsworth: Penguin, 1964), p. 213.

man causeth the ceremonies to be more strictly observed than they which under the precepts thereof . . . serve their bellies rather than Christ."[14]

This hypocritical delight in the epicurean pleasures of the flesh is shared not only by Fals-Semblant and the Summoner's Friar (not to mention the Monk of the General Prologue), but also by Spenser's "Idlenesse, the nourse of sin," who takes the shape of a "holy Monke," remains "still drownd in sleep," challenges liberty from all work "for contemplation sake," and nonetheless leads "his life . . . in lawlesse riotise: / By which he grew to grievous malady" (*Faerie Queene* 1.4.18-20). Finally, the official Tudor *Homilies* also perpetuate the attack on hypocrisy in the religious orders by linking them, as did Jean de Meun, with the arch-hypocrites of the Gospels:

> of them it might be most truly said, that which Christ spake unto the Pharisees [Matt. 15], You break the commandments of God by your traditions: you honour God with your lips, but your hearts be far from him. And the longer prayers they used by day and by night, under pretence or colour of such holiness, to get the favour of widows, and other simple folks . . . the more truly is verified of them the saying of Christ, Woe be unto you Scribes and Pharisees, hypocrites, for you devour widows houses, under colour of long prayers, therefore your damnation shall be the greater.[15]

Such Reformation views reveal the decorum that dresses hypocrisy in the habiliments of monks or friars. From Ariosto's hermit (glossed in Harington's translation as "an unchast hermit or hypocrite"), for example, Spenser develops his own monkish enemy to Holiness. Like Fals-

---

[14] *A booke called in latyn Enchiridion militis christiani and in englysshe the manuell of a christian knyght* . . . (London: W. de Worde, 1533), sig. C4^{r-v}.

[15] *Certaine Sermons or Homilies*, ed. Mary Ellen Rickey and Thomas B. Stroup, 2 vols. in 1 (1623; rpt. in facsimile, Gainesville, Fla.: Scholars' Facsimiles and Reprints, 1968), sig. D1^r.

Semblant, Archimago appears as a "hermit" who asserts that he "lives in hidden cell / Bidding his beades all day for his trespas." But in a self-contradiction apparent to us if not to Redcrosse Knight, Archimago in fact walks abroad "under colour of long prayers," attired like a member of the regular clergy (*Faerie Queene* 1.1.29).[16] If Spenser's hypocrite is among Fals-Semblant's most memorable literary offspring, John Webster's assassins, disguised as Capuchin friars, may well be the most horrible. In *The White Devil*, a play whose title translates "the hypocrite" and almost all of whose dramatis personae represent some degree of hypocrisy, the murderers' religious habits (at 5.3.134 ff.) would probably have seemed to an English audience shocking yet rhetorically decorous.[17]

While remaining important in Reformation antiregular satire, however, hypocrisy was no longer the primary focus of attack. The Reformers turned their attention instead to the theological foundations of all forms of religious vows. Although the relevant doctrines became common to all major Continental and English Reformers, Martin Luther originated and best illustrates Reformed opinion on monasticism. By means of three seminal pamphlets (*De captivitae babylonica ecclesiae, De libertate hominis christiani*, and *De votis monasticis*) that first became influential in England in the 1520s, Luther undermined, in the words of Dom David Knowles, "the whole system of the monastic and devoted life, and . . . [swept] away its characteristic observances and prohibitions in the names of Christian liberty, of the word of Scripture, and of early Christian practice."[18]

---

[16] Though called a "hermit," Archimago is associated with the religious orders not only by his attire and apparent life of solitary prayer, but also by the historical fact that hermits, too, lived under monastic rules—witness that most notable of Augustinian hermits, Martin Luther.

[17] Cf. also Marlowe's *Doctor Faustus* 1.3.25-28, and Miles, *Problem of "Measure for Measure*," pp. 169-70.

[18] Dom David Knowles, *The Religious Orders in England* (Cambridge: Cambridge University Press, 1959), 3:55.

Luther's opinions had an immediate and a lasting influence discernible in all major discussions of monasticism current in Shakespeare's time.

Central to Luther's argument is the notion that monasticism rests on false theological principles that involve a dethronement of faith because regulars seek their salvation through works rather than faith. "When thou beginnest to believe," Luther taught, "thou doest learn withall, that all things in thee are altogether blameworthy, sinful, and damnable." Hence, you realize that you can be "made free from all thy sins, and justified by the merits of Jesus Christ only."[19] In the section of the *De votis* entitled "Vows are against faith," Luther takes as his central proof texts Rom. 14:23 ("For whatsoever is not of faith is sin"), Gal. 3:12 ("The law is not of faith"), and Rom. 3:20 ("By the deeds of the law there shall no flesh be justified in his sight"). These texts apply to monastic vows because "vows and the works of vows are but law and works."[20] Here we may glimpse the essential and intimate connection between antimonastic polemic and a much larger class of texts concerning the law. We see also that Luther's attack on monastic life is a major corollary of the central Reformation doctrine that became article 11 of the Anglican faith: "We are accounted righteous before God, only for the merit of our Lord and Savior Jesus Christ by Faith, and not for our own works or deservings. . . . We are justified by Faith only."[21]

We tend often to forget today that this doctrine had a singularly important ethical consequence that required and received careful exposition in the writings of the Reformers, "lest," as the Tudor *Homily* points out, "carnal men should take unjustly occasion thereby to live carnally, after the appetite and will of the world, the flesh, and the devil."[22] Far from conceding anything to these primordial

---

[19] *A Treatise, Touching the Libertie of a Christian*, trans. James Bell (London: Ralph Newbery and H. Bynneman, 1579), sig. C5ᵛ.

[20] *Works*, 44:280.

[21] *The Thirty-nine Articles*, ed. cit.   [22] *Certaine Sermons*, sig. B3ʳ.

enemies of mankind, the Reformed doctrine of salvation aimed especially to destroy the last—the devil of pride. This aim is implicit in the very ordering of the Tudor *Homilies*. After an opening exhortation to the diligent reading of Scripture, the homilists turned directly to "A sermon of the misery of all mankind," which declares that "the Holy Ghost, in writing the Holy Scripture, is in nothing more diligent than to pull down man's vain glory and pride, which of all vices is most universally grafted in all mankind."[23]

The Elizabethans learned from the Epistle to the Romans that Paul had himself proceeded in the order adopted by the Tudor homilists. And Romans, according to Erasmus (and other prominent Reformers), is "the principal and most excellent part of the New Testament," which all men should have without book and should ponder daily. Paul begins, Erasmus demonstrates, by showing that "all men [are] sinners and children of wrath by inheritance, and how that to sin is their nature, and that by nature they cannot otherwise do than to sin, and therewith to abate the pride of man and to bring him unto the knowledge of himself, and of his misery and wretchedness, that he might desire help."[24] The good saint then points the way to that help (Rom. 3:23-24). Similarly, after the "Ser-

[23] Ibid., sig. A4[r]. Cf. [John Jewel], *An Apologie; or, Aunswer in defence of the Church of England, concerning the state of Religion used in the same* (London: Reginald Wolfe, 1562), sig. E1[v].

[24] *Paraphrase*, 2, fol. ✠ ✠ 1[v]. We do well to recall that this book is of unique importance for understanding Tudor Christianity. Two Tudor governments considered it essential to stabilizing their reforms. The "Injunctions for Religious Reform" of Edward VI ordered that it be so placed in all churches that the parishioners might have ready access to it. Elizabeth's "Injunctions for Religion" (19 July 1559) ordered that "every parson, vicar, curate and stipendiary priest . . . shall provide and have of his own . . . the New Testament both in Latin and in English, with [Erasmus's] Paraphrases upon the same [and shall devote some time to?] conferring the one with the other," *Tudor Royal Proclamations*, ed. Paul L. Hughes and James F. Larkin (New Haven: Yale University Press, 1969), 2:121; cf. 1:395.

mon on the Misery of Mankind" has firmly established that man unaccommodated by God's grace is no more than "ground, earth, and ashes," the homilists' subsequent "Sermon of Salvation" can properly explain the meaning of the doctrine that only faith justifies:

> this saying, that ye be justified by faith only, freely and without works, is spoken for to take away clearly all merit of our works, as being unable to deserve our justification at God's hands, and thereby most plainly to express the weakness of man, and the goodness of God, the great infirmity of ourselves, and the might and power of God, the imperfectness of our own works, and the most abundant grace of our Saviour Christ, and therefore wholly to ascribe the merit and deserving of our justification unto Christ only, and his most precious bloodshedding. This faith . . . beateth down the vain glory of man.[25]

The doctrine of *sola fides* asserts, in short, the kind of relationship between God and man that we have found to be figured in the imagery of *Measure for Measure*, scene 1. All human value is directly attributed to God himself. Nonetheless, good works remain essential to Christian life; one must use his powers. Although good works cannot merit salvation, they appear as inevitable outward manifestations of true faith. "For that faith which bringeth forth (without repentance) either evil works, or no good works, is not a right, pure, and lively faith."[26] Ultimately, therefore, the

[25] *Certaine Sermons*, sig. B4[r].

[26] *Certaine Sermons*, sig. B3[r]. By stressing this inevitable connection between good works and true faith, Protestants avoided the theological pitfall of antinomianism and preserved the doctrinal foundations of their characteristic emphasis on ethics. See Horton Davies, *Worship and Theology in England from Cranmer to Hooker, 1534-1603* (Princeton: Princeton University Press, 1970), pp. 18-19, and *Certaine Sermons*, sig. B4[v]. For a singularly lucid exposition of the Anglican doctrine of salvation, see Hooker, *Laws*, 1:206, 209.

In *The Basilicon Doron* (1:29-31), Shakespeare probably read the king's restatement of the conventional doctrine on works as followers of faith:

doctrine of justification by faith frees men not from the obligation to do good works, but from "the foolish presumption" that justification can be "purchased by means of works."[27] Like many another, this Protestant view originates with Paul, who insists that justification comes "not of works, lest any man should boast" (Eph. 2:9).[28]

To the Reformers, then, the sin of pride and what we might call a "works ethic" were inseparable, and in their view the "foolish presumption" that justification can be purchased by man's works was manifest—more obtrusively than in any other Catholic institution—in monasticism. Because they attribute merit to works like bodily chastity, the regulars, Luther says, "hold themselves in a class apart from all other Christians."[29] With transparent scorn, Calvin remarks that by instituting "a new and fained worshipping," the regulars seek "to deserve God's favor." "Forgetting their own weakness," they vow chastity, presumptuously shaking off "the universal state" of sexual frailty expressed in God's own assertion that it is not good for man to be alone (Gen. 2:18). This reveals not

---

"in two degrees standeth the whole service of God by man: interior, or upward; exterior, or downward: the first, by prayer in faith towards God; the next, by works flowing therefrom before the world: which is nothing else, but the exercise of Religion towards God, and of equity towards your neighbour."

[27] *Libertie*, sig. G8ʳ.

[28] The ethical point of this doctrine is insisted on by Milton's God:

Yet not of will in him, but grace in me
Freely voutsaf't; once more I will renew
His lapsed powers . . .
Upheld by me, yet once more he shall stand
On even ground against his mortal foe,
By me upheld, that he may know how frail
His fall'n condition is, and to me owe
All his deliv'rance, and to none but me.
[*Paradise Lost* 3.174-82]

[29] *Monastic Vows*, in *Works*, 44:263. Erasmus makes the same charge; see *Enchiridion*, sig. C5ᵛ.

only "arrogance and contempt of his gifts by too much trust in themselves," but also extreme stubbornness "when one being warned that he needeth marriage, and that the same is given him of the Lord for a remedy, doth not only despise it, but also bindeth himself with an oath to the despising of it."[30]

Similarly, William Tyndale assails "our hypocrites" for denigrating the "chastity of matrimony" and establishing "another wilful chastity which they . . . profess to give God, whether he will give it them or no."[31] The latter part of Tyndale's statement derives its acid tone from the doctrine we reviewed above: nothing good can originate in man himself. Every gift that men offer to God is originally received from him. Calvin urges therefore that "every man . . . have respect unto the measure of grace given unto him . . . vows must be tempered to the measure which the Lord prescribed thee in his giving."[32] Since chastity is a gift allotted to very few, monks and nuns are both foolish and presumptuous to vow it.[33] Such unanimity of opinion among the fathers of Anglican orthodoxy must be borne in mind as we witness Isabella's eagerness to become a votarist of St. Clare, "rather wishing a more strict restraint."

In sum, we may conclude that the pride that was so prominent a characteristic of Chaucer's regulars received a fresh theological explanation consequent on the Protestant dogma of *sola fides*. The themes embodied in Dame Abstinence-Streyned gained similar renewal in light of the doctrine of Christian liberty, itself a major preoccupation of Reformation antimonastic writings. This extremely in-

---

[30] *Institutes* 4.13.3-12; fols. 420ᵛ, 415ᵛ, 416ʳ, 422ᵛ.

[31] "Prologue to the Book of Numbers," in *Doctrinal Treatises*, ed. Henry Walter, Parker Society (Cambridge: Cambridge University Press, 1848), p. 430. Cf. p. 438.

[32] *Institutes* 4.13.3; fol. 415ᵛ.

[33] Cf. Erasmus, *The Dyalogue called Funus*, ed. Robert R. Allen (Chicago: Newberry Library, 1969), p. 43. William Fulke, *Stapleton's Fortress Overthrown*, ed. Richard Gibbings, Parker Society (Cambridge: Cambridge University Press, 1848), p. 101; and Tyndale, *Doctrinal Treatises*, p. 438.

fluential idea derives from a seminal passage in Paul, who chides the Galatians for desiring to return to the bondage of the law after once having known Christ. By observing "days, and months, and times, and years" (4:10), they return to "bondage under the elements of the world" (4:3) and so become once again enslaved children of Agar (4:22-31).[34] Christ had brought freedom from the law of external compulsion, and Paul exhorts the Galatians therefore to "stand fast . . . in the liberty wherewith Christ hath made us free, and be not entangled again with the yoke of bondage" (5:1). The terms of Paul's message deserve attention, because slavery to external laws is one of the charges Reformers constantly level against the regular clergy. In the following passage, Calvin illustrates how pride often results, paradoxically, from self-imposed bondage:

> our liberty should not be despised. . . . Since God hath made us Lords of all things, and hath so made them subject unto us that we should use them all for our commodity: there is no cause why we should hope that it shall be an acceptable work to God if we yield ourselves into bondage to the outward things which ought to be a help to us. I say this for a purpose, because many do hereby seek praise of humility, if they snare themselves with many observations, from which God not without cause willed us to be free and discharged.[35]

Thus Pharisaic pride derives from the Galatians'—and the regulars'—self-imprisoning revival of and elaborations on the law of Moses.

The view that the monastic life represents legalistic bondage achieved wide currency in sixteenth-century Eng-

[34] The Geneva gloss at 4.9-10 explains "The Galatians, of Pagans began to be Christians, but by false apostles were turned backward to begin anew the Jewish ceremonies . . . which beggarly ceremonies are most pernicious to them which have received the sweet liberty of the Gospel, and thrust them back into superstitious slavery."

[35] *Institutes* 4.13.3; fol. 416[r].

land. Thomas Becon's *Catechism*, for example, narrates the history of the monasteries that, he says, gradually degenerated from "free schools" to "prisons of antichrist" where even the most trivial human activities are subject to legislative tyranny.[36] The Reformers insist, too, on the kinship of such slavery with the bondage of the Old Law. This charge is amusingly made in Erasmus's popular *Praise of Folly*, when Folly claims the regular clergy for her own precisely because they substitute external forms—man-made rules that extend far beyond even the ceremonial provisions of the Old Testament—for religion's spirit. The monks and friars do everything, she says,

> by certain precedents of their orders, much like mathematical rules, which in no wise without offense they may alter, or swerve from. As for example, how many windows they must make to their shoes? What colour, and number of knots goeth to their girdles? With what difference, and whereof must their weeds be made? Of what breadth their leather thongs? How many bushelfuls their cowls? How many inches long, their knotted hair? And how many hours for sleeping?[37]

To "ceremonies and traditions" like these, the monks impute great merit. On Judgment Day, Folly imagines,

> one of them (may chance) will for his discharge show forth a trough stuffed full of all kind of fish. Another, will pour forth an hundred quarters of psalms. Another,

[36] *The Catechism*, ed. Rev. John Ayre, Parker Society (Cambridge: Cambridge University Press, 1844), pp. 376-77. Cf. also Bullinger *Decades* 5.10, Parker Society, 10:518; Philip Melanchthon, *Loci Communes Theologici*, in *Melanchthon and Bucer*, trans. Lowell J. Satre (Philadelphia: Westminster Press, 1969), pp. 60-61; Erasmus, *Enchiridion*, sig. C5ᵛ. Melanchthon's book, incidentally, was influential in England. As J. E. Neale points out, for example, "Elizabeth I had been brought up on Melanchthon's *Loci Communes*." See *Elizabeth I and Her Parliaments, 1559-1581* (London: Jonathan Cape, 1953), 1:71.

[37] *The praise of Folie*, trans. Sir Thomas Chaloner (London: Thomas Berthelet, 1549), sig. N1ʳ⁻ᵛ.

will number up millions of fastings. . . . But Christ inter-
rupting their selfboasts, which else would never take
end, whence cometh (he will say) this new race of Jews? I
do acknowledge but one law and rule for mine, whereof
I hear never a word spoken. For whilom plainly, and by
no shadow of parables, I promised my father's kingdom
not to cowls, nor rosaries, nor set fastings, but rather to
works of charity: nor I know none such, as too much
know their own good works.[38]

Like the Galatians in Paul's epistle, the monks represent
a "new race of Jews," and these Jews are metaphors for
legalists who seek salvation through external works of the
law rather than through faith in Christ and the charity that
manifests faith.[39] Their literalness denies them access to
the essential meaning, the fruit, of the New Law—the
meaning Paul urges the Galatians to recognize: "For all the
law is fulfilled in one word, even in this; Thou shalt love
thy neighbour as thyself" (Gal. 5:14).

The regular clergy's blindness to the central meaning of
the New Law assumes a local habitation and the name of
Corceca in Spenser's *Faerie Queene*. As the *Variorum Spenser*
notes, Corceca's name, "blind heart," derives from another
Pauline passage concerning those whose "understanding
[is] darkened, being alienated from the life of God through
the ignorance that is in them, because of the blindness of
their heart" (Eph. 4:18). Significantly, Corceca is the
mother of Abessa and is a practitioner of hyperbolically
strict monastic devotion:

> that old woman day and night did pray
> Upon her beades deuoutly penitent;
> Nine hundred *Pater Nosters* every day,
> And thrise nine hundred *Aves* she was wont to say.

[38] Ibid., sigs. N1^v-N2^r. Cf. Roland H. Bainton, *Erasmus of Christendom*
(New York: Scribner's, 1969), p. 6.

[39] The Tudor homilists ensured the currency of this hoary metaphor.
See *Certaine Sermons*, sigs. C6^v-D1^r.

And to augment her painefull pennance more,
  Thrise every weeke in ashes she did sit,
And next her wrinkled skin rough sackcloth wore,
  And thrise three times did fast from any bit:

[1.3.13-14]

This is indeed a frenzied attachment to the beggarly external elements of religion. Transparently enough, the spirit of charity is altogether absent, its place usurped by the superstition suggested by incantatory rhythms and a fetish for ritual threes and nines. And while Fals-Semblant had revealed his antipathy to charity by simple refusal to aid the poor, Corceca's opposition to that virtue is downright aggressive: She harbors Kirkrapine, a "sturdie thiefe" who robs "poore mens boxes of their due reliefe" (1.3.17). Both Fals-Semblant and Corceca aptly embody the "monks and cloisterers" who, Erasmus argues, live at war with charity because they never attain to a spiritual understanding of Scripture, "neither hear they Christ crying in the Gospel: the flesh, that is to say, the letter, or that ye see outward profiteth not at all. It is the spirit within that quickeneth or giveth life."[40]

Failure to live according to the spirit of charity is no slight charge. Englishmen in Shakespeare's era had not forgotten the medieval belief that love is the cause both of all man's good works and of all his sins. Echoing the medieval commonplace that received its most famous literary statement in *Purgatorio* 17, the *Homilies* maintain that "Of all things that be good to be taught unto Christian people, there is nothing more necessary to be spoken of, and daily called upon, than charity: as well for that all manner of works of righteousness be contained in it, as also that the decay thereof is . . . the banishment of virtue, and the cause of all vice."[41] It follows, therefore, that any institution that by its very nature impedes charitable activity is a notable abomination. Monasticism, according to the Reformers,

[40] *Enchiridion*, sig. I1r.   [41] *Certaine Sermons*, sig. D2v.

had just that effect. In his gloss on the Sermon on the Mount, Tyndale turns automatically to monasticism to illustrate lack of charity. In his view, the very nature of the monk's separation from the world and their dependence on endowments operates against the essential law of the New Testament.[42] Above all, in their pursuit of endowments, the monks compete directly with the legitimately poor. (This, in part, is the idea personified in Spenser's Kirkrapine.) Although monasticism in general receives the blame for this, Reformers sometimes point to the vow of obedience as a particular impediment to acts of charity. Echoing Luther, the Tudor *Homilies* point out that "for all [the monks'] riches, they might never help father nor mother, nor other that were in deed very needy and poor, without the license of their Father Abbott, Prior, or Warden, and yet they might take of every man, but they might not give ought to any man, no not to them whom the laws of God bound them to help."[43]

Such fugitive and cloistered virtue was very much at odds with the humanistic bent of Shakespeare's age. We therefore find implicit or explicit attacks on the monastic life in works only tangentially concerned with religious issues. In *The Basilicon Doron* King James, sounding very much like Duke Vincentio, makes the standard humanist point—and bolsters it, in equally standard humanist fashion, with marginal references to Aristotle and Cicero: "For it is not enough that ye have and retain (as prisoners) within yourself never so many good qualities and virtues, except ye employ them, and set them on work, for the weal of them that are committed to your charge: *Virtutis enim laus omnis in actione consistit*."[44] Francis Bacon makes the

---

[42] *Expositions and Notes on Sundry Portions of the Holy Scriptures*, ed. Henry Walter, Parker Society (Cambridge: Cambridge University Press, 1849), pp. 41-42.

[43] *Certaine Sermons*, sig. D1ʳ. Cf. *Monastic Vows*, in *Works*, 44:326.

[44] Previous scholars have noticed that this speech compares closely with Duke Vincentio's at 1.1.29-36. See Ernest Schanzer, *The Problem Plays of Shakespeare* (London: Routledge and Kegan Paul, 1963), p. 123.

point in more philosophic terms, arguing that Christianity, more than any other philosophy or religion, urges active virtue and condemns ethical inertia. The regular profession must therefore rest, he continues, "upon this defence, that monastical life is not simple contemplative, but performeth the duty either of incessant prayers and supplications . . .[45] or else of writing or taking instructions for writing concerning the law of God. . . . But for contemplation which should be finished in itself without casting beams upon society, assuredly divinity knoweth it not."[46] "Let your light so shine before men," Duke Vincentio's Christian counsel, figured prominently in the humanist credo.

In considerations such as these may lie the point of Venus's taunt (in *Venus and Adonis*) against "self-loving nuns" (l.752).[47] The practice of "contemplation which should be finished in itself" indicates, above all, self-love, charity's diametric opposite.[48] The self-love of Fals-Semblant becomes most clearly manifest, as we have seen, in his cupidity for "pitaunces" and for the solaces of his "lemman." The Reformed treatment of this monastic cupidity adds a corollary that returns us once again to the charge of monastic pride. This charge assumed tremendous significance in the Reformation because the search for legacies appeared to Protestants to transform monasteries into perverse economic institutions. The monastic "sects and religions," the Tudor homilists taught, "had so many hypocritical and feigned works in their state of religion . . . that their lamps as they said ran always over, able

[45] Bacon is more tolerant toward this office than many of his contemporaries could bring themselves to be.

[46] *Advancement of Learning* 2.20.8. Cf. Baldassare Castiglione, *The Courtier*, trans. Sir Thomas Hoby, in *Three Renaissance Classics*, ed. Burton A. Milligan (New York: Scribner's, 1953), p. 541.

[47] Except where I indicate otherwise, all quotations from Shakespeare's works (other than *Measure for Measure*) derive from *The Complete Works of Shakespeare*, ed. Irving Ribner and George Lyman Kittredge (Waltham, Mass.: Xerox College Publishing, 1971).

[48] See Latimer, *Sermons*, 1:434, for the commonplace that self-love, the original source of pride, is also "the root of all mischief and wickedness."

to satisfy, not only for their own sins, but also for all other their benefactors, brothers, and sisters of religion." Hence, their custom was to keep "in diverse places (as it were) marts or markets of merits."[49] The regulars, that is, deluded men with the notion that salvation was to be achieved by purchasing shares of stock in monastic corporations. In view of the Reformed doctrine of salvation, these merit markets imply an incredible pride. As usual, Luther expresses most trenchantly the spiritual implications of the monastic industry: "they all say, 'I am Christ'; they abstain from using the name, but arrogate to themselves the office, the work, and the person."[50] This view achieved currency in England through popular works such as Tyndale's *Obedience of a Christian Man*. For Tyndale, the pope and the religious orders appear to "say that they themselves are Christ. . . . For they, under the name of Christ, preach themselves, their own word and their own traditions, and teach the people to believe in them."[51]

The result of this monastic presumption was massive wealth, the booty of Kirkrapine. As we have seen, any threat to the sources of their wealth evoked wrathful vindictiveness from Jean de Meun's and Chaucer's friars. Similarly, in Latimer's view the regulars would stoop even to treason in defense of their financial interests, and "beside all this, they will curse and ban . . . even into the deep pit of hell, all that gainsay their appetite, whereby they think their goods, promotions, or dignities should decay."[52] After suffering some such injury, the regulars turn impulsively to vengeance, just as Corceca and Abessa, having found Kirkrapine slain, pursue Una "like two amazed deare, / Halfe mad through malice, and revenging will."

Like their medieval progenitors, these regulars excel at slander and at prayers for their enemies' misfortune:

[49] *Certaine Sermons*, sig. C6^v-D1^r.

[50] *Monastic Vows*, in *Works*, 44:286-87, 320. Cf. Luther's Thesis on Vows, #137.

[51] *Doctrinal Treatises*, p. 227.   [52] *Sermons*, 2:301.

Whom overtaking, they gan loudly bray,
  With hollow howling, and lamenting cry,
  Shamefully at her rayling all the way,
  And her accusing of dishonesty,
  That was the flowre of faith and chastity;
  And still amidst her rayling, she did pray,
  That plagues, and mischiefs, and long misery
  Might fall on her, and follow all the way,
And that in endlesse error she might euer stray.
                                        [1.3.23]

In his sardonically amusing image of Corceca alternating slanderous bellows with moments of malicious piety, Spenser illustrates that imprisonment to the letter, or the flesh, or "that ye see outward" ensures that regulars will manifest the wrath of "revenging will." He that is proud is lightly wroth, as Chaucer's Parson reminds us, and men unenlightened by faith remain eternally "children of wrath" (Eph. 2:3; cf. Gal. 5:20).

In addition to slanderous vindictiveness, Spenser's parodic monastics introduce a last important feature of monasticism as it appeared to Reformers. The gloomy frenzy of Corceca's superstitious observances, performed in the "eternal night" of her "darksome corner," represents an important variation on a recurrent theme of *The Faerie Queene*, book 1. Redcrosse Knight's "too solemn" sadness (1.2) finds varied correlatives in gloomy woods and caves and dungeons. It is personified above all in Sansjoy and in his psychological kinsman Despair. Ironically, Redcrosse Knight's proud self-reliance, itself akin to that of the monks, banishes all rest and engenders perpetual anxiety that sin will draw the sinner ineluctably to damnation. This fear, which leads Redcrosse to near suicide, may explain also the extreme fearfulness Corceca and Abessa exhibit in the presence of the lion, a beast whose flexible symbolic values include both the English king and his divine prototype (3.12-13; 19). Such anxiety results from a consciousness of only one aspect of the Deity—the judge who revealed himself amid smoke and thunderings on Mount Sinai.

Because it renewed "Jewish" legalism, monasticism renewed also a related anxiety. But the Protestant conception of salvation by faith alone offered a needful balm for tender consciences. Paul's proof text for the doctrine of justification by faith illustrates the paradox that pride yields terror whereas self-abasement brings freedom and rest: "Behold, he that lifteth up himself, his mind is not upright in him, but the just shall live by his faith" (Hab. 2:4; Rom. 1:17). The Geneva gloss adds: "To trust in himself or in any worldly thing, is never to be quiet: for the only rest is to stay upon God by faith."[53] The solemn sadness and sourness we often associate with Puritanism therefore manifests false doctrine and allied spiritual ills, for, as Erasmus says, true faith "maketh a man glad, lusty, cheerful, and true-hearted unto God and to all creatures."[54] The Protestant doctrine of justification could therefore serve an extremely important psychological and social function. It served such a function for its earliest Reformation proponent, Martin Luther, the tormented Augustinian hermit who was terrified that he could never suffer monastic austerities suffi-

---

[53] The Geneva "Argument" to Paul's Epistle to the Galatians gathers together the nexus of ideas—pride, anxiety, and ignorance—figured in Spenser's parodic convent. The false apostles whom Paul attacks in the epistle taught "that the ceremonies of Law must be necessarily observed, which thing the Apostle so earnestly reasoneth against, that he proveth that the granting thereof is the overthrow of man's salvation, purchased by Christ: for thereby the light of the Gospel is obscured: the conscience burdened: the testaments confounded: man's justice established." And see, especially, Rom. 5:1, for Paul's statement on the psychological comforts that derive from the doctrines of predestination and salvation by faith.

[54] *Paraphrase*, 2, fol. ✠ ✠ 1ʳ. Erasmus is joined in this cheerful view by a redoubtable father of English Puritanism, for William Perkins lists as a sign of one's justification "doing the works of the Spirit, with joy and cheerfulness of heart, as in the presence of God, and as his children and servants" (*Whole Treatise*, p. 77).

cient to save himself; who suspected that the merits of the saints could themselves be ineffective; who immediately after six hours of compulsive confessing recalled with horror sins previously forgotten; who in short reduced himself to desperation by the conviction that nothing he could do would merit salvation. Even this man found emotional peace, and made the same peace available to countless others, by depending without reservation on the merits of Christ alone.[55]

In concluding this review of common sixteenth-century attitudes toward the regular clergy, I should add that major Reformers did not promote absolute, blind prejudice against all monks, friars, and nuns. We saw above that Erasmus, Luther, Calvin, and Thomas Becon agreed that monasticism had begun as a benign and, according to some, even a necessary educational institution that succumbed gradually to the corrupting influences of wealth, ceremonies, and pride. Citing Augustine, Calvin goes so far as to provide a conception of true monastic life, a conception that accords with his reading of the Sermon on the Mount: "charity is chiefly kept: to charity the diet, to charity the speech, to charity the apparel, to charity the countenance is fitted." Despite all the corruptions of modern monasticism, Calvin also insists that there remain "some good men in their flock."[56] Still more generously, Erasmus believes that many good men, misled by honest error, remain under vows, and he frequently attributes their self-

---

[55] Roland H. Bainton, *Here I Stand: A Life of Martin Luther* (New York: New American Library, 1950), pp. 31-50. As Luther points out, the faithful believe they are pleasing to God despite their conviction of sin—Christ has rendered their sins irrelevant (*Monastic Vows*, in *Works*, 44:278, 279). Cf. Erasmus (*Enchiridion*, sig. K4^r), who explains that since most regulars live according to the flesh, they display "this so great infirmity of mind: trembling for fear where is no fear, and therein surety and careless where is most peril of all." See also Calvin *Institutes* 4.13.17; fol. 420^v. We should not forget, of course, that Pauline doctrine could produce a psychological hell of its own, as witness Bunyan's *Grace Abounding*.

[56] *Institutes* 4.13.15; fol. 420^v.

deception to childlike simplicity.[57] Similar positive and sympathetic views of the devoted life—of its original ideals and ideal practitioners rather than contemporary actualities—appear in salient literary works of reforming bias. We need think only, for example, of Spenser's House of Holiness, where monasticism becomes a metaphor for the proper interior ordering of individual souls. In Rabelais's Abbey of Thélème, the very elusive Alcofribas Nasier appears to cast an approving glance at a monastic society directed (not unlike Calvin's later idealization) by almost instinctive obedience to an honor dramatized as charitable good will.

This tolerance toward the ideals that inspired monastic endeavor suggests that the proverb *Cucullus non facit monachum* can apply in its opposite as well as its usual sense. Religious habits can act simply as straightforward indications of the wearer's devotion to God. Since this positive response is both immediate and, compared with the negative alternative, very simple, I need not labor it. We must be aware, however, that the cowl assures neither holiness nor hypocrisy in its wearer. Like most traditional literary symbols, the religious costume can bear multiple and even self-contradictory implications, and the poet is free to use it as he will.

Shakespeare elsewhere avails himself of this freedom. Under strained circumstances in which a lover collapses into hatred and malicious public slander, a father into vehement desire to see his daughter dead, and a pair of Shakespeare's most voluble comic characters into inarticulate helplessness, a friar alone can see truth where it lies hid. His is an act of judgment based on cautious observation of the facts before him, observation swayed by no private interest, but governed rather by the tenor of a book that originally inspired the foundation of fraternal orders:

[57] Erasmus in fact considered Jean Vitrier, a Franciscan, an ideal embodiment of the Christian priesthood (Knowles, *Religious Orders*, 3: 150-51). Cf. *Enchiridion*, sig. $K5^r$.

Call me a fool;
Trust not my reading nor my observation
Which with experimental seal doth warrant
The tenor[58] of my book; trust not my age,
My reverence, calling, nor divinity,
If this sweet lady lie not guiltless here
Under some biting error.
[*Much Ado* 4.1.161-67]

We recognize the Friar's rightness here and the generosity of spirit that proposes a plan that will harm none and *may*, in ways he specifies, benefit many. He is a figure of dignity and authority, and his authority is strengthened by his humility. He recognizes that any man's detailed prognostications are at best mere possibilities. Friar Francis knows, that is, both the powers and the limits of human reason and of its judgments:

doubt not but success
Will fashion the event in better shape
Than I can lay it down in likelihood.
[4.1.231-33]

The robe of Duke Vincentio and that of Isabella may therefore imply the same or opposite things. With this caveat, we can turn at last to *Measure for Measure* and Shakespeare's characterization of the enskied and sainted Isabella.

[58] I have restored the F reading; Kittredge emends to "tenure."

Chapter 3

A Thing Enskied and Sainted

Our first meeting with Isabella is carefully prepared. We are conditioned to respond to her appearance at the Convent of St. Clare by means of a decisive variation on the theme of law, a variation effected primarily through the introduction of Claudio, a figure whose thematic significance has never been fully explained. When the comic dialogue of Mistress Overdone and Pompey breaks off, Claudio's entry brings a sharp change in tone and a corresponding expansion of thematic horizons:

> *Claudio.* Thus can the demi-god, Authority,
>   Make us pay down for our offence by weight.
>   The words of heaven; on whom it will, it will;
>   On whom it will not, so; yet still 'tis just.
>   [1.2.112-15]

Claudio's sarcasm expresses bitterness natural for a man who feels arbitrarily handled, but the thematic resonance of his words transcends their local context. They recall the intimations of universal ordering communicated in the Duke's cryptic early speeches. Specifically, Claudio describes the demigod Authority by means of a transparent allusion to Rom. 9:15 (itself an echo of Exod. 33:19),[1] Paul's most prominent statement of the doctrine of predestination. In Claudio's view, human authority has assumed the inscrutable, seemingly arbitrary, yet immutable justice

---

[1] See Richmond Noble, *Shakespeare's Biblical Knowledge*, p. 222.

of the providence that determines human election and reprobation. We may see in this speech a rebellion against Angelo's human authority and probably also against the divine source of that authority.

The amplitude of the allusion serves above all, however, to provide a context necessary for the subsequent dialogue. It is here that the law first begins to appear in civil and political manifestations that, like God's incomprehensible predestinating power, wear an aspect of severity. The key word now becomes "restraint" in its most confining sense. "Why, how now, Claudio?" Lucio asks, "Whence comes this restraint?" (1.2.116). Claudio's opening line ("Fellow, why dost thou show me thus to th'world?" [1.2.108]), the Provost's response ("from Lord Angelo by special charge" [1.2.111]), and Lucio's subsequent comment ("To make him an example" [1.4.68]) indicate that Claudio is undergoing a form of punishment often used in Shakespeare's England for the correction especially of sexual offenders and for the edification of the public.[2] The restraint so apparent to Lucio is signaled perhaps by manacles, a white sheet, tapers, the usual paraphernalia of public punishments—as well as by the presence of the Provost and his officers. Whatever the details of staging, this visible "restraint" becomes a subject for poetically striking ethical discourse as Claudio makes clear that his external bondage follows from inner imprisonment to the natural impulses of man:

> From too much liberty, my Lucio, liberty;[3]
> As surfeit is the father of much fast,
> So every scope by the immoderate use
> Turns to restraint. Our natures do pursue,

[2] Millar MacLure, *The Paul's Cross Sermons, 1534-1642* (Toronto: University of Toronto Press, 1958), pp. 15-17.

[3] Lever's punctuation is idiosyncratic. F appears merely to omit a full stop after "liberty," a pause that the rhythm tends in any case to impose on the speaker. I have therefore restored Rowe's more modest emendation.

Like rats that ravin down their proper bane,
A thirsty evil; and when we drink, we die.

[1.2.117-22]

This justly famous passage aptly conforms to the com-
pressed, elliptical, suggestive style characteristic of the play
at large. It is preeminently "fraught with background," for
the fleeting personifications of "surfeit" fathering "fast"
merge swiftly into the parallel and paradoxical identification of scope and restraint. The lines forcefully realize the
elliptically put yet convincing paradox: immoderately
exercised political and social liberty transforms, by some
law of nature and of God, to license and ultimately to
bondage. Shakespeare elaborates this notion . . . in the suc-
ceeding generalization about human nature, a generalization carrying implications that far transcend the immediate
dramatic situation. The statement gains a sense of complex, almost muddled fullness from an ellipsis by which
the rats are imagined, despite the present tense ("ravin"),
already to have suffered arsenic poisoning and to be feeling the raging thirst it brings. Men ruled by their sexual
appetites share this thirst, whose very satisfaction leads to
death.

Claudio's gloomy assessment of human nature, though
novel in its dramatic metaphors and darkened by his de-
pressed emotional state,[4] is also Paul's reasoned doctrine.
By a law of his nature man ineluctably pursues sin, and sin
brings inevitable death of the spirit. Our perception of
Claudio's doctrinal accuracy is sharpened by his earlier allusion to predestination, and it is worthy of notice that the
twin concepts of predestination and of human depravity
are as closely related in theology as they are in Claudio's
speeches. For contemporary Protestants, at least for those
whose faith was firmer and whose emotional state was

---

[4] Though less striking, traditional metaphors are no more flattering to
natural man, who is dust, earth, ashes, a worm, the potter's clay, ephemeral grass, a breath, etc.

more positive than Claudio's, the doctrine of predestination was a "sweet, pleasant, and unspeakable comfort" (article 17; the point is Paul's, Rom. 8:29-39) precisely because human depravity allowed no qualification, no remedy except in "the everlasting purpose of God, whereby, before the foundations of the world were laid, he hath constantly decreed by his counsel, secret to us, to deliver from curse and damnation those whom he hath chosen" (article 17).

With Claudio's first appearance, then, civil law acquires a spectrum of implications that reaches from a dark aspect of the natural law that governs fallen mankind to the mysterious law of God that directs individual human destinies. Claudio's visibly emphatic physical restraint becomes forcibly symbolic. It recalls and elaborates in particularly constraining terms the imagery of limitations and human debility that appeared in scene 1. More immediately, it suggests spiritual subjection to the natural impulses of man. Claudio's inner imprisonment becomes extremely significant when we approach his sister for the first time.

This approach will itself be the more rewarding if we notice that in the markedly theological atmosphere of Claudio's first appearance, the liberty that physical excess turns to restraint suggests a final Pauline allusion. Useful for heuristic purposes even if it remains unrecognizable to many members of a given audience, this allusion recalls one of Paul's famous pronouncements on law and two opposing misuses of liberty from that law. To his exhortation castigating the Galatians for their return to "bondage under the elements of the world," Paul adds a warning against the opposite vice—one of special concern to theologians who promoted the doctrine of *sola fides*: "For, brethren, ye have been called unto liberty; only use not liberty for an occasion to the flesh" (Gal. 5:13). The scope provided by lax enforcement of civil law ministered occasion to Claudio's flesh, and that indulgence in liberty led him to restraint. The idea receives repeated attention, notably in the play's comic scenes. We shall shortly hear "that such a one and such a one were past cure of the thing you wot of, unless they kept very good diet" (2.1.110-11). And in a monologue that at first appears to be mere gratuitous comedy, we see a comic dramatization of the law that liberty of the flesh is self-imprisoning:

Pompey. I am as well acquainted here as I was in our house of profession: one would think it were Mistress Overdone's own house, for here be many of her old customers.

[4.3.1-4]

The subsequent, animated Jacobean rogue's gallery, though its members are literally imprisoned by Angelo's stern administration of civil law, suggests by its very comprehensiveness that all of Mistress Overdone's clients were imprisoned by misuse of liberty before they suffered literal incarceration: "one would think it were Mistress Overdone's own house."

This glance ahead to the comic business of act 4 reminds us that Claudio's theme of imprisoning restraint reappears constantly throughout the play. It is embodied most prominently in the prison, which provides a symbolic setting for much of the play's action. But diction and imagery concerning law in its imprisoning sense is epidemic, and the idea of confinement begins to permeate the play even before Claudio appears—in the play's second scene, where characters often repeat that Claudio is going "to prison" (1.2.56-57, 61-63, 79, 106-7, 109). This iterative diction receives support and elaboration from frequent references to the physical implements of incarceration—"gyves," "fetters"—and from varied synonymous phrases ("perpetual durance") that themselves reach an affective climax in Claudio's horrified vision of death. This is a particularly terrifying vision because Claudio imagines death as a grim imprisonment, his body remaining sentient even in the grave: "To lie in cold obstruction, and to rot" (3.1.118).

Obstructing imagery of confinement also informs important characterizations and determines corresponding local
settings. Angelo's strenuously cultivated self-restraint—

> one who never feels
> The wanton stings and motions of the sense;
> But doth rebate and blunt his natural edge
> With profits of the mind, study and fast.
>
> [1.4.58-61]

—finds an external correlative in his

> garden circummur'd with brick,
> Whose western side is with a vineyard back'd;
> And to that vineyard is a planched gate,
> That makes his opening with this bigger key.
> This other doth command a little door
> Which from the vineyard to the garden leads;
>
> [4.1.28-33]

It is appropriate that Angelo's earthly paradise, which is
entered suggestively through something of a "strait gate"
leading from a vineyard, be notable for its walls of impervious brick and for general difficulty of access. These characteristics are rendered emphatic by visible stage properties (the keys) and by Isabella's verbal stress on the heavily
planked gate and little door.

Imagery of confining limits extends also to the habitation
of Mariana: "St. Luke's," the Duke tells us, "there at the
moated grange resides this dejected Mariana" (3.1.265-66).
Again the emphasis is on enclosure. The grange is
"moated," and although editors customarily interpret
"grange" as farm, J. W. Lever correctly argues that "in con-
junction with 'St. Luke's,' " the word means " 'an outlying
farm-house belonging to a religious establishment' (*OED*,
2b)." Mariana's residence therefore links the imagery of
confinement to the play's persistent monastic concerns.
Together with the ubiquitous prison setting, the pervasive
imagery of confinement generates an atmosphere of claus-

trophobic repression that, until the end of act 5, dominates the play.

This atmosphere is intensified as we move from Claudio's bondage (1.2) through the Duke's temporary monastic retreat (1.3), to Isabella's convent of St. Clare (1.4). The transition from monastery to convent is rendered especially significant by means of another important scriptural allusion. This one describes Angelo's vaunted self-restraint: "Lord Angelo is precise," the Duke tells us,

> scarce confesses
> That his blood flows; or that his appetite
> Is more to bread than stone.
>
> [1.3.51-53]

Clearly enough, the Duke's statement indicates that Angelo believes himself exempt from basic human appetites. The scriptural allusion allows us to see broader significance in the Duke's indictment, significance that both predicts accurately the extent and nature of Angelo's ignorance of himself and guides our perceptions when Isabella appears within the next few lines. Every commentator since Noble has asserted that the Duke alludes to Matt. 7:9: "What man is there among you, if his son ask bread, would give a stone?" (Geneva). I seriously doubt that this can function as an allusion. It does indeed oppose bread to stone, but it does so in a context totally unlike the Duke's—Christ is speaking about the mercy natural to fathers. But there is a more famous scriptural opposition between bread and stone, one that appears in the narrative that leads directly to the Sermon on the Mount. It is part of a central episode in the drama of salvation, and it concerns a hungry man who denies his appetites by preferring stone to bread: "If thou be the Son of God, command that these stones be made bread" (Matt. 4:3). The point of the temptation is that only Christ, true man but also truly God, could perfectly overcome the temptation to bread that epitomizes all lusts of the flesh. The Duke's allusion implies therefore that Angelo's rigorous abstinence betrays an aspiration to, or assumption of, powers uniquely attributable to the Deity.

This suggestion directly precedes our first encounter with Isabella, who immediately introduces into the cloister of St. Clare the developing complex of ideas and images concerning restraint, self-restraint, and confinement:

Isab. And have you nuns no farther privileges?
Nun. Are not these large enough?
Isab. Yes, truly; I speak not as desiring more,
But rather wishing a more strict restraint
Upon the sisterhood, the votarists of St. Clare.[5]

[1.4.1-5]

Isabella is like Angelo in her desire to repress basic human drives, and the Duke's insinuation appears to attribute a measure of spiritual overreaching to both of these eager ascetics. But we accurately understand Isabella's restraint only when we notice that it is at once similar to and different from Angelo's. Isabella is certainly as absolute as the deputy, for she desires a restraint more "strict" (and this word retains something of its uncomfortable Latinate sense: drawn or bound tight) even than that imposed by an order famous for its harsh austerities. Although she chooses to submit to it, this restraint, unlike Angelo's, will entail external enforcement. Angelo is self-reliant, it seems, because he has felt no true passion before his confrontation with Isabella (see 2.2.186-87). It is a common error to assume that, because of her youth, Isabella knows nothing of the natural inclinations that Angelo seeks to suppress in himself and all Vienna. She has been Juliet's "cousin," Isabella later tells us, "by vain though apt affection" (1.4.46-48). The recognized vanity of that childhood attraction implies knowledge of the opposing reality, that

[5] I have restored the F2 reading. Lever suggests "sisters stood"; F reads "Sisterstood." Though it posits a plausible printing-house error, Lever's reading makes nonsense of the subsequent appositive.

which often results in a vice that most she does abhor and
most desires should meet the blow of justice (2.2.29-30).
She knows further that man is most assured that he has a
frail, a "glassy essence" (2.2.121), and that all men should
in their hearts "confess / A natural guiltiness" like Claudio's
(2.2.139-40). Isabella is fully aware, in short, that man's virtue is fragile and that "women are frail too":

> Ay, as the glasses where they view themselves,
> Which are as easy broke as they make forms.
>
> .   .   .   .
>
> we are soft as our complexions are,
> And credulous to false prints.
>
> [2.4.124-25, 128-29]

The unobtrusive and unintentional erotic symbolism (the
printing image; cf. 2.4.45-46) in these last lines indicates
that Isabella has known the yearnings of the flesh. Her determined espousal of the Poor Clares' "strict restraint"
therefore implies not purely virginal ignorance and inno-
cence, but a deliberate flight from the world. Like many
another sincere soul of Shakespeare's own and of earlier
ages, Isabella seeks freedom from feared natural impulse
in freely chosen religious bonds.

Isabella's emphasis on "restraint" recalls the restraint of
her brother Claudio and sparks our recognition that both
brother and sister are in different ways bound by the impulses of the flesh. To borrow Paul's helpful distinction, we
may say that Isabella and Claudio manifest different yet related and equally deviant relationships to law. Claudio uses
civil liberty as an occasion to the flesh and is made captive
to laws of society and nature. Isabella fails to heed the allied warning that concerns religious law: "Stand fast therefore in the liberty wherewith Christ hath made us free, and
be not entangled again with the yoke of bondage" (Gal. 5:1
and cf. 4:3).

That Isabella's chosen vocation *is* bondage becomes clear
not only from Shakespeare's use of symbolically charged

diction. In act 1 scene 4, the poet makes it very plain that this portion of his play belongs to the genre of antimonastic satire. The restraint explicit in the language becomes visible in stage imagery that recalls Claudio's more familiar bondage, for the very sight of Isabella enfolded in her novice's robe and of Francisca enveloped in the Poor Clares' traditional white habit intensifies our sense of confining rigidity. The generic identity of act 1, scene 4 becomes still clearer when Shakespeare presents a portion of the rule by which Isabella desires to be bound. When Lucio calls from the gate, Francisca entrusts Isabella with the key:

> It is a man's voice! Gentle Isabella,
> Turn you the key, and know his business of him;
> You may, I may not; you are yet unsworn:
> When you have vow'd, you must not speak with men
> But in the presence of the prioress;
> Then, if you speak, you must not show your face;
> Or if you show your face, you must not speak.
> He calls again: I pray you, answer him.
>
> [1.4.7-14]

The broken rhythms of Francisca's flurry of antithetical qualifications sound a note of deliberate mockery that suits the matter of her speech. Shakespeare's satiric tone is obvious, and it is easy to recognize a generic relationship to Erasmus's more broadly mocking assertion that regulars do everything "by certain precedents of their order, much like mathematical rules, which in no wise without offence, they may alter, or swerve from."[6] Both speeches imply that monastic devotion parcels out the unitary simplicity of the New Law into a complex series of trivial and artificial rules. Behind this panoply of regulation stands the prioress, their executor. Her virtual presence in the speech and the scene (cf. 1.4.86) further tightens Isabella's symbolic kinship with Claudio. His Provost balances her prioress, both emphasiz-

---

[6] *Folie*, sig. N1ʳ. See also chap. 2 above.

ing the prevailing atmosphere of constraint and compulsion.

In act 1, scene 4, that emphasis measures the distance between true worship of God and worship compelled by a human executor of factitious regulations, for Christian doctrine in general and the Sermon on the Mount in particular reveal that God's law, in Erasmus's words, "requireth the ground of the heart and love from the bottom thereof, and is not content with the outward work only: but rebuketh those works most of all which spring not of love, from the ground and low bottom of the heart."[7] As various scholars have said, this stress on intentions and motives rather than works implies that compelled sin can be considered no sin at all.[8] We should note in addition that the opposite can be equally true. Since the inner man is the essential concern of Christians and since only the exterior man is subject to compulsion, compelled virtue can never be virtuous. Hooker provides a lucid exposition of this commonplace: "What we do against our wills, or constrainedly, we are not properly said to do it, because the motive cause of doing it is not in ourselves, but carrieth us, as if the wind should drive a feather in the air, we no wit furthering that whereby we are driven."[9] In addition to the compulsion suggested by administrative surveillance, the atmosphere of imprisonment receives emphasis and refinement from vivid stage imagery and action. Shakespeare uses the convent's key—undoubtedly a sizable stage property—and Isabella's action of unlocking the gate to give the nuns' imprisonment visual force. When Lucio enters, moreover, Francisca possibly retires to one side and stands muffled in mute illustration of her rule. (Since the prioress is absent, we do not know how Francisca should act.) Her muffling pushes our sense of confinement to the

---

[7] *Paraphrase*, 1, fol. ✠ 4ʳ.

[8] Lever, pp. lxxx-lxxxi and Robert Grams Hunter, *Shakespeare and the Comedy of Forgiveness* (New York: Columbia University Press, 1965), p. 218. Cf. also *The Rape of Lucrece* ll. 1240-67.

[9] *Laws*, 1:186.

point of suffocation. Taken as a whole, act 1, scene 4 realizes in deft and original fashion the idea that monasteries are prisons where young Christians become slaves to needless and trivial regulation. Francisca's excerpt from her rule emphasizes, too, that one of its special purposes is to enforce the vow of chastity. What it aims specifically to imprison are the natural inclinations that Claudio has described.

This much is clear from Shakespeare's text and implied staging alone. Yet Francisca's rule appears likely also to inhibit obedience to God's law of true love. Familiarity with the conventions of antimonastic literature leads us to expect that monks and nuns may be guilty of yielding more careful obedience to the letter of their man-made laws than to the spiritual meaning of the Scriptures. The Tudor homilist directed his version of this attack especially against the vow of obedience: "But for all their riches, they might never help father nor mother, nor other that were in deed very needy and poor, without the license of their Father Abbott, Prior, or Warden."[10] Shakespeare appears to glance at this idea, to fulfill our genre-aroused expectations, when Isabella pauses before leaving her monastery "to give the Mother / Notice of [her] affair" (1.4.86-87). This detail reminds us of Francisca's "you may, I may not" and leads us to wonder whether Isabella's vows would have permitted her charitable mission in any circumstances. On the basis of the knowledge Shakespeare has provided, we can assume that at the very least, Isabella would have been obliged to hurry the prioress herself off to Angelo's court and to make her plea with veiled face.

Especially to a Protestant audience, charity would thus have seemed much encumbered by rules that appear, in the circumstances, frivolous. Enveloped in her novice's cos-

---

[10] See chap. 2 above. For a more balanced account of the monks' charitable activities, see H.P.R. Finberg, *Tavistock Abbey* (Cambridge: Cambridge University Press, 1951). Cf. Peter Heath, *The English Parish Clergy on the Eve of the Reformation* (Toronto: University of Toronto Press, 1969), chap. 9.

tume, Isabella therefore may function in act 1, scene 4 as a
visible image of the restraints by which monastic vows can
impede the true end of God's law. We can now perceive
therefore that the Duke's words to Angelo apply prolepti-
cally also to Isabella:

> Thyself and thy belongings
> Are not thine own so proper as to waste
> Thyself upon thy virtues, they on thee . . .
>   for if our virtues
> Did not go forth of us, 'twere all alike
> As if we had them not.
>
>   [1.1.29-35][11]

On the other hand, of course, Isabella's appearance in a
context drawn from antimonastic satire does not necessarily implicate her in all the evils Reformers attributed to
monasticism. She may be in that world, but not yet of it, for
she still holds the key to her freedom and may depart on
her mission of mercy. Yet despite its considerable particu-
larity, Shakespeare appears clearly to have developed
Isabella's character from typical contemporary conceptions
of monks and nuns. Isabella's name,[12] which is first mentioned and twice repeated (1.4.7, 18, 23) in the setting of
the convent, itself appears to suggest Catholicism, perhaps
specifically Spanish Catholicism. It may even allude directly to the "Isabella Rule" that governed the ascetic
branch of the Poor Clares (see Appendix). This aura of
Catholicism is elaborated as Lucio enters and indulges his
taste for turning religious phrases to jocular ends:

[11] As I pointed out earlier, this commonplace of Renaissance humanism
is repeated by King James in *The Basilicon Doron*. But we should notice also
that James imagines the unemployed virtues as "imprisoned": "For it is
not enough that ye have and retain (as prisoners) within yourself never so
many good qualities and virtues, except ye employ them, and set them on
work" (1:125).

[12] Although some think otherwise, I doubt that Shakespeare was much
concerned to honor his great-aunt Isabella, though that lady's name was
nicely suited to her own monastic profession.

Hail virgin, if you be—as those cheek-roses
Proclaim you are no less.

[1.4.16-17]

Lucio's irreverent and very ephemeral flattery of Isabella
relieves our growing sense of claustrophobia. At the same
time, his salutation mocks Catholic devotion to the Blessed
Virgin by echoing the familiar Catholic prayer and its
scriptural source (Luke 1:28). Though amusingly re-
tracted, Lucio's flattery momentarily confers sainthood on
Isabella. This mock canonization becomes explicit as Lucio,
again with sardonic irony, insists on his inviolate sincerity:

> I hold you as a thing enskied and sainted
> By your renouncement, an immortal spirit,
> And to be talk'd with in sincerity,
> As with a saint.
> *Isab.* You do blaspheme the good, in mocking me.

[1.4.34-38]

Although critics persist in reading Lucio's hyperbole as
empirical observation, Isabella knows a hawk from a hand-
saw and can recognize mockery when she hears it. The unceremonious "thing" jostles uncomfortably with its exalted
and exaltedly placed adjectives "enskied and sainted," and
this rhetorical exaggeration strengthens the literal sense of
the words—that Isabella has *made herself* a saint by renounc-
ing the secular world. The false "works ethic" doctrine contemporaries normally attributed to Catholicism is as precise here as the sarcasm is patent. To this, Isabella responds
as we expect a fresh devotee to do: her profession is "the
good." Although we are meant to enjoy Lucio's sarcasms,
we need not entirely disagree with Isabella—blasphemy is
blasphemy despite all controversy, and Lucio would doubtless treat devotion of any kind with equal contempt. It
would be unfair, no doubt, to ask that Isabella engage her
impudent visitor in a debate on the niceties of salvific
dogma. Yet while she takes no notice of his recognizably

papistical notion that monastic retirement confers sanctity,
the context of Lucio's remarks helps us to a more
perspicacious view. We begin to suspect that Isabella's religious ideas, in harmony with her costume, her name, and
her setting, are meant to differ sharply from those of a
largely Protestant audience.

In act 1, scene 4, this difference is implicitly related to the
complementary themes of human powers and universal
law. Consider, for example, the famous but often very
loosely interpreted lines on natural procreation:

> Your brother and his lover have embrac'd;
> As those that feed grow full, as blossoming time
> That from the seedness the bare fallow brings
> To teeming foison, even so her plenteous womb
> Expresseth his full tilth and husbandry.

> [1.4.40-44]

This view of sexuality is new to the play, and its refreshing
effect is heightened by contrast with the oppressive atmosphere of the convent. Sexuality and human procreation
become, in Lucio's poetry, functions of natural plenitude,
powers that are part of nature's beauty and, like all other
powers of nature and of man, descend from God. This is a
far cry from the suicidal thirst that Claudio described. It is
also an imperfect description of Claudio's relationship to
Juliet. Eager to encourage uninhibited intercourse, Lucio
employs his rhetorical skill to set out that sport in its
brightest colors. But his choice of illustrative material turns
ironically against him. His vision of the orderly unfolding
of the seasons stresses that aspect of the natural world
which has traditionally been taken as evidence of providential ordering and which here certainly implies that true fertility involves paradox, a *concordia discors* of restraint and
abandon. Lucio inadvertently reminds us that in violating
"outward order" Claudio and Juliet also violate the ultimate order that is reflected in marriage laws. Because it is a
power bestowed by the God of nature, sexuality, lawfully

indulged, can be the fruitful impulse Lucio describes. But when excessive liberty allows violations of divine and human law, sexuality becomes the thirst that leads to death. Though imperfect as a description of Claudio's error, therefore, Lucio's statement is thematically significant. It suggests an idea of sexuality that mediates between the excessive scope promoted by Lucio (whose very name implies, among other things, sexual wantonness—cf. Italian *luce* and its derivatives; see also *OED*, s.v. "light") and the repression of natural powers represented by Isabella and her monastic kin.

It is important to realize both that the topic of sexuality is an extension of the more general theme of human powers and that the scope of human power is a central theme in Lucio's bantering reference to merited sainthood. This theme resurfaces at the end of act 1, scene 4, when Lucio persuades Isabella to enter, at least temporarily, the active life. The speech also nicely illustrates Shakespeare's persistent effort to provide unequivocal standards by which to judge his characters' actions, for although Isabella's immediate mission is to gain human pardon for an infraction of human law, Shakespeare manipulates his diction to evoke larger meanings:

> your brother's life
> Falls into forfeit. . . .
> All hope is gone,
> Unless you have the grace by your fair prayer
> To soften Angelo.
>
> [1.4.65-70]

The diction is patently theological, and it hints that Isabella's role in the ensuing scenes will be that of an intercessor who comes by grace to soften the rigorous justice under which her brother will lose his life. Consciously or semiconsciously, we recognize that Isabella is being asked to assume a role akin to that of the Redeemer or, perhaps more naturally in this context, of his mother, heroine of Catholic

Mariolotry. She is to imitate, insofar as they are imitable, the greatest exemplars of self-denying intercession.

For the moment, this suggestion serves primarily to guide our response to the diffidence Isabella feels concerning her ability to aid Claudio:

Isab.   Alas, what poor ability's in me
          To do him good!
Lucio. Assay the power you have.
Isab.   My power? Alas, I doubt.
                              [1.4.75-77]

Because of the Christological (Mariological) suggestions in Lucio's request, Isabella's doubts are especially becoming. But despite her diffidence, Isabella is persuaded to approach Angelo, to

> let him learn to know, when maidens sue,
> Men give like gods; but when they weep and kneel,
> All their petitions are as freely theirs
> As they themselves would owe them.
>   [1.4.80-84]

The conventional association of magistrate and Deity here becomes once again explicit, and this convention lends special weight to the great scenes of intercession that occur shortly. Both Isabella and Angelo, we foresee, will be acting in ways that should make them appear (if we may Christianize the Homeric epithet) "godlike." In light of our own experience and of the play's earlier stress on human dependence and weakness, we know that men and women in this world are more likely to fall short of this standard than to attain it.

And in Isabella's name, in her costume and setting, in the nature of her provisionally espoused rule, in Lucio's doctrinally accurate sarcasms, in Isabella's tacit (and rhetorically decorous) acquiescence in his questionable doctrine, and in her announced need "to give the Mother / Notice of [her] affair" (1.4.86-87), Isabella is identified with typical contemporary criticism of the regular clergy. Her manner of embracing the godlike role of her brother's redeemer demands careful attention, and we expect that Shakespeare will include other traits typically associated with monks and nuns. Rather like Christ, the humanists, and Duke Vincentio, who all disapprove of "contemplation that should be finished in itself," we secular moderns normally expect contemplatives to exhibit inexperience and downright incompetence in the affairs of the world. That expectation is fulfilled in *Measure for Measure* as Isabella allows her diffidence in worldly affairs to mar her first plea for Claudio. Fittingly, her chilly timidity receives an injection of warmth from Lucio, spokesman for unrestrained natural emotions—emotions that may include love of kin and of friends. As she warms to the argument, Isabella's confidence grows impressively. She bursts finally into vituperation scarcely tolerable in so exalted a court:

> But man, proud man,
> Dress'd in a little brief authority,
> Most ignorant of what he's most assur'd—
> His glassy essence—like an angry ape
> Plays such fantastic tricks before high heaven
> As makes the angels weep.
>
> [2.2.118-23]

These thinly veiled attacks on the judge himself bespeak not only passionate devotion to Claudio's cause. They also reveal an accretion of confidence in Isabella's power to attain earthly justice, and this confidence parallels a still greater assurance in affairs of the spirit. We have noticed Isabella's conviction that her renouncement constituted "the good." This belief in the spiritual value of monastic observance receives further development in the same scene. For like her progenitors in antimonastic satire and their prototypes in the Bible, Isabella begins here to evince a somewhat superficial confidence in works of the Law. Our first hint—and it is only a hint—of this legalism appears when Lucio reports that Claudio has made Juliet pregnant. Isabella's automatic, impulsive response is "let him marry her!" (1.4.49). Although it is common, and probably true, to assert that Jacobean mores would have led Shakespeare's audience to concur in this solution, we should not overlook the possibility that his audience may also have recognized in Isabella's words a paraphrase of the Old Law itself.

The applicability of Moses' law to Isabella's words has been obscured by scholarly insistence that Moses prescribed death for fornication. This notion persists, in turn, because Shakespearean scholars assume that the Old Law confuses fornication and adultery. The evidence cited, for example, by R. G. Hunter, to prove that there was a contemporary Puritan drive to make fornication a capital offense (because it was so under the Old Law) in fact concerns adultery.[13] But whether Isabella knows it or not, she is accurately echoing the Old Law's provision for cases like Claudio's: "if a man entice a maid that is not betrothed, and lie with her, he shall surely endow her to be his wife" (Exod. 22:16; cf. Deut. 22:28-29). Although we know that marriage was officially recognized in Elizabethan England as a remedy for fornication, we nonetheless rightly feel a certain superficiality in Isabella's suggestion. This feeling is encouraged by the genre of antimonastic satire by which Isabella is in part created for us. It is rendered unavoidable because, just a few moments earlier, Claudio has described his physical bondage not merely as an effect of outward crime and Viennese law but of a universal law of human nature. Although it is drawn from her by eager concern for both Claudio and Juliet, Isabella's proposed solution carries an inadvertent hint that Claudio can be freed from his bondage merely by the fulfillment of legal precept. Unlike

---

[13] *Comedy of Forgiveness*, p. 211. Lever (pp. xlv-xlvi, but see also lxvi) joins Hunter in this confusion. Only one of his citations offers Hunter some support, for Stubbes in his rage includes fornication in a list of supposedly capital offenses.

spectators who have followed carefully the development of the play, Isabella betrays no awareness of the spiritual dimensions of the law or of Claudio's disease.[14]

But the pressure of dramatic events prevents us from dwelling on this very oblique hint of legal formalism, and after all, Isabella is no simple personification like Fals-Semblant. She is a type, but she is more than that. Represented by an actress (originally an actor) who can command immediate human sympathies, she is also a sincere young novice whose religious principles have begun to seem distorted in typically monkish ways. She betrays the inconsistency normal both to real people who find themselves in trying circumstances and to symbolic figures who appear in narrative genres. In her first meeting with Angelo, therefore, the religious idea that receives most emphatic statement is not law, but the grace that issued in undeserved redemption. In reply to Angelo's insistence that "Your brother is a forfeit of the law," Isabella's response reaches to the ultimate frontiers of the concept of law:

> Why, all the souls that were, were forfeit once,
> And He that might the vantage best have took
> Found out the remedy. How would you be
> If He, which is the top of judgement, should
> But judge you as you are? O, think on that,
> And mercy then will breathe within your lips,
> Like man new made.
>
> [2.2.73-79]

This speech paraphrases doctrine central to the play. Isabella asks Angelo to exercise his godlike judicial function in precisely the way the Sermon on the Mount prescribes: "first cast out the beam out of thine own eye; and then shalt thou see clearly to cast out the mote out of thy brother's eye" (Matt. 7:5 and see chap. 1). One who first re-

---

[14] We later discover that the Old Law to which Isabella alludes is identical with the Viennese law administered by Duke Vincentio. See chap. 6, below.

calls his own inherent sinfulness and gratuitous salvation will judge in a manner characteristic of the regenerate. According to the terms Isabella borrows from Paul, such a judge will put on the new man and his charity will issue in mercy. Similar implications inhere in Isabella's second paraphrase of the play's scriptural source:

> Go to your bosom,
> Knock there, and ask your heart what it doth know
> That's like my brother's fault. If it confess
> A natural guiltiness, such as is his,
> Let it not sound a thought upon your tongue
> Against my brother's life.
>
> [2.2.137-42]

Every judge who begins with sincere self-judgment will confess such "natural guiltiness" and will consequently forgive his debtors as he expects his own debts to be forgiven. For magistrates, this forgiveness need not result in a dismissed case. It leads instead to a softening of legalistic rigor and, consequently, to an enactment of the New Law's essence (cf. chap. 1, n. 49).

The ubiquitous but unobtrusive presence of the New Law in the language of act 2 deserves mention, for it invites us to judge the characters' actions by standards that are both firm and generous. Early in act 2, scene 1, Escalus alludes to Matt. 7:1-2 in words that again enforce the lesson that right judgment springs from the humane and accurate observation that all men—even the most precise—are likely to succumb to inevitable weakness:

> Let but your honour know—
> Whom I believe to be most strait in virtue—
> That in the working of your own affections,
> Had time coher'd with place, or place with wishing,
> Or that the resolute acting of your blood
> Could have attain'd th'effect of your own purpose,
> Whether you had not sometime in your life

Err'd in this point, which now you censure him,
And pull'd the law upon you.

[2.1.8-16]

Similar antitheses between "you" and "him" reappear in intensified form during Isabella's first plea for mercy:

If he had been as you, and you as he,
You would have slipp'd like him, but he like you
Would not have been so stern.

[2.2.64-66]

Rhetoric here imitates the idea it expresses, for thoughtful consideration of the other—an imaginative transposition of souls—is essential to loving one's neighbor as oneself. Hooker puts the point effectively—and bases his exposition on the measure-for-measure text. The law of charity, he says,

> hath brought men to know that it is their duty no less to love others than themselves. For seeing those things which are equal must needs all have one measure; if I cannot but wish to receive all good, even as much at every man's hand as any man can wish unto his own soul, how should I look to have any part of my desire herein satisfied, unless myself be careful to satisfy the like desire which is undoubtedly in other men, we all being of one and the same nature? To have any thing offered them repugnant to this desire must needs in all respects grieve them as much as me: so that if I do harm I must look to suffer; there being no reason that others should shew greater measure of love to me than they have by me shewed unto them.[15]

The constant, implicit presence of this essential law and of its assumption of human equality—equality of desires and depravity—becomes in act 2, scene 2 an important determinant of our responses to Isabella. Her fervent anger

[15] *Laws*, 1:180.

after line 107 may be altogether righteous, but it expresses
a level of assurance that soon modulates into self-
righteousness of the kind typically associated with monks
and nuns. As their interview comes to a close, Isabella offers to bribe Angelo:

> Not with fond sickles of the tested gold,
> Or stones, whose rate are either rich or poor
> As fancy values them: but with true prayers,
> That shall be up at heaven and enter there
> Ere sunrise: prayers from preserved souls,
> From fasting maids, whose minds are dedicate
> To nothing temporal.
>   [2.2.150-56]

This speech rings with the good will of an ingenuous
novice, zealous in the service of God. Yet Isabella considers
her bribe valuable not only because it is not "fond" gold,
but because the prayers are "true prayers." The final appositive forcefully implies that, for Isabella, prayers gain
value—become "true"—by virtue of monastic works performed in isolation from the world: "prayers from preserved souls, / From fasting maids." These works, she implies, render prayers worthy to enter heaven, perhaps with
some special priority conferred as well by early rising as by
allied monastic austerities, "That shall be up at heaven and
enter there / Ere sunrise." The speech recalls in a subtler
and more sympathetic form the tradition of the Summoner's Friar and his ill-founded confidence that the efficacy of fraternal prayer is enhanced by good works. One of
Erasmus's attacks on monastic presumption states a commonplace—treated at length in the Sermon on the Mount
(Matt. 6)—that is especially apropos: "There is no man further from true religion than he that thinketh himself to be
very religious."[16]

The metaphor of bribery yields further grounds for

---

[16] *Enchiridion*, sigs. C6ᵛ-C7ʳ.

criticism of Isabella because she characteristically employs commercial diction at unfortunate times—most notoriously when she considers her brother's death "cheaper" than the effects of having intercourse with Angelo (2.4.105). Although they indeed are not gold, and we gratefully share Lucio's relief (2.2.149), her prayers are offered as payment for a benefit. This betrays once more the subtly revealed naiveté that Isabella showed on hearing of Claudio's plight. Prayers are not to be offered as advance payment for favors granted by men. Prayers are to be made, the homilist says, "to declare therein as well the faith we have in Christ towards God, as also the mutual charity that we bear one towards another, in that we pity our brother's case, and make our humble petition to God for him."[17] Isabella's fee-for-service attitude betrays by contrast the disconcerting fact that her prayers will constitute, in a spiritual sense, bribery. She does not offer gold; yet she offers a commodity she judges still more valuable: prayers of the votarists of St. Clare. Isabella's description of monastic prayer concludes, moreover, with ringing irony. Our recollection of Francisca's fussy rules renders ludicrous the notion that the nuns' minds are "dedicate to nothing temporal." As externally coercive man-made additions to the laws of Christ, these rules are inherently subject to envious and calumniating time.[18]

A final point must be made concerning Isabella's confidence in the value of monastic prayer. Audiences trained in even the first principles of Reformed Christianity realize that prayer must be attempted only with profound humility. In the official catechism of the Tudor period, Alexander Nowell treats at length the question "with what confidence" mortal men in their prayers may call upon the immortal God. His answer is given in terms that echo the appraisal of unaided human power that was inculcated by

---

[17] *Certaine Sermons*, sig. Kk4ᵛ.
[18] See Erasmus, *Enchiridion*, sig. C3ʳ⁻ᵛ.

the Protestant doctrine of salvation. Insofar as they are in accord with that doctrine, they differ from Isabella's view:

> We are indeed every way most unworthy. But we thrust not ourselves in, proudly and arrogantly, as if we were worthy, but we come to him in the name, and upon trust of Christ our Mediator by whom the door being opened to us, though we be most base silly wretches, made of clay and slime, oppressed with conscience of our own sins, we shall not be forbidden to enter, nor shall have hard access to the majesty of God, and to the obtaining of his favour . . . our prayers stand in confidence, not upon anything in us, but upon the only worthiness of Christ, in whose name we pray.[19]

We ought always to pray, Nowell concludes, "leaving all respect of our own worthiness, and framing our prayers, as it were out of the mouth of Christ; which doing, as it is most agreeable to the truth of Scriptures, so is it most far from the fault of arrogancy and presumption."[20] Since she intends to live according to man-made laws and places her confidence in works of the devoted life, Isabella is unlikely to pray in a manner "agreeable to the truth of Scriptures" as the Reformers understood that truth. She intends to enter upon a life that by its very nature leads to the "arrogancy and presumption" that supplants Christ himself.

Forgetting the attractive self-doubt she shows in worldly affairs, Isabella implies in her first meeting with Angelo that she might assume a function utterly unique to Christ. As we have seen, a common argument in the attack on the religious orders held that they corrupted penance by claiming the power to "satisfy, not only for their own sins, but also for all their benefactors, brothers, and sisters of religion." This charge is epitomized in Luther's assertion that "they all say, 'I am Christ'; they abstain from using the name, but arrogate to themselves the office, the work, and the person."

[19] *Catechism*, p. 186.   [20] Ibid., p. 187.

Although she avoids outright blasphemy and although her intentions in themselves are generous and sincere, Isabella displays a clear kinship with monks and friars who exhibit this presumption. In their second meeting, Angelo poses his tendentious question:

> Might there not be a charity in sin
> To save this brother's life?
>
> [2.4.63-64]

While she altogether misses the drift of Angelo's question and consequently exhibits her inexperience in worldly affairs, Isabella's response also betrays belief in the notion that souls of the religious can substitute for those of other men:

> Please you to do't,
> I'll take it as a peril to my soul;
> It is no sin at all, but charity.
>
> [2.4.64-66]

Shakespeare deems this questionable doctrine worthy of repetition, for Isabella engages her invaluable prayers to make the substitution efficacious:

> you granting of my suit,
> If that be sin, I'll make it my morn prayer
> To have it added to the faults of mine,
> And nothing of your answer.
>
> [2.4.70-73]

On the surface, this appears to be merely the exuberant generosity appropriate to a youthful maiden pleading for her brother's life. She has just received a hint that Claudio can indeed be saved; she will do anything—even take upon herself another's sin. Yet Shakespeare chose to express that generosity in a way that manifestly recalls the false doctrine which sixteenth-century Protestant writers typically associate with monastic devotion. Isabella believes that Angelo's sin could be transferred to her. It is an opinion

Shakespeare's audience had been prepared to expect from a character enfolded in monastic robes, and it is a theme central to the Erasmian colloquy that appears to have left identifiable traces in Shakespeare's play (see Appendix). Even Isabella's urgent desire to accept Angelo's hypothetical sin numbers among the accumulating details that identify her with contemporary criticisms of the regular clergy.

Isabella's monastic errors and the full subtlety of her interrogation by Angelo in act 2, scene 4 are thrown further into relief by Shakespeare's deft manipulation of narrative structure. Act 2, scene 3 constitutes a prelude that conditions our responses to the more elaborate following scene, for it is entirely concerned with the Duke's parallel interrogation of Juliet. In this, his first appearance since act 1, scene 3, the Duke takes us rather by surprise. We have been expecting to see a disguised figure spying on Angelo's administrative activities. His appearance at the prison among people already incarcerated conflicts mildly with this expectation. The Duke's behavior again challenges interpretation. The scene's first lines offer us oblique assistance, for after a moment of comedy in which the Duke's familiarity with the Provost nearly betrays his disguise ("Hail to you Provost—so I think you are"), the new "friar" announces his errand:

> Bound by my charity, and my bless'd order,
> I come to visit the afflicted spirits
> Here in the prison.
>
> [2.3.3-5]

I believe we are to recognize in this announcement yet another allusion to the central law of God. The Duke obliquely describes himself as a monk whom even Calvin would have seen to be a "true" one—free yet bound by the charity that governs all men, as well as by his blessed order. Since he is literally enacting one of the conventional corporal works of mercy, this announced and dramatized

charity of intent sets the tone for the remainder of the
scene, where the Duke and Juliet extend and internalize
the play's theme of judgment. They do so by performing
an inner "arraignment" (2.3.21-23) and a trial that parallels the aborted judicial one (of Pompey and Froth) in the
previous scene. This successful arraignment begins with
charitable gentleness: "Repent you, fair one, of the sin you
carry?" (2.3.19),[21] and it aims to test Juliet's penitence to
find "if it be sound / Or hollowly put on" (2.3.22-23). The
Duke's test of Juliet's penitence begins as a test of her love:

Duke. Love you the man that wrong'd you?
Juliet. Yes, as I love the woman that wrong'd him.
                                         [2.3.24-25]

Juliet's paraphrase of the second precept of charity iden-
tifies her love with that which led the Duke to the prison.
Her claim is therefore a large one; its sincerity in turn is
put to the test:

Duke. So then it seems your most offenceful act
           Was mutually committed?
Juliet.   Mutually.
Duke. Then was your sin of heavier kind than his.
                                         [2.3.26-28]

Mutuality implies equality of guilt. Despite social conventions that charge the woman with special responsibility for
chastity in sexual relationships, the Duke's unexplained
conclusion seems a little absurd. We are made to feel that
Juliet's natural response, like our own, would be self-
justification—*he* is equally guilty. She surprises us too: "I do

[21] Miles (*Problem of "Measure for Measure,"* p. 178), perpetuates a common misinterpretation of the Duke's tone in this scene. The Duke, she asserts, "does not evince any sympathy for her plight . . . his assumed role
forces him into the position of strongly condemning her 'most offenceful
act' (III.iii.26). His attitude [is one] of moral superiority." Hawkins
(*Likenesses of Truth*, p. 71) is more strident, though her point is the same. I
fail to see how such interpretations square with line 19, or with the rest of
the scene. Reproof for error need not be harsh and inhumane.

confess it, and repent it, father" (2.3.29). As often, we are forced to analyze apparently irrational speech and behavior, to guess that the Duke's illogic is designed to expose love that masquerades as self-denying charity. Charity would indeed be violated if Juliet were to demand that Claudio share equally in her shame. Though it is "natural" to point the finger of accusation, it is no act of love. In this recognition, we are further reminded that charity is *not* ordinarily a "natural" response. Juliet's unnatural behavior is "against all sense," and she becomes, momentarily, a figure who typifies love in its ideal form. And although she is uninclined to justify herself, to rationalize her errors, or to show the aggressively witty individuality we admire in Rosalind and in Beatrice, she is rescued from insipidity by her intense love for Claudio. On being reminded of his approaching death, Juliet's apparent pain indicates that she shares intensely in his suffering (2.3.37-42). Her oxymoron "O injurious love" reminds us that the love which led to their mutual plight was an irrational earthly parody of the transcendent reality that now informs her character. "Injurious love" earlier received its definitive anatomy from Claudio. It is the thirst that soon drives Angelo to cry with terrible irony "Plainly conceive, I love you" (2.4.140).

Juliet shows herself capable of moral discriminations like these when the Duke tests her patience still further to discover whether it springs from love of God, the essential precondition for true love of neighbor, or from a worldly fear of shame:

Duke. 'Tis meet so, daughter; but lest you do repent,
As that the sin hath brought you to this shame,
Which sorrow is always toward ourselves, not
    heaven,
Showing we would not spare heaven as we love it,
But as we stand in fear—
Juliet. I do repent me as it is an evil,
And take the shame with joy.

                          [2.3.30-36]

In her repentance, she realizes once again a Christian ideal. According to medieval and contemporary authorities, "grief for sin, because it is sin" is an emotion inspired by divine grace.[22] Although Juliet's assertion that she finds joy in shame appears at first sight hyperbolical, it conceals the venerable paradox that adversity is always at bottom matter for joy. The Epistle to the Hebrews offers our most relevant locus classicus for the opinion that even "undeserved" suffering manifests divine love, and for the corollary that we must "run with patience the race that is set before us, Looking unto Jesus the author and finisher of our faith; who for the joy that was set before him endured the cross, despising the shame" (Heb. 12:1-2). If shame is to be our cross, Christ is to be our exemplar in taking shame with joyful expectation of eternal reward.

The cross in some form is unavoidable, and as modern scholars often forget, the suffering it brings is a necessary mark of election: "despise not thou the chastening of the Lord. . . . For whom the Lord loveth he chasteneth, and scourgeth every son whom he receiveth. If ye endure chastening, God dealeth with you as with sons. . . . But if ye be without chastisement, whereof all are partakers, then are ye bastards, and not sons" (Heb. 12:5-8). The same point is prominently made in the Sermon on the Mount (Matt. 5:11-12): It is the Christian's lot to suffer, and often in particular to suffer shame.[23] Juliet's joy in shame thus carries with it significant horizons of meaning that are perfectly suited to the religious subject of the entire scene. We perceive in her somewhat disconcerting words an implicit recognition that she ·has received punishment "lest," as the homilist puts it, she "should perish everlastingly." Her implied submission to the divine rod manifests faith in and obedience to divine providence, "the second law eternal."

With us, the Duke perceives these unspoken implica-

---

[22] See Perkins, *Whole Treatise*, p. 52. The implied corollary is that true sorrow for sin arises from the knowledge that God is offended.

[23] Cf. *Certaine Sermons*, sig. F2^{r-v}, and Rom. 5:3-5.

tions. Like the Friar in *Much Ado*, and as his own early self-judgment has led us to expect, the Duke recognizes the limits of his power to give moral counsel. The homily he was preparing to deliver proves needless, and in respect for Juliet's transparent integrity, he breaks off further instruction. In its context, his final benediction carries significant religious overtones. Literally, his words "There rest" advise Juliet to retain her ideal penitence. But the words also hint that submission such as hers is the ultimate source of rest, for, as we have seen, true rest is available only to those who avoid self-justification—who acknowledge their sinfulness and depend entirely on God. Meanings such as these are implicit in the laconic yet evocative language of this scene, and their presence alerts us to watch carefully for similar implications in the great, parallel confrontation that follows immediately.

The subtle moral introspection encouraged by Duke Vincentio in act 2, scene 3 suggests that scene's most important relationship to scene 4. Both draw heavily upon a rich and (in Shakespeare's age) flourishing subdivision of moral theology. This branch or phase of Christian philosophy was known as casuistry, the effort to relate imperatives of divine law to particular circumstances. Such efforts are ubiquitous in the standard genres of practical divinity, informing sermons, enchiridia, and the like. But casuistry also flourished independently in a popular sixteenth- and seventeenth-century genre known as "case-divinity," or cases of conscience.[24] Like the central confrontation scenes of *Measure for Measure*, such works invite readers to become intellectually and emotionally engaged in precisely defined ethical issues, to make careful distinctions among sins, to weigh the value of apparent virtue and the gravity of seeming vice, to wonder if in some circumstances there might be charity in sin, to believe that compelled sins might in fact be sinless. Having identified casuistry as the broad parent

[24] Perkins's *Whole Treatise* is perhaps the most famous English exemplar of this genre.

genre of Juliet's meeting with the Duke—the shared type
of language that allows them to say so much to each other
and to us in so few words—we are better prepared to comprehend the parallel debate between Isabella and Angelo.

Betraying his characteristic refusal to recognize degrees
of magnitude in crime, Angelo opens this confrontation by
asserting that fornication and murder are morally equivalent:

> It were as good
> To pardon him that hath from nature stolen
> A man already made, as to remit
> Their saucy sweetness that do coin heaven's image
> In stamps that are forbid. 'Tis all as easy
> Falsely to take away a life true made,
> As to put mettle in restrained means
> To make a false one.
>
> [2.4.42-49]

Although he is ostensibly stating a principle of legal administration, Angelo's terms anchor firmly in human experience. It is as "easy," he asserts, to commit murder as to
engage in illegitimate intercourse. This assertion defies
common sense, and I dare say our own individual experience, not to mention a basic assumption of the Old as well
as the New Law—the reasonable assumption that all sins
are not equally grave. As Erasmus (and others) had taught
English Christians, Moses clearly recognized sin's varying
gravity; the law that prescribes "eye for eye, tooth for
tooth, hand for hand, foot for foot," demands equivalence
between crime and punishment and seeks to ensure "that
vengeance should not go too far."[25] A murderer deserves
to lose his life, but, as we saw above (pp. 108-109), a for-
nicator should marry his partner. Angelo's statement de-
viates grossly even from the tenets of the Old Law, a law
that, as "Moses" himself repeatedly states and as English

---

[25] *Paraphrase*, 1, fol. F3^v.

authorities on human law sometimes reminded their countrymen, had been promulgated to govern "bondmen; yea, and them very obstinate, stubborn, and stiff-necked."[26]

But a further difficulty may lurk in Angelo's statement on the moral equivalence of murder and fornication. Readers conversant with Reformation theology sometimes suggest that Angelo alludes in these lines to the commonplace Protestant doctrine that all sins are equally heinous in God's eyes. Although his language does, as I have said, focus on human experience, this more abstract doctrinal consideration may be present as an overtone. If so, it complicates the issue by providing a theological rationale for an assertion that offends both common sense and our own experience of the world. Comprehensive attention to the play's theological sources and immediate backgrounds rescues us, I think, from this puzzlement and affirms my persistent tacit contention that Protestant theology is typically less doctrinaire, less remote from human realities than we expect it to be.

In point of fact, scholars are right to assert that for most Protestant theologians all sin was so offensive to God that it would lead (unless the sinner received gratuitous pardon) inevitably to hell. What is less well known, however, is that the same Protestant authorities who considered all sins

[26] *Utopia*, trans. Ralph Robynson (1551), in Milligan, *Three Renaissance Classics*, p. 130. A premier legal authority whose works were enjoying special vogue while Shakespeare was at work on *Measure for Measure* was of course King James. In *The Basilicon Doron* James speaks directly to this point, for he shows great concern for equitable adjustment of punishment to crime. He grounds his judgment, moreover, on divine law, cautioning that fornication ought not to be considered a negligible vice. One should weigh "every sin, not according to the light estimation, and common use of it in the world, but as the book of God counteth of it" (1:49). James later repeats the point (1:123), adding that the Old Testament reveals "what *praemium* or *poena* was accordingly given by God" (1:33) for particular acts of obedience and disobedience. Had Angelo shared the king's stern views, he might have recognized the spiritual gravity of fornication and yet have afforded Claudio the mercy of the Old Law. He might have required that Claudio marry Juliet.

damning often produced detailed and careful statements
that weigh, with minute attention to circumstantial detail,
the relative gravity of individual sins.[27] Even divines of
Puritan inclination argued that sins vary in gravity, and
William Perkins found evidence for this in a text that appears to have exerted direct influence on *Measure for Measure*. Perkins argues that when Christ asks "why beholdest
thou the mote that is in thy brother's eye, but considerest
not the beam that is in thine own eye?" (Matt. 7:4) he implies that sins can be as weighty as logs or as slight as motes.
Perkins then supplies a characteristically graphic illustration of his point:

> Christ makes a difference of sins: some are as motes,
> some as beams: every sin indeed is death and condemna-
> tion, and yet all are not equal, but far different in de-
> grees: as some men are drowned in the channel and
> middle of the sea, some by the shore side, which places
> differ in depth and danger, though all is one in regard of
> death: some men endure damnation in deeper measure,
> some in lesser, yet both are condemned.[28]

[27] This seeming self-contradiction is explicable if we attend to the
theologian's or the preacher's rhetorical purposes. If he aims to controvert the implication inherent, he thought, in Roman Catholic salvific
dogma, that venial sins do not damn the sinner, he asserts that all sins are
utterly damnable. He is equally absolute if he wants to stress the ethical
aims of the Protestant doctrine that men are saved by faith alone. We
must be saved, he argues, by sharing through faith in Christ's merits, because *any* sin should justly damn us—and we cannot of our own volition
do anything but sin. But when Protestant authors turned to pastoral care,
to teaching the faithful how to apply doctrine to daily living, the varying
gravity of sin assumed tremendous importance and received correspondingly elaborate treatment.

[28] *An Exposition of Christ's Sermon on the Mount*, in *The Workes of that Famous and Worthie Minister of Christ . . . M. William Perkins* (Cambridge: John
Legat, 1609), 2, fol. S2ʳ. See also *Whole Treatise*, pp. 33-34.

Perkins is no isolated case. William Tyndale (*Expositions and Notes*, p. 10)
and Hugh Latimer (*Sermons*, 2:7) adapt to Protestant uses the old Catholic
distinction of mortal and venial sins. Bullinger (*Decades* 3.10; Parker Society, 8:407-25) pronounces that "sins which are of their own nature mortal

Protestant doctrine therefore validates the surprise we feel when Angelo asserts that murder and fornication can be committed with equal ease and should be treated with equivalent judicial severity. Like the Duke's interrogation of Juliet, then, Angelo's offensive against Isabella opens with a startling assertion. Of course, Angelo intends his remarks about the equality of murder and fornication as a gambit to elicit Isabella's admission that some sins can be less damnable than others. Yet the idea matches Angelo's enforcement of Viennese law and can therefore be taken also as a statement of one of the deputy's private convictions, a rule by which he seeks to govern his life.

Unlike Angelo, Isabella does recognize differences of severity in earthly crime: " 'Tis set down so in heaven, but not in earth" (2.4.50). It is not impossible that these words paraphrase, tersely, the idea that, in God's eyes, all sins are equally damnable but that civil law ought to recognize crime's varying gravity. But in the experiential context established by Angelo's words, this interpretation seems somewhat remote. Because the velocity of the dramatic dialogue prevents auditors from settling the issue with any precision, we are likely to find Isabella's statement somewhat unsettling. Taken at face value, her words appear to

---

are through grace in faith of Jesus Christ made venial," that "sins do arise by steps, and increase by circumstances," and that anyone who considers all sins equal is infected by heresy derived from the Stoics. He supports his belief that sins vary in severity by referring to the Sermon on the Mount. Finally, although Calvin (*Institutes* 3.4.17-18; fols. 206^v-207^r) condemns the Roman tradition of dividing sins into various branches for purposes of auricular confession, he also urges that we not only must confess our general inherent sinfulness, we must also "record, how great and diverse is our filth of sins, not only that we be unclean, but what, how great, and in how many parts is our uncleanness; not only that we be debters, but with how great debts we be loaden." He adds (3.4.28) that although all sins deserve damnation, the sins of believers are venial, not because they are not deserving of spiritual death, but because, "by the mercy of God there is no condemnation to them that are in Christ Jesus. . . . [Yet] it doth not therefore immediately follow, that sins are equal, because they are altogether deadly."

imply that it is "set down" among God's laws that men will commit fornication and murder with identical ease, that there is no divine archetype of the earthly equity whereby crime receives measured punishment, and that God views fornicators and murderers with uniform severity. This implies that Angelo's iron law is God's law. As the debate proceeds, we recognize with growing conviction that Isabella's theology posits a God created in Angelo's image and similitude, an idea that conflicts with the vision of benign deity she had promoted earlier (2.2.73-79).

Our perception of Isabella's error should entail no smug censoriousness. A young woman subjected to insidious and aggressive cross-examination by an articulate and reputedly august magistrate should win no small measure of sympathy. She might also be expected to falter, inadvertently to misrepresent her true convictions. But while her errors cannot be viewed harshly, we should not overlook the fact that Isabella's misconception of the Deity remains firm throughout the scene. We begin to perceive this more clearly when, seizing on her hint that "in earth" crimes vary in magnitude, Angelo puts this question:

> Which had you rather, that the most just law
> Now took your brother's life; or, to redeem him,
> Give up your body to such sweet uncleanness
> As she that he hath stain'd?
>
> [2.4.52-55]

Angelo's diction seems calculated to perpetuate in our minds a conception of the Deity in his most beneficent aspect. To "redeem" her brother from "the most just law" by giving her body for satisfaction evokes insistent memories of Christ. On his part, Angelo's insinuation that Isabella's hypothetical sin might parallel the divine atonement is an outrageous exercise in false-seeming, a diabolical effort to make his sin appear to be her virtue. Yet the parallel is not utterly baseless, and in the context of moral subtlety that dominates this portion of the play, we are encouraged to concede the possibility that Isabella's sacrifice *could*, in its utter self-abnegation, constitute a shockingly unconventional *imitatio Christi*. (She is being asked, in a sexual sense, to "die" in order to "redeem" Claudio from the "law.") This possibility allows us to sense some rigidity in Isabella's reply, one that may carry an ironically inappropriate glance at Matt. 10:28,[29] "Sir, believe this: / I had rather give my body than my soul" (2.4.55-56). *If* Isabella's sacrifice were in some sense to parallel the Redeemer's, as the language here urges us to suspect, only the most implacable of deities would exact inevitable damnation. Angelo's rejoinder is not without point: Isabella's soul may not be directly at issue, for "our compell'd sins / Stand more for number than for accompt" (2.4.57-58).

This idea not only accords with native common sense, it is also a standard assumption of the moral theology that underlies and enriches this portion of Shakespeare's text. Its paternity can be traced from Augustine (*City of God* 1.1.16-18), through Aquinas (*S.T.* 2.1.73, art. 6) and Dante (where it determines the moral topography of *Inferno* and *Purgatorio*, passim), to contemporaries like Hooker (see the earlier quotation). The rationale behind Angelo's assertion is that sins diminish in severity in inverse proportion to the (interior *or* exterior) compulsion applied. Or conversely, as Perkins puts it, "the more free the will is, the greater is the sin."[30] Both common sense and ethical sophistication impel us therefore to recognize that Christian ethics would never readily condemn Isabella for choosing to "redeem" her brother by means of actions beyond the control of her will.

Unhappily, however, Angelo's aphorism on compelled sins is, as he himself realizes (2.4.59-60), only partially applicable to Isabella's circumstances. If she were to accept Angelo's as yet hypothetical proposal, her action would not be altogether beyond the control of her will. She could suf-

---

[29] "And fear not them which kill the body, but are not able to kill the soul: but rather fear him which is able to destroy both soul and body in hell."

[30] *Whole Treatise*, p. 18.

fer forcible rape while remaining perfectly sinless, but Angelo's temptation is especially diabolic because it requires complicity. Isabella must *choose* sin. Yet the dramatic situation obliges us to see that if Isabella should choose to give up her body to such sweet uncleanness, she could hardly be said to act "freely." Isabella will soon be placed under powerful compulsion to choose that particular sin—not only to rescue Claudio from death, but also to save him from the lingering torments with which Angelo embellishes his threat (2.4.164-66). The true complexity of Isabella's dilemma becomes apparent only when we recognize that she is faced neither with a voluntary decision to sin nor with a situation of absolute compulsion, but with something that lies in the gray region between—a paradox of voluntary compulsion. In this sense Angelo's proposition constitutes a demonic analogue of the slavery that Isabella freely wills upon herself by entering a convent.

Like those we encounter in the play's first scene, Angelo's insistent interrogatives solicit not only Isabella's responses but our own as well. The pressure of the dialogue allows no leisurely solutions, but fragmentary responses necessarily occur to us. Thinking perhaps of the fundamentals of Protestant salvific dogma, we might entertain the fleeting possibility that Isabella's hypothetical intercourse could never damn her—simply because good or evil works neither save nor damn. We might wonder, too, if Isabella might not, in this case, commit sin because her motives are pure; that is, she might sin so that good would result, for sin lies in the intent, not the act. Yet the proposition that ends justify means always arouses discomfort, and auditors of any theological sophistication would know that moral authorities are likely to condemn as a Satanic temptation the idea that men may freely sin if their ultimate aims are good.[31] Although we do not have time to resolve

[31] See, for example, John Downame, *The Christian Warfare* (1604; rpt. in facsimile, Amsterdam: Theatrum Orbis Terrarum, 1974), pp. 91-92. Cf. Rom. 6:1.

Isabella's dilemma is fraught with further difficulties. One of the most

these conundrums while watching the play, we probably reach a more or less conscious consensus on two points. First, that Isabella's decision to commit fornication *would* be sinful; second, that that sin could be judged with unmitigated severity only by a malicious God.

Protestant theologians who discuss situations analogous to Isabella's support these intuitive guesses. According to Perkins, one who is forced to choose sin (for example, to deny his religion) does indeed sin, but the less free his will is, the lighter his sin.[32] Hooker makes a similar point: "some things we do neither against nor without, and yet not simply and merely with our will, but with our wills in such sort moved, that albeit there be no impossibility but that we might, nevertheless we are not so easily able to do otherwise. In this consideration one evil deed is made more pardonable than another . . . [and] so much more pardonable, by how much the exigence of so doing or the difficulty of doing otherwise is greater."[33]

Hurried though we be, our position is, in comparison with Isabella's, one of Olympian disengagement. As Angelo's true intent becomes increasingly apparent, Isabella will be correspondingly less able to perceive clearly the theological subtleties of the issue before her. Anyone in her position can be expected to fall back on habitual responses and long-cherished principles, and that, I believe, is precisely what Isabella does. We begin to divine what these principles might be when Isabella greets Angelo's axiom about compelled sins with shocked disagreement

---

interesting was raised centuries ago by Pierre Bayle (*Dictionary*, s.v. "Acindynus"). Discussing a situation analogous to Isabella's, Bayle points out that the woman in question purchases a mere "temporal and perishable good," her husband's life, at the price of breaking God's law against fornication. And God's law, he maintains, matters more than mere life. Whatever conclusion one should reach in the case Bayle cites, Shakespeare eludes the difficulty by providing compelling evidence that Claudio is in despair and therefore lies in danger of damnation as well as death. See 3.1.117-27.

[32] *Whole Treatise*, pp. 18-19.   [33] *Laws*, 1:186.

(2.4.58). Although we cannot yet be certain, her disagreement may not rest entirely on her recognition that the case in question involves only partial compulsion. It may also arise from an exaggerated valuation of religious law, the same misconception that underlies Isabella's desire to serve God constrainedly. While the perennial wisdom of Christianity, epitomized in the Sermon on the Mount, stresses God's concern for the "ground of the heart" rather than for physical deeds, Isabella appears to believe that physical acts, even those done under powerful if not absolute compulsion, are liable to merciless divine wrath. This not only betrays her misconception of the Deity, it also manifests her habitually excessive concern for outward works—an inability to understand that virtue and vice are primarily qualities of the soul and that Angelo's compulsion would much diminish the gravity of her sin. Isabella appears, in short, to betray habits of mind appropriate to her monastic profession; her impending vow of chastity, defined as strict physical virginity, seems to assume for her a stature reserved in Protestant theology for much loftier, less physical laws.

Isabella's overly literal notion of sin becomes still clearer as Angelo edges toward a declaration of his desire. He suggests that there "might be a charity in sin" if the sin is committed in order to save a "brother." In the persistently theological milieu of *Measure for Measure*, even Isabella's blood relationship with Claudio acquires symbolic significance. The sister's natural affection for her kinsman in itself begins to represent the love that is a theological virtue. We therefore sense the real likelihood that there *could* be virtue in sin, and this possibility becomes yet more insistent when Angelo inches close to posing his case of conscience with unflinching lucidity.

> Admit no other way to save his life—
> As I subscribe not that, nor any other,
> But in the loss of question—that you, his sister,

> Finding yourself desired of such a person
> Whose credit with the judge, or own great place,
> Could fetch your brother from the manacles
> Of the all-binding law; and that there were
> No earthly mean to save him, but that either
> You must lay down the treasures of your body
> To this suppos'd, or else to let him suffer:
> What would you do?
>
>   [2.4.88-98]

The symbolic amplitude that both "brother" and "the all-binding law" have acquired by this point in the play helps us to recognize the controlling idea of this passage. In the very texture of the language, we feel once again the presence of the great Redemption that Isabella is urged to imitate by sacrificing her physical "treasures." This symbolic presence implies that Isabella may be somewhat too absolute in the way she rejects both the proposition and the example.

The terms of her refusal gain significance from their clear echo of the interrogation of Juliet. Isabella says that she would do

> As much for my poor brother as myself;
> That is, were I under the terms of death,
> Th'impression of keen whips I'd wear as rubies,
> And strip myself to death as to a bed
> That longing have been sick for, ere I'd yield
> My body up to shame.
>
>   [2.4.99-104]

The conclusion of the speech throws emphasis on "shame," and it is important that Isabella thinks of her sin in terms of that euphemism. We recall that Juliet accepted shame with exemplary joy—shame arising, of course, from sin previously committed. Isabella's speech begins, moreover, with a disconcerting echo of Juliet's claim to charitable love. For Isabella does not say that she loves her brother as herself,

but that she would do as much for him as she would for
herself. But her desire to enter the order of St. Clare argues a standard of outward behavior more punctilious
than God demands, and it is clear that Isabella's charity toward Claudio will be determined by her needs and desires
rather than his.

To demand, as Isabella eventually does, that Claudio become a martyr for her virginity's sake may be to measure
another man's ineluctable desire "to receive all good, even
as much at every man's hand as any man can wish unto his
own soul" by a very high standard indeed. It is also, and
more certainly, Isabella's own good that she considers—
what *she* would do if she were "under the terms of
death"—not what the yet hypothetical dilemma asks of her.
This self-centered standard for determining her behavior
toward a brother is symptomatic of self-love. We begin to
perceive that Isabella's refusal of Angelo's proposition
springs not only from fear of sin, but from a cupidity[34]
peculiarly her own, a cupidity as strikingly as it is aptly expressed in her startling metaphor for martyrdom:

> Th'impression of keen whips I'd wear as rubies,
> And strip myself to death as to a bed
> That longing have been sick for.

The powerful sexuality of this imagined martyrdom implies that Isabella and Claudio, with all other men, are the
closest of kin. Her religious desires are as truly (if not as
fully) informed with a passionate self-indulgence as is his
passion for Juliet, Angelo's for Isabella, Lucio's for Kate
Keepdown (or whomever).

In short, Isabella's famous metaphors express with
pointed irony the legalistic character of her religiosity. Her
adherence to external laws of religion is in essence a

[34] In its theological sense: an inordinate, egocentric desire; the opposite
of *caritas*, defined as the love of God and of self and neighbor for the sake
of God.

spiritual manifestation of the disease that physically afflicts Claudio, Lucio, and the inhabitants of the Viennese underworld. If we resurrect the theological connotations of the words, as Shakespeare's language urges us to do, we may say that Isabella's well-meaning religious convictions are shot through with "carnality," adherence to the "flesh" considered not merely as the body (Mistress Overdone's concern) but as the depraved spiritual nature of man. With this striking insight Shakespeare at once expresses and transcends in powerfully original terms an idea always implicit in antimonastic polemic. He reveals that monastic devotion can be a sham, a logical contradiction, a religion of externals. Yet he presents this conception in a character whose good intentions and unwarranted sufferings win our persistent, if not consistent, sympathy. The unspoken implication is that all good intentions are tainted by impurities that derive from man's diseased nature. The aesthetic adjunct of this conception is a marked tightening of the play's thematic structure. All the major characters, in different ways, are implicated in an identical and fundamentally human error.

Isabella's spiritual carnality receives its climactic expression when she asserts,

> Better it were a brother died at once,
> Than that a sister, by redeeming him,
> Should die for ever.
>
> [2.4.106-8]

Under any circumstances, even in an act of "redemption," she believes, fornication will damn her. The notion is deeply engrained, and Isabella soon voices the vaguely menacing threat that Claudio too would be justly damned if he should ask her to accept Angelo's terms:

> Yes, brother, you may live;
> There is a devilish mercy in the judge,
> If you'll implore it, that will free your life,
> But fetter you till death.

Claudio.   Perpetual durance?
Isab.   Ay, just, perpetual durance; a restraint,
          Though all the world's vastidity you had,
          To a determin'd scope.

[3.1.63-69][35]

The passage contains powerful irony, for while predicting Claudio's ultimate spiritual bondage, Isabella employs terms ("fetter," "durance," "restraint," "determined scope") that describe her own spiritual and intended physical slavery to the external forms of religion. This slavery is nowhere more apparent than in the assumption that whatever sin she might commit in redeeming Claudio would lead to certain damnation. This conviction contradicts the fundamental Reformation doctrine of salvation. Isabella believes that an unlawful work, rather than faith, will determine her eternal scope. She has forgotten her Redeemer, just as her monastic costume perpetually suggests she will. For that reason she, like her brother, can be considered "faithless."

But the audience is never allowed to share Isabella's amnesia. In addition to the reference already cited, Shakespeare provides further oblique allusions to the Redemption:

Ignomy in ransom and free pardon
Are of two houses: lawful mercy
Is nothing kin to foul redemption.

[2.4.111-13]

"Redeeming," "ransom," "free pardon," "lawful mercy," and even "foul redemption" (the shame of the cross) are all terms and paradoxes obliquely applicable to Christ's willing sacrifice as well as the human analogue that Isabella is refusing. Isabella is correct, of course, to argue that a grant of free pardon on Angelo's part would differ from the ignoble redemption he proposes. But the simultaneous and

[35] Editors often place a period after "just," thereby obscuring Isabella's belief that Claudio's "perpetual durance" would be "just."

ubiquitous allusions to Christ's sacrifice undermine Isabella's conviction that her action would necessarily entail damnation. The allusions recall the act that made all human works irrelevant to salvation.

As we well know, the doctrine of salvation by faith does not exempt men from moral responsibility, but it does free scrupulous souls from the potentially terrifying sense that their own actions could damn them. The excessive sober sadness, the inability to kill Sansjoy, and the ultimate despair of Redcrosse Knight result paradoxically from a spiritual self-reliance akin to that displayed by Isabella. Since she shares with Spenser's hero religious principles of the old Duessa, we should expect Isabella to react with special terror to Angelo's assault. Accordingly, we may perceive in Isabella's final soliloquy in act 2, scene 4 the rationalizations of terror—terror founded not only, as A. P. Rossiter says, on the "unknown violence and violation of lust," but also on the conviction that eternal damnation follows the loss of virginity. Like all scared souls, Isabella has reason to be a small soul, reduced "to a tiny rod of iron principle which is all she can think."[36] Isabella therefore wins our sympathy as she hastily convinces herself that Claudio's honor will convince him to sacrifice himself for her. But because we also know that sin varies in severity, that salvation is not to be bought for the ready money of vowed virginity or lost through voluntary yet compelled sin, we recognize the powerful irony of her epigrammatic conclusion

> Then, Isabel live chaste, and brother, die:
> More than our brother is our chastity.
> [2.4.183-84]

Unlike virginity, chastity is no purely physical virtue, and Isabella's night with Angelo could not, on a commonplace principle of which Angelo earlier reminds us ("Look what I

---

[36] A. P. Rossiter, *Angel with Horns*, p. 160.

will not, that I cannot do," 2.2.52), altogether violate her chastity. Isabella's epigram not only epitomizes the unthinking terror appropriate to a young girl in a crisis; it also reveals that her terrified reaction is both exaggerated and shaped by her monastic tendency to concentrate on works and vows at the expense of love for her brother and the spiritual nature of virtue. We therefore experience sympathy not void of judgment, and our sympathy is magnified, not lessened, because we recognize that Isabella's anguish, expressed in her brutal epigram, could be diminished if her situation would allow her to share at all in our relative detachment.

Moreover, Isabella's power to elicit our sympathy in this scene is very strong. It is increased by her manifest concern for the condition of Claudio's soul. Her recurrent references to his state encourage us to expect that her visit to the prison will provide him needed spiritual counsel:

Spare him, spare him!
He's not prepar'd for death.
            [2.2.84-85]

. . . I beseech you . . .
            He may be so fitted
That his soul sicken not.
            [2.4.39-41]

I'll tell him yet of Angelo's request,
And fit his mind to death, for his soul's rest.
            [2.4.185-86]

The last of these quotations predicts an aim quite proper to any clerical vocation considered in the Reformation worthy of the name. As the professor of a truly devoted life, Isabella ought to minister to the souls of the dying according to their needs. In his disguise, the Duke does this at the beginning of the next scene. Significantly, his ministration to Claudio's "afflicted spirit" occurs immediately after Isabella expresses her aim to undertake the cure of her brother's soul and immediately before the violent outburst that actually results from their meeting. The contrast is deliberate, and history suggests that Shakespeare's original audience may have recognized in this an immediate social relevance. Preparing men to face death was considered so important an office in sixteenth-century England that clerics found themselves bound by royal injunction to devote to it special care. The injunction accurately describes Claudio's spiritual state: "those persons which be . . . in peril of death be often times put in despair by the craft and subtlety of the devil, who is then most busy, and specially with them that lack the knowledge, sure persuasion, and steadfast belief that they may be made partakers of the great and infinite mercy which Almighty God of his most bountiful goodness and mere liberality, without our deserving, hath offered freely to all persons that putteth their full trust and confidence in Him."[37]

Since to an impartial observer Claudio's desperate, godless vision of the afterlife provides ample evidence that he is in despair because he lacks "knowledge, sure persuasion, and steadfast belief" in his share in God's mercy, there is in Isabella's flood of abusive epithets one that is apt. In his present state, Claudio is "faithless." It therefore behooves Isabella as a Christian and a "sister" (in both senses) to provide "such comfortable places and sentences of Scripture as do set forth the mercy, benefits, and goodness of Almighty God towards all penitent and believing persons." As we have seen, such knowledge "is the only stay of man's conscience."[38]

Not only does Isabella fail to provide the expected comfort, but the recent advocate of mercy becomes, as many have said, a most merciless judge and exhibits in the process an astounding lack of charity.[39] Yet in a play that shares

---

[37] *Tudor Royal Proclamations*, 1:399.   [38] Ibid.

[39] See David L. Stevenson, "Design and Structure in *Measure for Measure*," *ELH* 23 (1956):277; and Hunter, *Comedy of Forgiveness*, pp. 217-18.

the moral subtlety characteristic of contemporary casuistry, we should be more precise. Because of her understandable terror of sexual violation and her exaggerated fear of damnation, Isabella suffers an emotional collapse that issues in explosive anger. Her penchant toward anger, apparent in earlier scenes, and the extreme to which it drives her here, suggest another correspondence with the family of Fals-Semblant, Frere Wolf, Corceca, and Abessa—their collective talent for verbal abuse:

> O, you beast!
> O faithless coward! O dishonest wretch! . . .
> Take my defiance,
> Die, perish! Might but my bending down
> Reprieve thee from thy fate, it should proceed.
> I'll pray a thousand prayers for thy death;
> No word to save thee.
>
> [3.1.135-46]

Since Isabella is, unlike Corceca and the rest, no allegorical counter but a figure impersonated by a living actor, our emotional response here will be correspondingly complex. We sympathize with her anger—a girl in her plight would be angry. But the type from which Shakespeare developed her appears to have determined the precise manifestation (the slanderous name-calling) and the fierce extent of that anger. The injustice of Isabella's cruelty is heightened because this outburst follows directly on Claudio's powerful evocation of death's palpable terrors. We recognize the human terror and despair that Isabella's passions conceal from her.

In a play that is informed by central doctrines of the Sermon on the Mount, Isabella's extreme anger has important implications. For Christ's spiritualizing reinterpretation of the Old Law treats, at length, rage like Isabella's:

Ye have heard that it was said by them of old time, Thou shalt not kill; and whosoever shall kill shall be in danger

of the judgment: But I say unto you, That whosoever is
angry with his brother without a cause shall be in danger
of the judgment: and whosoever shall say to his brother,
Raca, shall be in danger of the council: but whosoever
shall say, Thou fool, shall be in danger of hell fire.

[Matt. 5:21-22]

There is no doubt that Isabella has cause for anger, even
righteous anger. Not only has Claudio disappointed her by
refusing the rescue she desperately sought, he has revealed
his willingness to value life above the avoidance of sin and
is quite ready even to urge that Isabella sin in his behalf.
Yet Isabella's anger is extreme, and it is manifest in
epithets that easily transcend "Thou fool" and plainly appear to qualify their speaker for hell fire. (Anger may have
legitimate cause, but angry name-calling never does.)
Erasmus helps to explain the rationale for this apparently
extreme punishment: "what homicide is in the old law, the
same in the new law is the vehement motion of the mind to
be revenged. For the first degree to homicide is to be angry. For such an one hath not yet actually committed
homicide, but now he beginneth to go towards homicide.
Therefore he that willeth ill to his brother, even now hath
committed a grievous offence before God his judge. . . .
But he is near unto homicide, whosoever is fallen from
brotherly charity."[40] Shakespeare makes the connection
between anger and homicide, as well as the essential identity of anger and vengefulness, transparently clear: "I'll
pray a thousand prayers for thy death / No word to save
thee" as we see Isabella proposing revenge of the spirit if
not of the body. The admonition from the Sermon on the
Mount reminds us that Isabella has committed an offense
as damnable as homicide before the judge "who is the top
of judgment."

From the perspective of the central law that is perpetu-

---

[40] *Paraphrase*, 1, fol. E8ᵛ. Cf. Calvin, *Harmonie*, sig. L6ᵛ, and Perkins,
Whole Treatise, p. 513.

ally at issue in the play, Isabella commits nothing short of
fratricide in this scene. Her victim, moreover, is a brother
whose chief error was an act of fornication with a woman
who was in some sense "fast [his] wife." Unwittingly, therefore, Isabella in her anger precisely enacts a role described
in the play's scriptural source. Having a beam in her eye,
she condemns, mercilessly, her brother's mote. As we shall
see more fully in the next chapter, a very common moral
failing forbidden in the "judge not" passage explains
Isabella's abuse of Claudio. For the kind of judgment
Christ condemns "doth always draw with it this sin, that we
condemn every light offence, as though it were a most
grievous fault,"[41] or we proceed by "making very much of
things that be light and small."[42] Just so, Isabella magnifies
intercourse with an intended bride into professional
whoremongering:

> Thy sin's not accidental, but a trade;
> Mercy to thee would prove itself a bawd;
> 'Tis best that thou diest quickly.
>
> [3.1.148-50]

Perhaps as significant as the harshness of this judgment
is its scope. " 'Tis best that thou diest quickly" assumes
that further life would serve merely to involve Claudio further in sin. The notion echoes Angelo's earlier argument
that Claudio's execution is in reality an act of pity:

> For then I pity those I do not know,
> Which a dismiss'd offence would after gall,
> And do him right that, answering one foul wrong,
> Lives not to act another.
>
> [2.2.102-5]

Judgments as sweeping as this appear elsewhere in Renaissance literature. A notable one is made by Spenser's Despair:

[41] Calvin, *Harmonie*, sig. O1[r].
[42] Erasmus, *Paraphrase*, 1, fol. G1[v].

> The lenger life, I wote the greater sin,
>> The greater sin, the greater punishment. . . .
>> Is not enough thy evil life forespent?
>> For he, that once hath missed the right way,
> The further he doth goe, the further he doth stray.
>
> Then do no further goe, no further stray,
>> But here lie downe, and to thy rest betake,
>> Th'ill to prevent, that life ensewen may . . .
>>> [1.9.43-45]

Despair encourages suicide whereas Angelo seeks his victim's death according to law, but their arguments are equally overweening. For Shakespeare's contemporaries, as for us, human judgment even in its institutional forms had clearly defined limits. Hooker explains the conventional sixteenth-century terms of this circumscription. Magistrates, he says, have authority only to "examine and judge our deeds," and, he proceeds, in secret actions man's conscience constitutes the only immediate judge. As for ultimate judgment, none "can in this case be looked for from any other, saving only from Him who discerneth and judgeth the very secrets of all hearts; therefore He is the only rewarder and revenger of all such actions; although not of such actions only, but of all whereby the Law of Nature is broken whereof Himself is author. For which cause, the Roman Laws, called The Laws of the Twelve Tables, requiring offices of inward affection which the eye of man cannot reach unto, threaten the neglecters of them with none but divine punishment."[43]

Human judgment concerns only what "the eye of man" can reach unto; it judges the "external actions," the "deeds" of men. Spenser's Despair, Isabella, and Angelo all arrogate to themselves judgments that far surpass the deeds of men; they propose to end Claudio's life in order to avoid future sins that they choose to consider inevitable.

---

[43] *Laws*, 1:187.

Since sin, as Isabella had earlier argued, can be avoided by none, both she and Angelo utter judgments as apposite to themselves as to Claudio. This in itself betrays arrogance and self-ignorance; but by judging Claudio as if the "very secrets of his heart" were open to them and they could perceive in his heart intentions of future ill, they usurp the particular judgment that can never be expected, "saving from Him who discerneth and judgeth the very secrets of all hearts."

In her anger, then, Isabella once again forgets her Redeemer and claims an office peculiar to him. Just as her religion exceeds its proper scope by attributing to men powers appropriate only to God, so her chief exercise of human judgment far surpasses the limits appropriate to it. Both of these errors conform with rigorous logic to the type of character Shakespeare has created. For whatever her individual traits (her naive, youthful idealism, her ability to use reason and discourse, her fear of sexuality, her barely sublimated erotic desire for martyrdom, her sometimes fierce irascibility), Isabella is consistently developed in ways Shakespeare's original audience would have found consonant with her continuing appearance in the robes of the order of St. Clare. Her physical appearance, her speeches, and her actions repeatedly remind us that she has been developed from a special category of type figures. The essence of her nature lies in her allegiance to a system of man-made laws that are fundamentally at odds with other, transcendent laws to which the play's language persistently alludes.

Chapter 4

Venomous Tongues

So far we have seen that Isabella's well-meant though distorted understanding of religious truth ironically both fosters pride and reflects it. Primary symptoms of this spiritual ailment are her implicit confidence that the good works of monastic devotion can lead to merited salvation, her terror that her own sin could cause damnation, and her presumptuous judgment of Claudio's hidden intentions. A further—and much less determinate—symptom of pride now demands consideration. This one appears to link Isabella still more closely to common attitudes toward monasticism. More important, it leads us to consider another pervasive manifestation of the play's dominant theme of law.

As we saw in chapter 2, Fals-Semblant attributed even his colleagues' good works to their desire for worldly honor (*RR* ll.6909-10). The theme is echoed by Calvin (the monks seek "praise of humility") and by other Reformers, virtually all of whom agreed with the homilist's assertion that monks use "long prayers by day and by night" as a "pretence or colour" often employed to reap the material rewards that accrue to specious holiness. As often as not, however, false holiness aimed simply to acquire the praise of one's fellowmen. Milton includes this traditional criticism in his mockery of the monks and friars who, along with other vanities, populate his imagined limbo:

> all things vain, and all who in vain things
> Built their fond hopes of Glory or lasting fame,

Or happiness in this or th'other life.
All who have their reward on Earth, the fruits
Of painful superstition and blind Zeal,
Naught seeking but the praise of men.
[Paradise Lost 3.448-53]

The spiritual progenitors of these vainglorious monks are
the biblical hypocrites who appear prominently, as Milton's
direct echoes reveal, in the Sermon on the Mount: "do not
sound a trumpet before thee, as the hypocrites do in the
synagogues and in the streets, that they may have glory of
men. . . . They have their reward" (Matt. 6:2).

Although she seeks, paradoxically, to entomb herself in
the convent of St. Clare, and although she consciously
seeks rewards far more substantial than the praise of men,
Isabella frequently seems to betray conspicuous if inadvertent anxiety about her appearance in the world. We notice
this because the word "shame" begins to appear in her language at moments of high intellectual and emotional intensity, moments when we normally expect "sin" or its cog-
nates. This occurs when Isabella prefers martyrdom even
to a "shame" that would save her brother's life (2.4.104). In
the emphatically theological context of this passage and of
the play as a whole, this predominantly social conception
seems oddly out of place. And although we might at first
(especially in the instance under discussion) consider
"shame" merely a metonymic substitution for "sin," Isabella's repeated and insistent use of the word prevents our
making that assessment with absolute assurance. Her
thoughts anchor much too insistently not only on shame,
but on its opposite, the sense of honor she desperately
wants to lead Claudio to her rescue:

I'll to my brother.
Though he hath fall'n by prompture of the blood,
Yet hath he in him such a mind of honour,
That had he twenty heads to tender down
On twenty bloody blocks, he'd yield them up

Before his sister should her body stoop
To such abhorr'd pollution.

[2.4.176-82]

To stir Claudio's honorable enthusiasm, Isabella repeatedly threatens him not only with vague hints of eternal
damnation, but also with dishonor. Consenting to Angelo's
terms, she asserts,

Would bark your honour from that trunk you bear,
And leave you naked.

[3.1.71-72]

These metaphors are suggestive. Honor that can be lost as
a tree loses its bark seems curiously material, external, and
ephemeral. This implication is soon brought into relief, as
Isabella expresses her fear lest Claudio

a feverous life shouldst entertain,
And six or seven winters more respect
Than a perpetual honour.

[3.1.74-76]

To die in the interest of one's sister is to gain no ephemeral
husk, but a durable, even an eternal honor. Yet, as their
interview reaches its emotional climax, Isabella once again
reveals that her fear of vice is somehow commingled with
fear of dishonor. Her words imply, too, that her honor,
like Claudio's metaphorical "bark," can be lost by accepting
Angelo's shameful proposal:

O faithless coward! O dishonest wretch!
Wilt thou be made a man out of my vice?
Is't not a kind of incest, to take life
From thine own sister's shame?

[3.1.136-39]

As he did at act 2, scene 4, line 104, Shakespeare here gives
special rhetorical stress to the idea of shame. Isabella seems
now to be concerned somewhat more explicitly about a

"brittle social code," more about shame than about vice—
which is always nonetheless the first cause of her fear.[1]

Like other ill-explained shifts of direction and emphasis
in *Measure for Measure*, this aberration in Isabella's language demands active intellectual participation. And just
as the context of moral casuistry led us to ponder what sin
Isabella would actually commit if she were to accept
Angelo's terms, we are asked by the very prominence—at
the play's emotional climax—of ideas of honor and shame
to consider what "honor" might lie in jeopardy. Isabella offers some assistance, for a living idea underlies her distinction between ephemeral and perpetual honors. These two
kinds of honor (or fame) had been distinguished throughout the Middle Ages, true and lasting honor being a spiritual quality defined as God's favorable opinion, false and
ephemeral honor by contrast being an external thing—the
opinion of one's fellowmen.[2] Renaissance discussions of
honor normally repeat, extend, or take for granted this
medieval distinction, as can be seen in Montaigne's essay
"Of Glory,"[3] in Erasmus's *Enchiridion*,[4] in Spenser's *Faerie
Queene* (the pursuit of Gloriana as opposed to Philotime), in
Primaudaye's *French Academie*,[5] and in Shakespeare's *Henry*

---

[1] See Lever, pp. lxxix-lxxxi, and Alice Shalvi, *The Relationship of Renais-
sance Concepts of Honour to Shakespeare's Problem Plays* (Salzburg: Institut für
Englische Sprache und Literatur Universität Salzburg, 1972), chap. 8.
Both authors discuss the language to which I refer, but their judgments of
Isabella seem harsh because they imply that her fear of dishonor is some-
how independent of her fear of sin. My quotation is from Lever.

[2] B. Koonce, *Chaucer and the Tradition of Fame: Symbolism in "The House of
Fame"* (Princeton: Princeton University Press, 1966), chap. 1. Cf. D. W.
Robertson, Jr., "The Idea of Fame in Chrétien's *Cliges*," *SP* 69 (1972):
414-18. In my own discussion of these topics, I often use the terms
"honor," "glory," and "fame" as near synonyms. This procedure reflects
the nonchalance of my primary sources. Cf. Shalvi, *Renaissance Concepts of
Honour*, pp. 55-57.

[3] See *The Essays of Montaigne*, trans. John Florio (New York: Modern Library, 1933), p. 560.

[4] Sigs. R8^v-S1^r.

[5] Trans. T. B. (London: George Bishop, 1594), sig. R3^v.

IV, Part 1 (especially 1.3.80-82; 1.3.201-7; 5.1.127-39; 5.4.80-87, 99-101). The most prominent source of this conventional distinction is, of course, the New Testament, where Christ and Satan exemplify two kinds of fame—one sought for the glory of God and found in his goodwill, the other sought for its own sake.[6]

These conventional ideas of honor help guide our responses to Isabella. For although she reminds us that there is an honor that can be lost only through sin, Isabella nonetheless implies that accepting Angelo's proposal will utterly destroy the honor of both brother and sister. On the strength of our understanding of the nature of sin, we may speculate that only worldly honor is vulnerable to Angelo's assault and that Isabella's true loss would probably be a minor one. Her concern seems exaggerated, corresponding to her assessment of the magnitude and consequences of her hypothetical sin. We may begin to suspect, therefore, that Shakespeare has endowed Isabella with a touch of the vainglory characteristic of the type to which she belongs.

Let me be perfectly clear on this point. We are probably meant to recognize this as a trait characteristic of her type. But since it belongs to a figure of considerable individuality and of unfeigned religious zeal, we ought to see that Isabella's chief concern is fear of sin. Yet this laudable fear of sin—like all human motivation—is impure, to some extent polluted by merely social motives. As I have shown, the evidence for such an inference is both plentiful and obvious, but it can never ground a firm conviction either that Isabella is conscious of any impurity in her motives or that a desire for worldly honor bulks very large in her spiritual composition. Our decision on the issue must be to judge sparingly. As he does so often in the play, Shakespeare obliges us to attempt judgments for which the evidence provided is disconcertingly inconclusive. Isabella's language of

---

[6] Koonce, *Tradition of Fame*, pp. 16-17. See also Matt. 4:8-9; Gal. 1:10.

honor and shame therefore forces us to participate in the
play's leitmotiv of judgment. At the same time, it demonstrates that the evidence needed for such judgment, in the
play as in life, is seldom sufficient.

Yet because the question of Isabella's honor will lead us
to consider a dominant and neglected theme in the play,
we may fruitfully dwell on the subject a bit longer. As my
earlier quotation from Milton suggested, Isabella's scriptural forebears were unambiguously addicted to worldly
honor: "they have their reward" here and now—glory in
the eyes of men. They therefore forego all reward from
the "Father which seeth in secret" and shall Himself reward openly (Matt. 6:1-6). How this typical monastic trait
might relate to Isabella begins to become clearer if we recall the stress given, both in the Sermon on the Mount and
in early sections of *Measure for Measure*, to human debility
in contrast to God's glory (see chap. 1, pp. 24-30). To seek
any honor as an end in itself, according to the implications
of the candlestick metaphor, of the petition "forgive us our
debts," of the accusation of universal human hypocrisy
(Matt. 7:3-5), *and* of the analogous passages and themes in
Measure for Measure, is a direct offense to God. The larger
contexts of both works establish that excessive concern for
personal honor manifests, inevitably if inexplicitly, a faith
essentially awry: "How can ye believe, which receive honour one of another, and seek not the honour that cometh
from God only?" (John 5:44). Salient admonitions such as
these indicate that "the gate of faith is shut against all
those, whose minds are possessed with a vain desire of
earthly glory."[7]

It is helpful to consider exactly how faithlessness and the
search for worldly glory interrelate. Anyone concerned excessively with the opinion of other men makes them, their
reason, and their fallible perceptions the measures of his
righteousness. The inevitable result of adopting this an-

[7] Calvin, *Harmonie*, sig. I2^r.

thropomorphic standard is "wicked confidence," a psychological fact discussed usefully in Calvin's *Institutes*:

> To this . . . we must apply our mind, if we will profitably
> enquire of true righteousness, how we may answer the
> heavenly judge when he calleth us to accompt. Let us
> think him to be a judge, not such a one as our own un-
> derstandings do of themselves imagine: but such a one as
> he is painted out in the scripture, with whose brightness
> the stars shall be darkened, by whose strength the hills
> do melt away, by whose wrath the earth is shaken, by
> whose wisdom the wise are taken in their subtlety, by
> whose pureness all things are proved unpure, whose
> righteousness the Angels are not able to bear, which
> maketh the innocent not innocent, whose vengeance
> when it is once kindled pierceth to the bottom of hell. If
> he (I say) sit to examine men's doings, who shall appear
> assured before his throne?[8]

For this awesome judge, Isabella (and everyone who pursues worldly honor) seeks to substitute not only the indefi-
nite "eyes of men," but more precisely her own reason and
a prioress who would judge her on the basis of obedience
to the rule of St. Clare. Under such conditions, she might
acquit herself honorably. When men alone are the standard of measurement, we all readily fall into the trap of believing everything handsome about us. True faith, by contrast, establishes a judge who is infinitely more exacting.[9]

   This judge is also absolutely uninclined to share any part
of his honor—according to a doctrine fundamental in
Protestant theology. As one of two major corollaries of the
doctrine of salvation by faith, Calvin explains at length that
only a Pauline salvific system assures "that there may remain to the Lord his glory undiminished." "The righteousness of God is not sufficiently set out," he asserts,
"unless He alone be accounted righteous, and does com-

---

[8] *Institutes* 3.12.1; fol. 245^r.   [9] Ibid. 3.12.2; fol. 245^{r-v}.

municate the grace of righteousness, to them that deserve it not."[10]

From this brief excursus on conventions concerning divine and human glory, we may speculate that Isabella's unconscious and inadvertently revealed concern for "honor" follows aptly from her theology. In contrast to the self-abasement instilled by Protestant orthodoxy, she places her confidence in works performed according to law. This confidence leads her to overvalue man's worth and capacity for honor, just as she overvalues man's ability to work out his own salvation and to judge his fellowmen. In short, a desire for honor is implied by the very nature of Isabella's intended monastic profession. Her hint of concern for an honor that can be lost because it resides in the opinions of men represents a *social* manifestation of her fundamental carnality. And it is therefore a trait that few, even those with the best of intentions, can escape.

Although we may greet with some surprise the language that suggests Isabella's concern for honor and her concurrent fear of shame, and although we can draw from that language no unshakable critical judgments, we nonetheless sense that these topics belong to the very life of Shakespeare's larger design. Honor and shame, reputation and slander, apparent virtue and inner depravity are themes touched on repeatedly from the play's opening scene onward. We have already considered Claudio's punishment in act 1, scene 2 as a prominent example of institutionalized shame, a judicial tool commonly employed in Shakespeare's England. We have noted, in addition, Juliet's thoughtful distinction between shame which breeds selfish sorrow and that which springs from love of "heaven." These and numerous other examples of the polar themes

---

[10] Ibid. 3.13.1; fol. 247[v]. The dominance of this doctrine in England explains the Anglican liturgy's extreme concern for God's glory—a concern that sometimes (as in the communion service) seems oddly prominent.

of shame and honor support the more comprehensive
theme of law in all its aspects. As a dramatic focus for that
often implicit theme, Shakespeare devotes much explicit
attention to the execution of human law. This of course involves frequent judgments of men by other men, and
critics have been well aware that judgment is one of the
central activities of the play. No one, however, has pointed
out that judgment is the central unifying motif of the play's
action. Judgments of a quasi-juristic cast, most of which
touch on the honor of their subjects, occur everywhere, all
the time, not simply when the Duke, Angelo, or Escalus
holds court or when Isabella meets Claudio in prison.

Judgments begin, as we noted earlier, when Duke Vincentio first measures his own political powers against those
of Escalus and judges himself the less competent (1.1.3-12).
He then asks Escalus, and us, to judge the likelihood of
Angelo's success as substitute. More obliquely, the Duke's
opening judgment also concerns his own honor—he is
careful to condition our own and his fictional colleagues'
judgments of him—to avoid seeming "t'affect speech and
discourse" (l.4). Later, addressing himself directly to the
question of honor, he assigns to Nature all glory for human
talents (l.39), and in his subsequent assessment of Angelo,
he initiates an important pattern of metaphors that liken
character assessment to reading:

> There is a kind of character in thy life
> That to th'observer doth thy history
> Fully unfold.
>   [1.1.27-29]

This is clearly a special kind of judgment that political
leaders especially are obliged to make. To govern well they
must accurately "read" the behavior of those around them,
to assess their worth and their frailties. Having publicly illustrated this function in scene 1, the Duke bestows "honors" on his deputies (1.1.52), but he displays an odd shy-
ness about receiving honors due to him:

I'll privily away. I love the people,
But do not like to stage me to their eyes:
Though it do well, I do not relish well
Their loud applause and *Aves* vehement;
Nor do I think the man of safe discretion
That does affect it.

                                            [1.1.67-72]

Scholars often limit themselves to a topical interpretation
of this passage, arguing that Shakespeare pointedly compares Duke Vincentio to King James, specifically to the latter's distaste for crowds. So far as it goes, this interpretation could be accurate, for it is only one among several
traits that Londoners in 1604 might have identified as belonging to their new king.[11] Yet even if it is correct, the
particular allusion should not be allowed to obliterate
meanings both more apparent and more general. The
Duke disapproves less of crowds per se than of "staging"
himself to draw "applause and *Aves* vehement." In context,
the passage presents the Duke's rationale for declining a
ceremonial departure proposed by Angelo: "Yet give me
leave, my lord, / That we may bring you something on the
way" (1.1.60-61). The Duke suggests that such a departure
would be a mere "scruple," an overnice observation of the
minutiae of protocol (1.1.62-64). By means of the metaphor of staging, he expresses disapproval of regal his-

---

[11] Schanzer, *Problem Plays*, pp. 120-25. See also David L. Stevenson, *The
Achievement of Shakespeare's "Measure for Measure"* (Ithaca: Cornell University Press, 1966), appendix, and Lever, pp. xlvii-l. The evidence assembled by these scholars is extensive. We cannot therefore discount the
probability that Shakespeare sought to stress certain similarities between
the Duke and the king. In a play chosen for performance before the king
himself, this possibility alone tells strongly against the numerous scholarly
arguments that attempt to convict Duke Vincentio of unmitigated folly, to
transform him into a Machiavel, or to suggest that he represents a satiric
portrait of the king. As the experiences of Jonson, Chapman, and others
illustrate, political satire on the Jacobean stage was unsafe at best. To present personal satire before the royal butt himself would have been a most
un-Shakespearean indecorum.

trionics such as those employed by Henry Bolingbroke, a man whose discretion—as Shakespeare presents it throughout the sequence of three plays—was made unsafe by desire for the power and glory of the English throne.[12]

By contrast to Bolingbroke, his enemy Hotspur, and numerous other Shakespearean characters, Duke Vincentio exhibits a marked carelessness about the honors due to his place in the state. In short, he manifestly avoids seeking the praise of men. By stressing this trait in the first scene, Shakespeare begins to endow the Duke with an attitude toward personal honor that the New Testament, Boethius, the medieval fame literature, Spenser, Montaigne, Calvin, Erasmus, and the early Shakespeare himself had urged men to admire.

During the Duke's absence in the play's second scene, Shakespeare employs his covey of rakes not only to introduce the theme of religious law, but also to enact on a comic level repeated judgments of their fellowmen. These judgments introduce an important subcategory of the action's central motif. In their negative tone, they adumbrate a tendency toward slanderous judgment that becomes extremely persistent later in the play.

> *Lucio.* I think thou never wast where grace was said. . . .
> thou thyself art a wicked villain, despite of all grace. . . .
> *1 Gent.* And thou . . . art good velvet; thou'rt a three-
> piled piece . . . I had as lief be a list of an English kersey,
> as be piled, as thou art pilled, for a French velvet. Do I
> speak feelingly now?

---

[12] By being seldom seen, I could not stir
But like a comet I was wonder'd at. . . .
And then I stole all courtesy from heaven,
And dress'd myself in such humility
That I did pluck allegiance from men's hearts,
Loud shouts and salutations from their mouths,
Even in the presence of the crowned King.
                    (*I Henry IV* 3.2.46-54)
The metaphors here, which are deliberately stagey, condemn Bolingbroke out of his own mouth.

Lucio. I think thou dost: and indeed, with most painful feeling of thy speech. I will, out of thine own confession, learn to begin thy health; but whilst I live, forget to drink after thee.

[1.2.18-37]

This badinage continues, in the same vein of slanderous comedy, until Mistress Overdone arrives, gives something of an economic cast to her own summary judgment ("There's one yonder arrested and carried to prison, was worth five thousand of you all" [1.2.56-57]), and, with her news, breaks up the game of trading slander for slander.

When he returns in act 1, scene 3, the Duke takes up the themes both of honor and of slander. In so doing, he reveals that his nonchalance about personal honor has limits. He does repeat, however, his aversion to empty or self-aggrandizing ceremony:

My holy sir, none better knows than you
How I have ever lov'd the life remov'd,
And held in idle price to haunt assemblies,
Where youth, and cost, witless bravery keeps.[13]

[1.3.7-10]

These lines suggest that the Duke frequently resorts to the solitude of the monastery, and his suggestion unites him, at least in inclination, with Isabella, Angelo, and Mariana, all of whom are in some ways associated with the life of the cloister. But the Duke's association with monasticism stresses solitude, freedom to enter and depart, the consequent liberty to discharge obligations to society, and temporary withdrawal from a carefully defined world "Where youth, and cost, witless bravery keeps."[14] The

---

[13] Cf. Lucio's later remark: "A shy fellow was the Duke; and I believe I know the cause of his withdrawing" (3.2.127-29). Despite the concluding slur, the statement reminds us of the Duke's preference for the life removed.

[14] Some critics, quite wrongly I think, elevate the Duke's preference for solitude into an "aversion to marriage and society"; see Miles, *Problem of "Measure for Measure,"* pp. 181-89.

Duke does not disapprove the valid demands of personal honor and public ceremony, he rejects instead the "witless bravery," the useless, costly, and childish ostentation of court life.

Yet he also exhibits an undeniable sensitivity to the demands of personal honor, for shortly after his condemnation of "witless bravery," the Duke explains that his current seclusion results from a desire to avoid "slander":

> Therefore, indeed, my father,
> I have on Angelo impos'd the office;
> Who may in th'ambush of my name strike home,
> And yet my nature never in the fight
> To do it slander.
>
> [1.3.39-43][15]

It is insufficient, I think, to attribute this and the Duke's later assertion of the gravity of slandering a prince (5.1.521) to King James's "notorious sensitiveness to slan-

[15] I have adopted Hanmer's conjecture, "it," for F's "in," as the most likely reading. Lever follows F but offers no convincing defense of that reading.

Scholars sometimes identify the Duke's action as a "Machiavellian" ploy, parallel to that used by Cesare Borgia, of delegating unpopular duties to subordinates, but the situation in Shakespeare's Vienna differs from those cited by Machiavelli (see *The Prince*, chaps. 7 and 19, trans. Edward Dacres, in Milligan, *Three Renaissance Classics*, pp. 27-28, and 71). As Machiavelli relates their actions, the French king's institution of a political buffer between warring factions and Borgia's notorious employment and murder of a ruthless deputy arise from purely amoral or merely self-interested motives. In these instances, the French ruler is concerned to preserve his own position in the face of antagonistic political factions; Borgia aims to consolidate his holdings in order to continue a policy of political self-aggrandizement. By contrast, Duke Vincentio's aims remain in part stubbornly elusive, but the ones we do know are that he wishes (1) to protect himself from the slander of seeming tyrannical, and (2) to allow Angelo, in the interest of public order, to enforce the laws. His manifest concern for the moral health of his people (1.3.27-39) has nothing in common with the aims often attributed—especially in Shakespeare's era—to disciples of Machiavel. Cf., for example, the "Prologue" to Marlowe's *Jew of Malta*.

der."[16] The topical reference may be there, but Shakespeare in all likelihood had more in hand when he chose to make his entire plot spring from Duke Vincentio's desire to reform Vienna while avoiding "slander" of his nature.

Glancing ahead, too, we may see places at which the Duke, though a "shy fellow," defends his honor with dignity and force (e.g., 3.2.137-42) and in two soliloquies expresses his concern about a prince's inability to control subjects who defame his character (3.2.179-82; 4.1.60-65). The Duke's solicitude about his honor appears most strikingly of all in his elaborate ceremonial reentry into Vienna:

> Go call at Flavius' house,
> And tell him where I stay. Give the like notice
> To Valencius, Rowland, and to Crassus,
> And bid them bring the trumpets to the gate:
>
> [4.5.6-9]

This quotation fills nearly the whole of act 4, scene 5, a scene whose sole purpose is to reveal the Duke's careful provision for his ritual of return. In act 4, scene 6, emphasis again falls on the ceremonial aspect of the occasion:

> *Friar Peter.* Come, I have found you out a stand most fit,
> Where you may have such vantage on the
>   Duke
> He shall not pass you. Twice have the trumpets
>   sounded.
> The generous and gravest citizens
> Have hent the gates, and very near upon
> The Duke is ent'ring: therefore hence, away.
>
> [4.6.10-15]

The Duke's overall attitude toward honor and its accompanying ceremonies appears, in short, ambivalent if not

---

[16] This sensitivity did lead "to the passing of a Scottish Act of Parliament in 1585 that made slander of the King a treasonable offence, punishable with death," and "several people were, in fact, executed under this act, one in 1596 for calling James 'ane bastarde.' " My quotations here are from Schanzer, *Problem Plays*, p. 125.

downright schizophrenic. In a play consistently elliptical in mode, we do well to seek an aesthetic and thematic cause for this ambiguity. If Shakespeare introduced the Duke's early remarks on public ceremony primarily to imitate James's dislike of crowds, he has erred in the latter part of the play, for the original distaste has turned, as Schanzer says, to evident relish.[17] Most might wish to view this simply as evidence of authorial despair, haste, forgetfulness, or despondency. Before capitulating to these (not a priori impossible) explanations, I suggest that we seek in Shakespeare's sources hints of a rationale for the Duke's apparently inexplicable behavior, a rationale we may be deliberately left to supply in part for ourselves. In this case, understanding the play's genesis yields vital assistance in comprehending its meaning.

The sources most relevant here are *The Basilicon Doron* and, once again, the Sermon on the Mount. In considering the king's book, we should note at the outset that it belongs to an established genre of treatises concerning the institution of Christian monarchy. In its clear concern for the administration of law in society and for the relationship between the nature of the ruler and the adequacy of his government, Shakespeare's play also is related to the genre to which King James had contributed. Having failed to understand this fully, the many scholars who have studied the influence of *The Basilicon Doron* on *Measure for Measure* failed also to perceive that James's treatise includes in book 1 a compendious summary of the major doctrines of the Christian faith.[18] Its opening paragraph sets a tone of deep piety by locating "the true ground of good government" in the fear and the love of God and in his direct control of political events. "Neither can any thing in [a king's] gov-

[17] Ibid., p. 114.

[18] Lever, p. lxiv, for example, misrepresents the fundamental character of the book by insisting that "Cicero's *De Officiis* and Seneca's *De Clementia*, rather than the Pentateuch or the Gospels, were the decisive authorities invoked in . . . James I's *Basilicon Doron*."

ernment succeed well with him (devise and labour as he list) . . . if his person be unsanctified: . . . the blessing of God hath only power to give the success thereunto" (1:25).

The same paragraph takes up the topic of regal honor. It defines "the true glory of Kings" as the proper use of worldly glory: "Remember then, that this glistering worldly glory of Kings, is given them by God, to teach them to press so to glister and shine before their people, in all works of sanctification and righteousness, that their persons as bright lamps of godliness and virtue may, going in and out before their people, give light to all their steps" (1:27). "Sanctification" here and in the former quotation is a precise theological term accurately employed by a learned if sometimes smug and pretentious theosopher-king. Sanctification is a divine gift—the progressive mortification of the lusts of the flesh and a corresponding desire to obey the law—that follows from God's original gift of justifying grace and its ineluctable adjuncts, faith and the indwelling Spirit.[19] Such sanctity reveals itself in the good works that are, as James shortly reminds us (1:31), the fruits of true faith.

Throughout its first book, as in its first paragraph, the lessons of *The Basilicon Doron* rest on the conviction that all good comes from God alone. Even faith, "the golden chain that linketh the faithful soul to Christ . . . groweth not in our garden, but *is the free gift of God*" (1:37). In view of this doctrine of utter human debility, it is appropriate that the king preserves and enjoins an attitude of controlled contempt for the "glistering worldly glory of Kings." This attitude receives detailed expression in the concluding paragraph of book 1: "delight more to be godly and virtuous in deed, than to be thought and called so; expecting more for your praise and reward in heaven, than here: and apply to all your outward actions Christ's command, / to pray and

[19] Cf. Calvin *Institutes* 3.14.9; fol. 252ᵛ. See also Hooker's *Learned Discourse of Justification*, printed with *Laws*, 1:22, and "An Homilie concerning the comming downe of the holy Ghost," *Certaine Sermons*, sig. Ss3ʳ.

give your alms secretly: So shall ye on the one part be inwardly garnished with true Christian humility, not outwardly (with the proud Pharisee) glorying in your godliness: but saying, as Christ commandeth us all, when we have done all that we can, *Inutiles servi sumus* [Luke 10:17]" (1:51).

But this inward garnishing is only one part of the king's duty. "On the other part," James continues, "ye shall eschew outwardly before the world, the suspicion of filthy proud hypocrisy and deceitful dissimulation" (1:51). This attention to the outward as well as the inward and the correspondence or contrast between them is as persistent a concern in *The Basilicon Doron* as it is in *Measure for Measure*. The king is no less careful of his honor than is Shakespeare's Duke, and his published reasons are far from vainglorious. All the actions and qualities of the king, James persistently maintains, must be conditioned by the immense responsibilities of his office (1:205-7).

Honor is to be used as a means toward the due and faithful discharge of that office. In a polity still based in part on feudal reverence for the person of the sovereign (and more generally on direct personal ties among nobles and gentry, on the one hand, and servants, laborers, and farmers on the other), reputation remained an important tool for ensuring effective political control. In a seminal contribution to the genre of humanistic treatises on kingship, Erasmus, following Aristotle (*Politics* 5.10), explains the political significance of the prince's reputation. Hatred and contempt of the sovereign, he asserts, are two factors that have played the greatest roles in overthrowing empires. The prince must therefore study to avoid the hatred most readily bred by tyrannical behavior. He must cultivate especially the benign virtues of "clemency, affability, fairness, courtesy, and kindliness."[20]

The criterion of fairness would be violated, we may sur-

[20] *The Education of a Christian Prince*, trans. Lester K. Born (New York: Columbia University Press, 1936), pp. 208-209. See *The Basilicon Doron* (2:83) for evidence that Erasmus's treatise directly influenced the king's.

mise, if a ruler should suddenly begin to enforce laws that
he had allowed to lie in desuetude for fourteen years (as
Duke Vincentio had done, 1.3.21), or should fail to reward
faithful servants of the commonwealth (as the Duke conspicuously does not fail to do, 5.1.525-28). Clemency and
forgiveness, virtues especially germane to the events of
Measure for Measure, are said to inspire "to better efforts
those who are aware of their faults" and to extend "hope to
those who are now eager to make recompense by virtuous
conduct for the shortcomings of their earlier life."[21] Unlike
hatred, the contempt that destroys governments arises
usually from "a penchant for the worldly pleasures of lust,
for excessive drinking and eating." Such contempt can be
counteracted by virtues like wisdom, integrity, and self-
restraint.[22]

But it is never enough merely to have these qualities.
The prince's public behavior must advertise his virtue. And
since courtiers and public ministers are living symbols of
his character, the king ought to win to his love and place in
positions of highest authority "the best men . . . that he may
be accepted by those who are lauded by all. . . . By this
means everyone will come to have an excellent opinion of
the prince."[23]

[21] Historians have begun to recognize that this principle was applied,
with great effectiveness, in the administration of English law. As Douglas
Hay argues (*Albion's Fatal Tree: Crime and Society in Eighteenth-century England* [New York: Pantheon, 1975], pp. 17-63), the draconian nature of
early English law was mitigated by selective but liberal use of pardons and
other forms of judicial mercy. This combination of "justice" and mercy,
well advertised by the elaborate public ceremonial of the courts, effectively helped to preserve and reinforce a spirit of consent and submission
that fosters social and political order. Hay's study concerns a period when
the contrast between harsh laws and judicial clemency was particularly
marked. But the principles of legal administration Hay describes were
well known to James I. His famous last-minute reprieve of condemned
conspirators (see Lever, p. l.) reveals a conception of law's didactic purpose that George III made part of his routine administration of the law
condemning highwaymen (see Hay, p. 52).

[22] *Education*, p. 209.

[23] Ibid., p. 207.

This calculated aim to magnify the honor of the prince need not be, as it is for Henry Bolingbroke, for Machiavelli himself (in some moods), for the typical stage Machiavel, and for the public-relations men who inhabit modern capitals, an instrument of political self-aggrandizement. It is a tool necessary to the tamest of monarchs and civil magistrates.[24] And the magistrates' honor, according to Sir Thomas Elyot, must be cultivated especially through proper use of public ceremonies—coronations, processions, progresses, and the like, "that by reason of the honourable circumstances then used, should be impressed in the hearts of the beholders perpetual reverence: which . . . is fountain of obedience." The expensive ceremonial of governments, vain in itself, is justified as a means to compensate for the limited capacities of men: in Elyot's words, "we be men and not angels: wherefore we know nothing but by outward signification. Honour, whereto reverence pertaineth, is . . . the reward of virtue, which honour is the estimation of people, which estimation is not everywhere perceived, but by some exterior sign, and that is either by laudable report, or excellence in vesture, or other thing sembable."[25] In short, kings, who as Christians must avoid "glorying in their godliness" and seeking the reputation of virtue for its own sake, must for the good of their republics both avoid the dishonor that arises from tyranny or luxury and advertise their virtues through the manipulation of external appearance and the promotion of public ceremony. Properly employed, these things foster the obedience that preserves civil harmony.

[24] This was widely recognized. Cf. Sir Thomas Elyot, *The Boke Named the Governour* (London: n.p., 1544), sig. A4ᵛ. Machiavelli treats this theme with characteristic cynicism or "realism." See *The Prince*, chaps. 18, 21.

[25] *Governour*, sig. T1ᵛ. Elyot's argument for the necessity of political ceremony was being debated in Shakespeare's age in the heated controversy over religious ceremonies. See Hooker, *Laws*, 1:361-62. In *The Illusion of Power* (Berkeley: University of California Press, 1975), passim, esp. pp. 42-43, Stephen Orgel argues that the Stuart masques served, above all, to reflect and glorify the king's divinely established and godlike role in society—and to justify his political theories and policies.

Besides its political utility, attention to the king's reputation has an ethical justification. This is hinted by King James's exhortation that deeds of righteousness be performed to encourage similar behavior among the people. James's awareness of the king's obligation to promote his subjects' spiritual health appears in fact in the first paragraph of his book. This early hint receives expansive treatment as James explains that since kings are set, as it were, "upon a public stage, in the sight of all the people" (1:12), they must be especially careful of their behavior. "A mote in anothers eye, is a beam in yours,"[26] because "any sin that ye commit" is an exemplary sin that encourages "the whole multitude to be guilty of the same" (1:27). This idea is repeated persistently throughout the king's book (1:39, 53, 103-5, 117-19, 137, 161, and 163).[27] Thus, despite his contempt for honor sought for its own sake—or to use his scriptural metaphor, alms given in the sight of men—James urges repeatedly that kings attend even in details of food and clothing to the effects such normally indifferent matters may have on their reputation among men (cf. 1:163-67, 175). Since subjects "cannot judge of you, but according to the outward appearance of your actions and company" (1:111), tyranny and luxury—and the appearance of these vices—must be avoided if hatred or "contempt, the mother of rebellion and disorder" (1:163) is to be prevented.[28]

Throughout his treatise on monarchy, then, James both condemns vainglory and encourages the use of reputation as an instrument of policy. His attitude toward "slandering a prince," we can now see, represents no mere personal

[26] This is the first of James's five echoes of Matt. 7:1-5. See *Basilicon Doron*, 1:45, 67, 77, 157. On p. 45, the king quotes a Pauline echo (1 Cor. 11:31) of the passage. Cf. Pope, "Elizabethan Background," p. 75, and Stevenson, *Achievement*, p. 153.

[27] See Erasmus, *Christian Prince*, pp. 156-57; Elyot, *Governour*, sig. A4ʳ; *Basilicon Doron*, 2:80; and Castiglione, *Courtier*, in Milligan, *Three Renaissance Classics*, p. 545.

[28] See also *Basilicon Doron*, 1:57-59.

quirk, as Schanzer and others suggest. Even in the much-quoted passage where James criticizes the Scots' eagerness "to judge and speak rashly of their prince," his concern for orderly government rather than royal vanity is clearly implied. Besides enforcement of the laws, he advises his son to quell slander by governing justly—to enforce the law sternly, thereby awing "unjust railers," and to employ judicious clemency, thereby earning the praise of "good and loving subjects" (1:93). In context, then, James's punishment of slander and encouragement of honest praise and ceremony support his regal and Christian ideal of self-denying service to the commonwealth.[29]

Taken as a whole, the correspondence between Duke Vincentio's and King James's attitudes toward the honor of rulers may be at once more comprehensive and less narrowly biographical than scholars have so far realized. The purposes of Duke Vincentio's self-contradictory attitude toward his honor—sometimes disdaining ceremony, at other times orchestrating it himself, modestly revealing his faults to the Friar but warmly defending his "bringings-forth" against the slanders of Lucio—remain unstated. But our incursion into the parent genre of treatises on monarchical behavior reveals an identical ambivalence and suggests an inexplicit rationale. And the play sometimes supplies unobtrusive but explicit reminders of relevant portions of the conventional wisdom. Angelo recalls, for example, the ethical importance of a magistrate's manners: "thieves for their robbery have authority, / When judges steal themselves" (2.2.176-77). This suggests the real danger of allowing vice to make mercy (4.2.110-11) *and* of acquiescing in Lucio's slanders: "He had some feeling of the sport; he knew the service; and that instructed him to mercy" (3.2.115-17). With equal potency, the reality and the slanderous fabrication breed vice. At the beginning of

[29] I do not mean to imply that the king always practiced his published ideals. He must have found in these theories convenient excuse for his personal sense of pique.

act 5, furthermore, the Duke reveals his conviction that
public display must show the worthy receiving due recognition:

> Give me your hand,
> And let the subject see, to make them know
> That outward courtesies would fain proclaim
> Favours that keep within.
>
> [5.1.14-17][30]

Like actual sixteenth-century rulers, Duke Vincentio
must preserve appearances to avoid the loss of confidence
that could erode political power. Reverting to his explanation to Friar Thomas (1.3.35-43), we can see the same principle in operation. As the Duke says quite plainly, he cannot afford the reputation of tyranny. He therefore puts
Angelo in charge of Vienna, not only to enforce the laws
more rigorously than he had himself and to fulfill other,
more obscurely hinted ends (1.3.48–54), but also to protect
his own "nature" from the "slander" of tyranny. This action has been forced on the Duke by an admitted error. Of
that, I shall have more to say.

I offer this rationale for the Duke's departure not as an
absolute certainty, but as the kind of informed guess that
Shakespeare's deliberate obscurantism forces upon us.
Such guesses provide a context for understanding the
Duke's character and motives as the play proceeds, a context that can be validated or exploded by events. And although it has its most profound effects on the chief participants, Isabella and Angelo,[31] we should notice here that
the Duke's ceremonial return appears to have broad public

---

[30] In line 14, I restore the F2 reading "me your." Lever conjectures "we
our"; F reads "we your."

Queen Elizabeth I knew well that her private thanks for diligent service
ought to be completed by "outward courtesies." See the letter quoted by
Norman Council, *When Honour's at the Stake* (London: George Allen and
Unwin, 1973), p. 20.

[31] I discuss these effects in chapters 5 and 6.

motives analogous to those suggested by King James. The exposure of vice in high places powerfully builds the monarch's reputation for justice—both among the "generous and gravest" citizens of Vienna and among Londoners at the Globe—when that exposure is highlighted by ceremonies that political authorities of Shakespeare's age believed to be essential instruments of policy. Setting aside for now the vexing question of the ethical purity of the Duke's motives in "leaving" Vienna, we are, I think, intended to admire the *political* wisdom of a ruler who takes opportunistic advantage of the events caused by his absence in order to work a popular reprieve for the mildly guilty Juliet and Claudio, catch out an amusing yet potentially dangerous slanderer, and expose to corrosive public shame a deeply corrupt chief magistrate. These benefits result from the Duke's original non-Machiavellian but politically realistic desire to correct, without permanently damaging his ability to govern, the corruption his indulgent administration had encouraged. The Duke's solicitude and wisdom in these actions deserve the respect that fosters public order.[32]

In these considerations, we find the key to the Duke's seemingly inconsistent attitude toward public ceremony. His departure from Vienna, by contrast to his return, would have been a ceremony of little substance. On the basis of our knowledge of honor and ceremony as instruments of governance, we may view the Duke's ceremonial return not as mere self-dramatization or authorial inconsistency, but as an action tacitly calculated to benefit the commonwealth as well as the immediate participants. This can be, I repeat, a suggestion only, for Shakespeare adamantly refuses to tell all. But while we cannot utterly disperse the mystery that envelops the Duke, we can deter-

---

[32] Of course, one of the chief controversies of *Measure for Measure* criticism concerns the Duke's treatment of offenders *after* he exposes their guilt. I discuss this problem in chapter 6.

mine probable reasons for some of his actions. These probabilities, as I argue in the next chapters, aid us to accept the certainty that our judgment too has its limits, that ultimately we are meant to submit to mystery—in *Measure for Measure* as in life, where many things occur "against all sense."

This proleptic observation leads us to another important point: James's repeated expression of the power of princely example echoes an authority much more widely familiar than *The Basilicon Doron*, contemporary best seller though it was. The metaphor of the king's "glistering worldly glory," which is used "so to glister and shine before their people" that they become "bright lamps of godliness" (1:27), is twice repeated in slightly varied forms (1:137, 161) in the course of the book. In a treatise that begins with a compendium of Christian doctrine and is strewn throughout with biblical echoes and citations, it is not difficult to perceive in this metaphor the persistent influence of the original great summary of Christian law and of its familiar passage about candlesticks.

In stating his interpretation of that passage, Calvin corroborates the interpretation I proposed above and summarizes the reading conventional in his own age and implicit in the king's book. Christ's meaning is, he says, that "we be all children of the light after that we be lightened with faith, and are commanded to bear burning lights in our hands, lest we wander in darkness, and also to show the way of life to others." The greater our portion of divine gifts, furthermore, the more necessary that they be seen by men. The candlestick metaphor applies primarily but not exclusively, therefore, to the ecclesiastical and civil leaders of society, and in a passage closely parallel to that of James, Calvin interprets the doctrine of Matt. 5:16 as signifying that such leaders should live as if they were on constant display, since they foster evil by their highly visible perversities and virtue by their equally visible good works. Christian leaders especially are therefore commanded to join the pursuit of Gloriana, the glory that follows virtue and rightly belongs to God alone.[33]

The theme of honor, moreover, is no less pervasive in the Sermon on the Mount than it is in James's treatise and in Shakespeare's play. And as Erasmus's paraphrase nicely illustrates, the sermon insistently exhibits the same ambivalence toward worldly honor that we have found in *The Basilicon Doron* and in *Measure for Measure*: "So ye ought not to seek, how to purchase a fame and opinion among men: but only be ye careful·that ye darken not the light, which I have lightened in you, and that ye persevere and continue upon the candlestick, where I have set you."[34]

Although a persistent concern for honor and similar commands to eschew Philotime recur often in the Sermon on the Mount,[35] we should remember in particular that the sermon's first words promise heavenly felicity to those who have utterly subjected themselves to the will of God, a state that precludes all selfish vainglory. Erasmus explains the opening of the sermon by allusion to the seven deadly sins: Because fierceness and arrogance are the most dangerous diseases of the mind, "the fountain, from whence ... spring all deadly offenses: First of all Jesus healeth this, saying: 'Blessed be the poor in spirit.' " And by "poor in spirit" he means the ideal Reformed Christian who "distrusting

[33] *Harmonie*, sigs. L3ʳ-L3ᵛ. The Bible, Calvin, and other commentators demonstrate that modern scholars, notably Norman Council (*When Honour's at the Stake*, p. 26), are wrong to imply that Calvin saw human honor as a purely deleterious goal and that "Aristotle's ethics of mediocrity is the origin of all sixteenth-century justifications of a moderate desire for honour" (pp. 18-19). Council's book is, nonetheless, a useful antidote to the oversimplifications of Curtis Brown Watson, *Shakespeare and the Renaissance Concept of Honor* (Princeton: Princeton University Press, 1960).

[34] *Paraphrase*, 1, fol. E6ʳ. The speaker, of course, is Christ. Cf. Calvin, *Harmonie*, sig. L3ʳ.

[35] See esp. Matt. 6:1-18. The famous dicta "Where your treasure is, there will your heart be also" and "no man can serve two masters" (Matt. 6:21, 24) also touch by extension on the theme of worldly honor. See Calvin, *Harmonie*, sigs. N5ʳ-N6ʳ.

himself, putteth his trust in God, and distrusting the succour of man, doth depend wholly of heaven. . . . God ad-
vanceth unto his kingdom those chiefly, which do most
humble themselves."[36] As we shall see in chapter 5, this
doctrine concerning the self-glorifying effects of self-
effacement is essential to our understanding of the Duke's
corrective schemes.

More immediately, we should turn from these seminal
discussions of honor, which are also among the play's direct sources, to the text itself and especially, once again, to
Isabella's terrified, angry judgment of Claudio. In addition
to its lack of mercy and its exaggerated scope, we ought to
notice that Shakespeare realizes in Isabella's judgment
another typically monastic trait, one dramatized in the
comic railing of Chaucer's Summoner's Friar and of
Spenser's Corceca and Abessa. Isabella's judgment of
Claudio is an attack precisely on his honor; although it is
not publicly proclaimed, this judgment comprises a brace
of terrible slanders:

> What should I think?
> Heaven shield my mother play'd my father fair:
> For such a warped slip of wilderness
> Ne'er issued from his blood.
>
> [3.1.139-42]
>
> Thy sin's not accidental, but a trade;
> Mercy to thee would prove itself a bawd.
>
> [3.1.147-48]

In Isabella's judgment, Claudio is reduced to whore-
monger and bastard. And in recognizing that her cruel
words are slanderous judgments, we perceive that the
play's climactic judgment involves the persistent themes of
honor and dishonor, glory and shame.

[36] *Paraphrase*, 1, fol. E4ᵛ; cf. also Calvin, *Harmonie*, sig. K7ᵛ, and Luther,
Works, 21:10-17.

An even more apparent, and at first glance, somewhat gratuitous intrusion of these themes appears shortly after the play's climax, in Lucio's puzzling—and under the circumstances wonderfully comic—attacks on the reputation of the Duke. These begin shortly after Isabella's meeting with Claudio, and it is important to realize that they are immediately preceded by a comic parody of that meeting. Pompey hopes for help, specifically bail, from Lucio. But in a flight of levity unrestrained even for him, Lucio pours out all he knows about Pompey's "mystery": "imprison him. If imprisonment be the due of a bawd, why, 'tis his right. Bawd is he doubtless, and of antiquity, too: bawd born" [3.2.64-66]. Like Isabella's, Lucio's amusing stream of abuse, essentially true, is exaggerated. Its conclusion directly echoes Isabella's parting assertion that she will pray for Claudio's death:

Pom.   I hope, sir, your good worship will be my bail?
Lucio.   No, indeed will I not, Pompey; . . . I will pray,
      Pompey, to increase your bondage.
                                        [3.2.70-72]

The comic exaggerations in Lucio's abuse of Pompey become extraordinarily amusing slander when his attention is diverted to the deputy: "it is certain that when he makes water, his urine is congealed ice; that I know to be true" (3.2.105-7). When he turns to the Duke himself, his slanders sometimes become even more imaginative ("Yes, your beggar of fifty; and his use was to put a ducat in her clack-dish," 3.2.122-23); sometimes they turn to dull epithet-hurling ("a very superficial, ignorant, unweighing fellow," 3.2.136); but sometimes they are so appalling as to lead us to admire that Duke's almost superhuman patience: "The Duke, I say to thee again, would eat mutton on Fridays. He's past it; yet, and I say to thee, he would mouth with a beggar though she smelt brown bread and garlic" (3.2.174-78). Although scholars often remark that the Duke later treats Lucio with excessive harshness, any auditor capable of imagining his own responses to such slanders will wonder at the Duke's restraint, both here and in act 5.[37]

While their relevance is not immediately apparent, these comic Duke-baiting interludes contribute to the play's central themes. They are all judgments of varying degrees of accuracy and gravity, and all violate not only the essence of Christian law, but also the text from which the play's title comes. As we have seen, Isabella accurately enacts the errors of hypocrites who judge mercilessly despite the weighty beams in their eyes—she violates the lawful manner of judging prescribed in Matt. 7:3-5. But the relationship between Matt. 7:1-2 and the slanders that are rife in Vienna has yet to be noted.

In the larger context of the Sermon on the Mount, that passage enjoins, as I argued in chapter 1, charity in judging. But in explaining a more specific sense of the passage, commentators of Shakespeare's age stressed especially its negative implications. They recognized that Christ specifically intended to prohibit the often harmless yet cruel acts of judgment that issue in slanderous thoughts and words. Calvin summarizes this conventional interpretation: "Christ doth not in these words precisely restrain from judging: but his will was to heal that disease, which is settled almost in all. For we see how . . . every man is a severe censor against others. . . . This wicked delight in biting, carping, and slandering doth Christ refrain, when he saieth *Judge not*."[38]

This reading is not peculiar to Calvin. Erasmus's is similar, though it stresses the arrogant vainglory of censorious

---

[37] It appears sometimes that commentators believe that Lucio *is* whipped and hanged. In fact, he is simply made to marry the mother of his own child.

> Thou shalt marry her.
> Thy slanders I forgive, and therewithal
> Remit thy other forfeits.
>
> [5.1.516-18]

[38] *Harmonie*, sig. O1ʳ.

judges. The men Christ condemns in the passage that pro-
hibits "judgment," Erasmus explains, are men like the
scribes and Pharisees who censure others to secure a reputation for righteousness and who do it not out of love but
from a desire merely to destroy and to slander. Having a
beam in his eye and perceiving the mote in his neighbor's,
"one slandereth his brother because he weareth a loose
garment, where he himself is full of envy. Another
speaketh evil of his brother, because being overcome with
weakness of the flesh he useth a concubine, whereas he
himself is wholly the servant of avarice and ambition."[39] If
we set avarice and (literal) ambition aside and read "intended bride" for "concubine," it becomes clear that Erasmus describes in his last sentence a situation not unlike that
of Isabella and Claudio. The latter has fallen to frailty of
the flesh, the former, perhaps, to excessive concern for the
reputation of virtue and, certainly, to the anger that, under
the New Law, is murder.

In his commentary on Matt. 7:1, Luther stresses that
slanderous judgment is an entirely natural human impulse
that, when indulged, is likely to be repaid in equal measure. We are all inherently prone to support our egotism by
magnifying the faults of others. Consequently, he says, "I
am ready to despise and condemn a man as soon as he
stumbles a little or makes some other mistake. He treats me
the same way, giving me the same measure I give him, as
Christ says here. . . . By such behavior love is suppressed."
When men thus insist on seeing only their neighbors'
faults, "the only consequence must be slander and judging
back and forth."[40]

To the most influential Reformation commentators,
therefore, "to judge" meant to scan one's neighbors' deeds
with a censorious eye.[41] Most seriously, slanderous judg-

[39] *Paraphrase*, 1, fol. G2ᵛ.
[40] *The Sermon on the Mount*, in *Works*, 21:214-15.
[41] Cf. Fenton, *St. Matthew*, p. 109; and see the Geneva note to Matt.
7:1-2: "He commandeth, not to be curious or malicious to try out and

ment violates the ultimate law, "by such behavior love is suppressed." This is most obviously the case in Isabella's outrageous, angry judgment of Claudio. But on a comic level, such judgment is the very substance, in Shakespeare's Vienna, of street-corner gossip. Hence, the excessive mercy resulting from the Duke's fatherly affection (1.3.23) becomes, in Lucio's witty, uncharitable judgment, matter for slander: "He had some feeling of the sport; he knew the service; and that instructed him to mercy" (3.2.115-17). The Duke's preference for the life removed is transformed into vague innuendos hinting at secret assignations or equally secret resorts to the sweating-tub:

Lucio.   A shy fellow was the Duke; and I believe I know
the cause of his withdrawing.
Duke.   What, I prithee, might be the cause?
Lucio.   No, pardon: 'tis a secret must be locked within
the teeth and the lips.

[3.2.127-32]

Slanders such as these violate the law of Vienna, and all harsh judgments violate the transcendent law from which every other law derives. As Luther's explanation shows with special clarity, our inclination to defame others arises from a universal egotism that includes an eagerness to magnify faults, just as Isabella in her anger exaggerates Claudio's intercourse with an intended bride into habitual whoring. But besides magnifying minor evils into grave ones, the kind of judgment prohibited by Christ also finds unmitigated evil in things capable of less unfavorable construction: "sinistrally expounding things that be doubtful,"[42] or breaking forth into a "perverse boldness, so that we do proudly judge ill of every matter, although it may be

---

condemn our neighbours' faults." The Geneva running title on the page that bears Luke's version of the passage (Luke 6:37-38) reads "Rash judgement." Arthur Kirsch, "Integrity of *Measure for Measure*," notes (p. 102) that Perkins associates Matt. 7:1-2 with the vice of slander.

[42] Erasmus, *Paraphrase*, 1, fol. G1ᵛ.

taken in good part."[43] Either Angelo or Isabella, if he or she had been less self-involved and had truly considered Claudio's relationship to Juliet, could have taken his or her sin in good part and admitted, without scruple, that mitigation of the death penalty would be consistent with justice human and divine.

This admission would follow from obedience to the law of charity, a law that, as Hooker explained, grants measure for measure in a positive sense—measuring other men's desire for equitable treatment by the standard of one's own identical desire. This idea underlies Calvin's summary statement of the meaning of the measure-for-measure passage, a statement that returns to the wider implications of Matt. 7:1: "Now we see to what purpose Christ's counsel tendeth: that is, that we be not too desirous, or overthwart [i.e., angry, perverse], or malicious, or else curious in judging our neighbours. But he that judgeth by the word and law of the Lord, and directeth his judgement according to the rule of charity, doth always begin his judgement at himself, he doth observe the right manner and order of judging."[44] Echoing Paul's famous definition of charity (1 Cor. 13), Erasmus puts a similar interpretation in more positive form: "the judgements that ye have, must savour of the evangelical charity, which readily doth forgive, which misdeemeth no man rashly without cause, which doth expound every doubtful thing to the best, which desireth rather to heal than to punish, which considering

---

[43] Calvin, *Harmonie*, sig. O1^r. In urging that we should avoid the habit of seeing unmitigated evil in things possibly indifferent, Erasmus and Calvin touch on an implication that Augustine had considered central to Matt. 7:1. Since Augustine's *Commentary on the Sermon on the Mount* heavily influenced the Reformer's own interpretations, and since Augustine included in that work a narrative analogue of *Measure for Measure*, his remarks may be of value to us. See his *Commentary on the Lord's Sermon on the Mount with Seventeen Related Sermons*, trans. Denis J. Kavanagh (New York: Fathers of the Church, 1951), pp. 169-70. Cf. Perkins, *Whole Treatise*, p. 515.

[44] *Harmonie*, sig. O1^r.

her own infirmity and weakness, so judgeth other men's offences as she would be judged offending herself."[45]

In arguing that such warmly humane judgment should
include self-judgment, the glosses of Calvin and Erasmus
glance forward to the verses about the hypocrite with the
beam in his eye. Although it has often been recognized that
these verses describe Angelo, and although I have demonstrated their relevance to Isabella, they are also relevant to
Duke Vincentio. For despite the common assertion that his
admission of excessive laxity in enforcing the laws detracts
from his position as the play's ethical standard, this scriptural passage (which is woven deeply into the play's linguistic texture), the readings of contemporary commentators,
and our own ethical common sense suggest that he is correctly preparing himself for the exercise of charitable
justice. Before coming to judge the sins of others, as he
does especially in act 5, the Duke casts out the beam that
has rested for fourteen years in his own eye:

> We have strict statutes and most biting laws,
> The needful bits and curbs to headstrong jades,
> Which for this fourteen years we have let slip.
>> [1.3.19-21]

He further—and rightly, too—insists on accepting responsibility for the sins others committed during this period of
excessive leniency:

> Sith 'twas my fault to give the people scope,
> 'Twould be my tyranny to strike and gall them
> For what I bid them do: for we bid this be done,
> When evil deeds have their permissive pass,
> And not the punishment.
>> [1.3.35-39]

[45] *Paraphrase*, 1, fol. G1^v-G2^r. Cf. Luther, *The Sermon on the Mount*, in *Works*, 21:213.

This confession illustrates the fact, later attested by Escalus
(3.2.226-27), that the Duke sought always to know his own
faults—and this is the ideal proposed both by Christ and
His commentators.[46] The Duke's confession, therefore,
can be judged, if *we* are disposed to judge charitably, as
figuring a behavioral ideal, not as a warrant for self-
righteous condemnation. His confession, that is, can be
taken in good part; in heedlessly doing otherwise, we may
be guilty of "sinistrally expounding things that be doubtful." Whether we should take all his actions equally in good
part is another question; one treated to some extent above,
and to be discussed more fully in a later chapter.

By contrast to the Duke, as many have argued, Angelo
remains the unalloyed though tormented hypocrite who
passes judgment on Claudio's mote while himself retaining
a cartload of sturdy beams. Although it is his office to judge
offenders before the law, the deputy's first appearance as
presiding judge reveals that he administers the law in
exactly the way Christ forbade. He is, in Calvin's words,
desirous, overthwart, and malicious in his judgments of fellowmen. To emphasize this in a context devoid of the problematic yet specious justifications Angelo employs in his arguments with Escalus (2.1.17-31) and Isabella (2.2.79-106),
Shakespeare introduces a sour and revealing remark into
the delightfully comic arraignment of Pompey and Master
Froth:

> I'll take my leave,
> And leave you to the hearing of the cause;
> Hoping you'll find good cause to whip them all.
> [2.1.134-36]

As his humorless sourness had earlier led us to expect,
Angelo's judgments savor of outright malice. And as we
are reminded by King James, even when a magistrate con-

---

[46] This continuing effort at self-knowledge, and its bearing on judicial
behavior, is treated in one of the Duke's epigrammatic precepts: "More
nor less to others paying Than by self-offences weighing" (3.2.258-59).

forms outwardly to the letter of the law, he is guilty before
God if he enforces that law "for satisfying any particular
[i.e., private] passions" rather than "for love to justice"
(1:63). In addition, as Angelo himself reveals in soliloquy
(2.4.9-10), the Duke and Claudio are correct in suggesting
that he seeks by his gravity to receive glory of men. There
is no doubt, moreover, that in Claudio's case, he is sinistrally expounding things that are doubtful. He clearly corresponds, in detail, to those hypocrites to whom Christ ad-
dressed the measure-for-measure passage, those who "seek
for a name of righteousness, because they be very stout and
sore against other men's faults." He also appears to "do it
neither for the love of [his] neighbours (whom [he desires]
rather to be destroyed than corrected, and to be slandered
openly, rather than amended) neither for hatred of vice,
whereas [he maintains] and [pardons his] own vices far
greater than the others'."[47] And we should recall that the
offenses Angelo has pardoned in himself include more
than the unspecified general sinfulness of all men. For although he believes himself sinless and immune to temptation, we soon discover that he once resorted to a subterfuge
that lowers him to the moral level of the amoral Lucio. He
viciously slandered Mariana to escape an unprofitable
marriage.

On the basis of the evidence so far collected, the theme
of honor and the related topics of slander and public
ceremony appear to have broad significance in *Measure
for Measure*—significance related intimately to the central
theme of law. We can begin to perceive *Measure for Measure*
as an aesthetic unity based on a very careful thematic structure. We now perceive that Lucio's slanderous activities in
the subplot—and especially in the oft-maligned fourth
act—represent a comic variation of the very sin that both
Isabella and Angelo commit in their separate judgments of
Claudio. All three precisely enact the sin specifically pro-

hibited by the measure-for-measure text. All therefore manifest in their judgments the carnality they betray, as we have seen, in other prominent ways. They reveal once more the mind of the flesh and the consequent lack of charity that the Sermon on the Mount as a whole condemns. At its most serious, this lack may lead to the unjustified death of men; at its most trivial, it results in the slanderous exaggerations of comic and ineffectual gossip. But in a play that refers, subtly and persistently, to central ideals of Christian life, lack of charity threatens the ultimate death of souls. As act 5 begins, therefore, the chief characters in *Measure for Measure*, with the possible exception of the Duke, find themselves in a most parlous state.

Chapter 5

A Satisfaction and a Benefit

With the emotional crisis of act 3, scene 1, we reach the play's climax, and from the moment of his reappearance at line 151, the Duke's new ascendancy leads us to expect an escape from the dilemma that seems insoluble to those involved in it. Our previous relationship with the Duke is reestablished immediately. His motive in lying to Claudio (3.1.160-69) is suppressed at the same time that we are eager to know why he should direct Claudio to expect only death, a death that can, we now know, be readily averted. The Duke brings with him, in short, the air of mystery he has generated from the outset. He brings also—and this is what *his* friar's habit has begun to symbolize—a recollection that his role in two previous appearances was entirely that of charitable and sophisticated spiritual counselor. His first words suggest that Isabella herself may soon join the clientele he has been building since he assumed the robes of a friar: "the satisfaction I would require is likewise your own benefit" (3.1.154-55).

As Lever's note points out, "satisfaction" implies the "performance of a penance enjoined by one's confessor"; it hints therefore that the Duke's ministrations will include a measure of purgatorial suffering. This hint, together with the Duke's previous efforts to know the precise nature of his subjects' crimes that he might "minister to them accordingly" (2.3.7-8), suggests that the plot Duke Vincentio now begins to administer aims as much to treat Isabella's ills as to rescue her brother and to "scale" the corrupt deputy. As usual, we are obliged to piece together for ourselves the logic of this treatment. To perceive how the Duke's purgatorial machinations work is to understand how the themes I have been exploring determine the shape of Shakespeare's plot after act 3, scene 1, line 151 and, conversely, how the plot brings the play's major thematic tensions to a satisfying resolution.

From the argument he overhears between brother and sister, Duke Vincentio has learned Isabella's most comprehensive malady. He has received ample evidence of the literalism, born of spiritual naiveté, that leads her to locate virtue in precise obedience to rules of outward behavior and therefore to believe that fornication will result in inevitable damnation. Having ourselves accurately diagnosed Isabella's malady, we may recognize the striking precision of the Duke's first words of advice: "The hand that hath made you fair hath made you good. The goodness that is cheap in beauty makes beauty brief in goodness; but grace, being the soul of your complexion, shall keep the body of it ever fair" (3.1.179-83).

The Duke has "read" Isabella with characteristic accuracy. Beneath her hysterical anger and exaggerated fear of damnation he recognizes ill-directed efforts toward goodness. Isabella's visible actions participate in the play's large pattern of false-seeming, for however distorted by her current hysteria, there is something of devotion in them. The Duke's opening statement recalls theological implications that are central to Isabella's case of conscience, and unknown to her. All goodness, and all beauty, come directly from the hand of God. The lesser good of physical attractiveness ("the goodness that is cheap in beauty") can often make beautiful women "brief in goodness" because it arouses perpetual temptation in a world populated by Lucios, Overdones, Pompeys, and Angelos. But "grace" being the soul of Isabella's "complexion"—the word signifies primarily emotional temperament and quality of spirit—can preserve even the "body," the incarnate manifestations of that complexion, "ever fair."

This is the Duke at his cryptic best (or worst). But whatever difficulty we may have with specific details, their drift is clear: essential goodness is a quality of the soul, the soul's goodness is a graciously imputed divine gift, and it is therefore ultimately inviolable. We may thus infer that in extreme circumstances like Isabella's, the presence of grace and the consequent will to do good make physical virginity almost a matter indifferent. The Duke's aphoristic remark depends upon and economically restates doctrine implicit in the play's first scene, that all goods are God's own. This restatement initiates a series of lessons that both urge the accurate attribution of value and efficacy to their grand source and promise the comforts that result from complete dependence on that source.

The Duke's educative manipulations of Isabella begin in startling fashion, for he here introduces the palpable absurdity of what is usually called the "bed trick." Like the obscurities and mystery elsewhere evident in the play, and like the extravagant and superficially inexplicable actions that normally appear in symbolic narrative, the bed trick is meant to startle us into an analytical frame of mind. We ought to be surprised by the Duke's suggestion, but before consigning the whole affair, as many do, to Shakespeare's surrender to unwieldy materials, we should seek what analysis might yield.

Our analysis must begin with the disconcerting fact that Isabella appears, as a result of the Duke's persuasion, to waver in her heretofore rigidly held ethical and religious principles. Scholars would sometimes persuade us that the logic at work here depends on our own and Isabella's knowledge that Angelo's contract with Mariana takes the form of a *sponsalia per verba de futuro*, and that sexual intercourse between them would therefore complete a legally binding marriage.[1] This historical information serves, however, to distract attention from the text and the facts it presents. The Duke promises no legal certainties; he offers instead a bare "if": "If the encounter acknowledge itself hereafter, it may compel him to her recompense" (3.1.251-53). All the happy results anticipated are avowedly mere possibilities, remote ones for anyone unaware of the Duke's identity.

This remoteness strengthens our perception that Isabella's principles have become surprisingly supple when she agrees uncritically with the notion that "the doubleness of the benefit defends the deceit from reproof" (3.1.257-59). Just moments earlier, Isabella had given clear evidence of her conviction that sin committed under duress would bring her own damnation. Now she acquiesces unhesitatingly in a strange plan to arrange an act of extramarital intercourse. Many readers—most stridently Arthur Quiller-Couch—have considered this inconsistency morally offensive. And despite the fact that intercourse between espoused parties would not be prosecuted in the English courts, Elizabethan authorities on marriage nonetheless considered such action sinful (see chap. 6, below). These authorities simply reinforce our discomfort— discomfort encouraged by the moral subtlety that has so far characterized the play—with the facile idea that if intercourse is legal it would also necessarily be sinless. Our scruples are further aroused by the entry, immediately after the Duke and Isabella strike their agreement, of Pompey, newly arrested because he "will needs buy and sell men and women like beasts" (3.1.271-72). This juxtaposition demands that we perceive the outward similarity between the Duke's plot and a habitual activity of the play's boisterous bawd. We are justified in concluding that Isabella here accepts the Duke's reasoning somewhat too readily because she earnestly wishes to believe it. She con-

---

[1] Lever reviews the evidence, pp. liii-liv; see note 15, below.

sequently gives no thought to the potential damnation of the substituted bedmate.

If the Duke's assurance that there is a contract (of some sort) between Angelo and Mariana has forestalled Isabella's concern for Mariana's soul, then our previous experience of Isabella suggests that we are to see here further evidence of her legalistic spirituality. Unlike us, she is willing to equate legality and moral purity. However we choose to read her behavior, Isabella's ready acceptance of the Duke's proposal appears to fulfill expectations raised by traits we now recognize as fundamental to her character. This observation is itself reinforced by the most visible reason for Isabella's readiness to accept the Duke as spiritual authority—his friar's robes. With little resistance, Isabella submits to an authority we know to be beneficent, but she does so for reasons we suspect to be poor ones: his appearance of piety and his ability to offer what she desperately wants, an escape from her dilemma *and* the assurance that everything will remain strictly legal.

Once the Duke persuades Isabella to join him, the plot of the latter half of the play builds gradually to its artfully protracted and dramatically effective climax in act 5. Our preparation for this climactic act, however, provides important reminders that Isabella is herself to expect a penitential experience. This is true, for example, of the final scene of act 4, where Isabella ponders the Duke's written instructions for pleading her cause and voices scrupulous doubts about the role he has assigned her:

> To speak so indirectly I am loth;
> I would say the truth, but to accuse him so
> That is your part; yet I am advised to do it,
> He says, to veil full purpose.
>
> [4.6.1-4]

Displaying as a stage property the elaborate scenario written by Duke Vincentio, Isabella expresses confusion both in her words and in her syntax. Although as members of a

theater audience we may miss the precise implications of
her words, it will become plain in act 5 that "to accuse him
so," which is Mariana's part, is to accuse him of the act of
fornication arranged by Isabella and the Duke. But
Isabella is herself advised to confess to that act for a patently unconvincing reason, "to veil full purpose."

As before, the vagueness of this reason engages our interest, interest further whetted by the cryptic addition:

> Besides, he tells me that, if peradventure
> He speak against me on the adverse side,
> I should not think it strange, for 'tis a physic
> That's bitter to sweet end.
>
>   [4.6.5-8]

This confusing preparation ensures that we adopt an attitude of anticipation, devoid of all certainty. What remains
absolutely clear, however, is the repeated suggestion that
Isabella will receive some medicine that promises her
good—something "bitter to sweet end."

We soon discover what this bitter physic entails. Having
taken Mariana's advice to adopt a new "rule," to "be rul'd
by him" (4.6.4), Isabella confesses to the act she had not
done:

>   the vile conclusion
> I now begin with grief and shame to utter.
> He would not, but by gift of my chaste body
> To his concupiscible intemperate lust,
> Release my brother; and after much debatement,
> My sisterly remorse confutes mine honour,
> And I did yield to him.
>
>   [5.1.98-104]

While we listen to this bogus confession, the stage, crowded
with "generous and gravest citizens" (4.6.13), reminds us
that the Duke has arranged that Isabella confess her "grief
and shame" before a large and distinguished audience.
Having once submitted herself to his will (3.1.174, 238),

Isabella on the mere strength of his written instructions surrenders the reputation for chastity she had previously preserved with unusual care. Under the Duke's tutelage, Isabella has begun to abjure an important symptom of her proud religiosity. She has progressed, without understanding why, from an excessive eagerness to preserve the appearance of virtue to a willing acceptance of public shame.

Having arranged that she accept this shame, the Duke next leads Isabella to comprehend the rationale for her own action. Isabella's vehemence on first meeting the Duke supplies Angelo with a temporary defense:

> My lord, her wits I fear me are not firm.
> She hath been a suitor to me for her brother,
> Cut off by course of justice. . . .
> And she will speak most bitterly and strange.
>
> [5.1.35-38]

When the Duke pretends to agree, Isabella counters with a powerful attack on the false-seeming represented, primarily but not exclusively, by Angelo.

>   Make not impossible
> That which but seems unlike. 'Tis not impossible
> But one, the wicked'st caitiff on the ground,
> May seem as shy, as grave, as just, as absolute,
> As Angelo; even so may Angelo,
> In all his dressings, caracts, titles, forms,
> · Be an arch-villain.
>
>   [5.1.54-60]

She concludes that reason must be employed to pierce the veil of hypocrisy:

>   let your reason serve
> To make the truth appear where it seems hid,
> And hide the false seems true.
>
>   [5.1.68-70]

This is a forceful if unoriginal attack on the hypocrisy that Angelo represents. As she pursues this attack, Isabella's reasoning tacitly destroys the basis for her own adherence to worldly honor, a commodity awarded indiscriminately by Dame Fortuna to the worthy and the unworthy alike. Surely, to borrow Mistress Overdone's phrase, "here's a change indeed," if not in the commonwealth, at least in Isabella's little world of man. Her former frenzied concern for honorable appearance must already have partly dissipated, we are left to conclude, since she can voice this new and compelling sense of the radical divergence between the inner and the outer, the spirit and the letter. In response to the Duke's pretended inclination to the opinion of his reputable deputy, therefore, Isabella has begun to disengage herself from the seeming virtues she had once anxiously sought. In so doing, she has begun to abandon her more fundamental adherence to the phenomenal world of mutable and deceptive appearances.

After this mild beginning, the Duke's medicinal adversities increase in rigor until they destroy all vestiges of Isabella's honor in the eyes of Vienna's assembled society. As his responses to Isabella's plea gradually destroy her hope of redress, we must keep in mind that Duke Vincentio is to Isabella, as to the majority of characters in the play, "the good Duke" (3.1.190). In that character, he contrives to turn Isabella's plea against her by means of the very principles that she has so eloquently urged. He seeks to let his reason "serve / To make the truth appear where it seems hid" by giving as reasonable a judgment of Isabella's plea as the evidence before him warrants.

> By heaven, fond wretch, thou know'st not what thou
>   speak'st,
> Or else thou art suborn'd against his honour
> In hateful practice. First, his integrity
> Stands without blemish; next, it imports no reason
> That with such vehemency he should pursue
> Faults proper to himself. If he had so offended,

He would have weigh'd thy brother by himself,
And not have cut him off. Someone hath set you on:
Confess the truth, and say by whose advice
Thou cam'st here to complain.

[5.1.108-17]

In the circumstances, this is no unreasonable judgment.
The widely held opinion of Angelo's unblemished integrity
is indeed a stronger argument for his honesty than Isabella's mere appearance is of her own. Moreover, the accusation of conspiracy must in the light of Isabella's limited
knowledge seem an astute perception. Isabella is receiving
a pointed lesson in the limitations of human justice even
when it is administered by reason allied with goodness.

The lesson soon turns bitter as the Duke, again with apparent reason, accuses her of attempting to escape and orders her to prison (5.1.123-24). This is an extraordinary
blow to one inclined to preserve a reputation for righteousness. Isabella's public shame grows still greater when
not only Mariana and Friar Peter but also the disguised
Duke himself, who deliberately acts the part of a leader of
conspiracy, receives angry treatment from the characteristically moderate Escalus: "Away with him to prison!
Where is the Provost? Away with him to prison! Lay bolts
enough upon him: let him speak no more" (5.1.342-45).
Isabella and her friends have now been utterly "disvalued
in levity" in the eyes even of moderate and intelligent justice: "Away with those giglets too, and with the other con-
federate companion!" (5.1.345-46). We need no unusual
powers of sympathy to feel something of the immense
weight of shame that the Duke has imposed on Isabella. He
has reduced her from a "thing enskied and sainted" to a
"giglet" in the eyes of the world. And this shame merely
adds to the pangs of a supposed bereavement.

The sum of Isabella's suffering is therefore enormous,
and like the Duke's initial advice, it is carefully fitted to her
needs. The pride that manifested itself partly in her addic-
tion to worldly honor is most appropriately humbled by

this intense subjection to shame before the eyes of Vienna's assembled nobility. The results of this treatment will become apparent as we proceed.

While depriving Isabella of her worldly honor, however, Shakespeare subtly reminds us of the more pervasive, apparent, and purely religious manifestations of her pride. This reminder operates by means of the persistently implied parallel between the divine laws that are (or should be) Isabella's primary concern and the social ones administered by Angelo. Isabella's confidence that she can earn salvation from God is matched by her assurance that she can "wring" justice from God's earthly image:

> O worthy Duke,
> You bid me seek redemption of the devil.
> Hear me yourself: for that which I must speak
> Must either punish me, not being believ'd,
> Or wring redress from you.
>
> [5.1.29-33]

As her confident bearing (5.1.23-25) and the ensuing arguments reveal, Isabella has at this point little doubt that the latter alternative will in fact occur.

This self-assurance before the bars of human and divine justice recalls a particular manifestation of Isabella's lack of faith (see pp. 125-33, 141 above), a manifestation that acquires great significance in act 5. As we saw earlier, when men arrogate to themselves the power to effect their own salvation, they offend against the glory of God, for salvation comes only by faith, and faith follows the providential grant of justifying grace. It is appropriate, therefore, that Isabella's failure of faith in the Redemption is matched by unobtrusive but recurrent indications of a corresponding lack of faith in the efficacy of God's providence. On hearing the Duke's recital of Angelo's past cruelty to Mariana, for example, Isabella exclaims: "What merit were it in death to take this poor maid from the world! What corruption in this life, that it will let this man live!" (3.1.231-33).

Isabella's feelings here are natural enough. But just before relating her story, the Duke has suggested that Mariana's particular sufferings could result in general good: "I do make myself believe that you may most uprighteously do a poor wronged lady a merited benefit; redeem your brother from the angry law; do no stain to your own gracious person; and much please the absent Duke" (3.1.198-202). The Duke promises, in short, a providential action—or rather a series of actions patterned on the prototypical *felix culpa*. This preface and the Duke's powerful, beneficent, and ubiquitous presence, as well as our memories of Juliet's symbolic joy in suffering, forestall ready acquiescence in Isabella's view, however natural that view might be. Shakespeare has disposed his materials in a manner designed to reveal with particular force that Isabella's judgment rests on imperfect knowledge. We recognize in her an archetypal predicament of man, ever denied the omniscience that alone can perceive in particular events manifestations of the power that shapes our ends, rough-hew them how we will.

The point is reiterated in Isabella's passionate reaction to the Duke's report of Claudio's execution:

Isab. Nay, but it is not so!
Duke. It is no other. Show your wisdom, daughter,
         In your close patience.
Isab. O, I will to him and pluck out his eyes!
Duke. You shall not be admitted to his sight.
Isab. Unhappy Claudio! wretched Isabel!
         Injurious world! most damned Angelo!
                                      [4.3.116-22]

Isabella has every right to feel and to express outrage and horror. But Shakespeare has given her reaction specific content and emphasis. Isabella's emotions move from incredulity to vengeful wrath, to a moment of sympathy for her brother, to self-pity, to outrage against the world, and back to wrath. Sorrow for her brother's suffering receives relatively short shrift, angry vindictiveness is given much greater stress, and her outburst against the injurious world follows hard upon the Duke's promise to draw heavenly comforts from despair (4.3.109). By arranging his material in this way, Shakespeare displays in Isabella the folly that is often implied when characters in Christian literature cry out against the evils of fortune. Theirs is a judgment as presumptuous as Isabella's is to Claudio, a judgment founded on imperfect knowledge, by judges who pretend to an inappropriate omniscience.

Faith in providence represents an essential part of the Christian's larger faith in the omnipotence, the wisdom, and the goodness of God. As such, faith in providence is prominently urged both in *The Basilicon Doron* and in the Sermon on the Mount. In his explanation of prayer, King James advises that prayers which appear to remain unanswered should be accepted as one variety of life's many medicinal adversities (1:41). The king's argument springs from fundamental Christian doctrine, for the truly faithful never doubt that "all things work together for good to them that love God" (Rom. 8:28). This doctrine receives one of its most engaging expressions in a passage of the Sermon on the Mount that directly precedes the injunction forbidding judgment: "Ye cannot serve God and mammon. . . . Behold the fowls of the air: for they sow not, neither do they reap, nor gather into barns; yet your heavenly Father feedeth them. Are ye not much better than they?" (Matt. 6:24-26).

As other parts of the sermon make clear, this passage is meant to discourage excessive concern for the necessities of life, mammon's unsatisfying wages. The cure prescribed for this endemic disease is faith in providence. Thus, as Calvin explains, "the sons of God, though they be not free from labour and care" are not "careful for the life: because that they reposing themselves in the providence of God, do quietly take their rest." Christ forbids only the cares that grow from distrust, and he cites the example of the birds "that we might learn to rest upon the providence of God: for infidelity is the mother of all these excessive cares."[2]

Infidelity argues a fault commonly annexed to immoderate concern for the goods of mammon, and consequently Christ adds the words "Which of you by taking thought can add one cubit unto his stature?" (Matt. 6:27). The fault condemned here is "that a mortal man taking upon himself more than is lawful for him, doubteth not through sacrilegious boldness . . . to promise himself anything of his own industry and power."[3] Inasmuch as she depends on her own industry and power even for salvation, it comes as no surprise that Isabella betrays a corresponding lack of faith in the providence that predetermines salvation and damnation. This infidelity constitutes another element of Isabella's multifaceted but essentially uncomplicated essence. As glossed by contemporaries, the familiar texts from Shakespeare's scriptural source help us perceive in Isabella's distrust of providence another adumbration of her essential carnality—and a clearer explanation of the anxiety that dominates her character at moments of dramatic crisis.

The unconscious pride and infidelity implied especially by her notions concerning salvation are reflected in Isabella's confidence that she can force justice from God's earthly representatives. Pride and infidelity, moreover, are the particular faults that explain the harsh treatment the Duke imposes upon her—the satisfaction he requires. As a treatment for pride, he forces her to recognize the deceptions of appearance and the consequent implied hollowness of worldly honor. This treatment is followed by the bitter and painful loss of her own reputation through an imposition of immense public shame. To this intense suffering, the Duke adds a simultaneous illustration of the

---

[2] *Harmonie*, sig. N7^r-N7^v. Cf. Davies, *Worship and Theology*, p. 20, who explains the related Lutheran concept of *fiducia*, the "staking one's whole life in trust."

[3] *Harmonie*, sig. N7^v.

limitations of human justice even when it is administered by good and intelligent men. Isabella's resulting awareness of the incapacity of men and of human laws is expressed briefly, but her sense of disillusionment is profound. Like Kent's agonized question ("Is this the promised end?"), Isabella's words indicate deep dismay at the apparent failure of the justice that she believes her case merits: "And is this all?" (5.1.117).

The sequel represents a profound and thorough shift in the sources of Isabella's strength. Here, for the first time, she places her trust beyond the mutable world and beyond her own powers:

> Then, O you blessed ministers above,
> Keep me in patience, and with ripen'd time
> Unfold the evil that is here wrapt up
> In countenance!
>
> [5.1.118-21]

It is to be noted especially, first, that the blessed ministers above are accurately credited with providing the gift of patience, the quality exemplified by Juliet and sorely needed by the often vengeful Isabella. Next, she expresses for the first time a manifest confidence that providence will at the appropriate moment reveal the evil that she herself has failed to expose. Finally, by recalling the pervasive imagery of clothing and disguise, the passage reaffirms Isabella's new sense of the immensely powerful and pervasive deceptions of false-seeming: "the evil which is here wrapt up / In countenance." In short, the Duke's manipulations of Isabella result in a loss of all hope in worldly aid and a consequent real and utter dependence on divine ordinance. Her outward appearance of piety and her inner spiritual state have begun at last to correspond. She here begins to comprehend, and subsequently to submit to, the ideas of human scope expressed in the imagery of the play's first scene.

The Duke has, in fact, actualized in Isabella the poverty

of spirit toward which the Sermon on the Mount, in its insistence on universal sinfulness, persistently urges. As Erasmus reminds us, the man who is "poor in spirit," exactly like the new-made Isabella, is one who "distrusting the succour of man, doth depend wholly of heaven."[4] While providing essentially the same intepretation, Calvin suggests still more clearly the relationship between the Duke's harsh treatment and Isabella's new inner state. In calling them blessed who are poor in spirit, he says, "Christ pronounceth them happy, which being tamed and subdued with troubles, do submit themselves wholly unto God, and being inwardly humbled, they commit themselves into his custody; others do interpret them poor in spirit, which do arrogate nothing to themselves, but throwing down all trust in flesh, they acknowledge their own need."[5] Either of these alternatives fits Isabella's condition at the moment when she surrenders all hope of human aid and commits herself to the blessed ministers above. This new reliance on divine ordinance and the accompanying willingness to suffer evil patently suggests that Isabella's inadvertent infidelity has itself begun to weaken. For it is a sign of true faith when one "suffreth himself to be exercised, according to the will and pleasure of God, because cleaving firmly to his promises, he doubteth not but that he is true, just, wise, and will do, dispose, and govern all things for the best."[6]

Shortly after she expresses her new accession of faith in providence, Isabella willy-nilly "suffreth [her]self to be exercised, according to the will and pleasure" of the Duke. At some convenient moment between the Duke's order, "An officer! To prison with her!" (5.1.123-24) and line 241, Isabella is indeed carried off to prison. There is dramatic irony in this, for Shakespeare's visual, linguistic, and

---

[4] *Paraphrase*, 1, fol. D4^v.

[5] *Harmonie*, sig. K7^v. For the divine application of cruel adversity specifically as a cure for Pharisaic pride, see Hooker, *Laws*, 1:6-7.

[6] Luther, *Libertie*, sigs. D1^v-D2^r. Cf. Melanchthon, *Melanchthon and Bucer*, p. 113.

thematic parallel between Vienna's prison and St. Clare's convent reminds us that imprisonment of body and soul was Isabella's original aim. In this we perceive a hint of the inexorable, providential justice frequently represented in Christian literature. Such justice routinely punishes sinful men by granting their own desires, abandoning Grill to his trough (*Faerie Queene* 2.12.86-87) and confining Paolo and Francesca, lovers who willfully abandoned themselves to the storms of passion, in the circle of eternal whirlwinds.

The rationale that underlies such ironic justice is not altogether foreign to the text "with what judgment ye judge, ye shall be judged: and with what measure ye mete, it shall be measured to you again" (Matt. 7:2), and this text appears in yet another way to have influenced Shakespeare's treatment of Isabella. In her appeal to the Duke, Isabella's proclivity toward vengefulness breaks out in flashes of anger, and her anger is expressed in name-calling akin to that she had formerly lavished on her brother. Angelo has behaved with incredible wickedness, and we share Isabella's outrage. Yet her ire exaggerates even his wickedness:

> That Angelo's forsworn, is it not strange?
> That Angelo's a murderer, is't not strange?
> That Angelo is an adulterous thief,
> An hypocrite, a virgin violator,
> Is it not strange, and strange?
> [5.1.40-44]

Angelo may indeed be a murderer in the eyes of God, but in the eyes of the law, his execution of Claudio would have been strictly legal. The charge of murder therefore requires some qualification, as more certainly do those of adultery, theft, and, perhaps, the suggestion of habitual rape that lurks in the phrase "virgin violator." This inclination to exaggerate recurs as Isabella begins her narrative: "I went / To this pernicious caitiff Deputy" (5.1.90-91); the Duke corrects this liberty by taking the phrase as evidence of Isabella's imputed madness (5.1.92). Isabella is indulging once again in the censorious—and therefore essentially slanderous—judgments forbidden by Matt. 7:1-2. To bring her to judgment in the public street and to convict her of slanderous conspiracy represents a precise accord between crime and punishment. Her anger and slanderous judgments of others receive a seasoned judgment that draws with it the temporary loss of her own reputation.

Her punishment brings unjust slander as well, for Shakespeare's comic Blatant Beast, true to the pun expressed by his name—moves lightly[7] from an attitude of sympathy toward Isabella (4.3.150-51) to his normal role of witty slanderer. When Escalus requests permission to interrogate the accused Isabella, he unintentionally provides Lucio with repeated opportunities to exercise his forte:

Esc.   Pray you, my lord, give me leave to question; you
         shall see how I'll handle her.
Lucio. Not better than he, by her own report.
Esc.   Say you?
Lucio. Marry, sir, I think if you handled her privately she
         would sooner confess; perchance publicly she'll
         be ashamed.
Esc.   I will go darkly to work with her.
Lucio. That's the way; for women are light at midnight.
                                                    [5.1.270-78]

This return of shame and slander upon a repeated slanderer is clearly adumbrated in Matt. 7:1-2. Once more, Calvin fully elucidates Christ's obliquely expressed meaning. Men who are "rigorous censors" of others' faults, he says,

> shall be nothing gentler entreated of [them]. . . . As there
> is nothing more dear or precious to us than our name; so
> there is nothing more sharp or bitter than to be con-

---

[7] As an adjective, "light" means: (1) frivolous, (2) sexually wanton, and (3) pliant, unsteady, or fickle. Lucio himself puns on the second and third of these as well as the normal substantive meaning at 5.1.278. Cf. 3.2.172.

demned and subject to the reproaches and infamy of
men: and through our own fault we procure ourselves
that, which we of our own nature do so much abhor. For
which is he amongst many, which doth not search more
narrowly into other men's deeds than is convenient?
Which dealeth not hardlier with light offenses? Which
doth not more overthwartly improve that which is of itself indifferent?[8]

Isabella clearly typifies this vice of uncharitable judgment,
the deep affection for her own reputation, and the ironic
procurement of equally slanderous judgment of herself by
others. Lucio's role arises naturally from Calvin's accurate
(and timeless) reading of Matt. 7:1-2. This is most apparent
because, as the second verse implies, "there shall not want
revengers, which shall punish wicked and slanderous men
with the like poison or rigor."[9] These revengers are themselves in no way justified, but like all other evils, they are
instruments unwittingly furthering the ends of a benign
providence.

It might be objected that my entire interpretation of
Isabella's change places excessive stress on her short apos-
trophe to the blessed ministers above. That objection
would be valid if Isabella's subsequent actions gave no indication that she had indeed changed in the ways her apos-
trophe suggests. But her actions in the remainder of the
play do in fact corroborate the hypothesis I have proposed.
Immediately after Isabella receives her "bail" from the
Duke (5.1.355), for example, the play's language begins to
borrow trappings from the popular contemporary genre
of revenge plays. Because irascibility and vengefulness as

---

[8] *Harmonie*, sig. O1ᵛ.

[9] Ibid.; cf. Luther, *The Sermon on the Mount*, in *Works*, 21:214-15. In addition, Calvin adds a qualification that the overall context of the Sermon
on the Mount implies: "If that men cease, so that they escape punishment
in the world, which have been too desirously bent to condemn their brethren, yet they shall not escape the judgment of God."

well as fear have dominated her behavior in moments of crisis, this efflorescence of revenge-play rhetoric provides one of the chief indexes of Isabella's spiritual renewal.

We are reminded of her penchant for vengeful anger when, at the beginning of act 5, Isabella's desire for justice betrays the vindictiveness that had been her most emphatic response to the news of Claudio's death (4.3.119, 121-22):

> O worthy prince, dishonour not your eye
> By throwing it on any other object,
> Till you have heard me in my true complaint,
> And given me justice! Justice! Justice! Justice!
>
> [5.1.23-26]

Lever's note relates this to a famous scene in *The Spanish Tragedy*, where the mad or nearly mad Hieronimo employs a similar repetition of the word "justice" in his futile effort to reach the ear of the king. Whether or not Shakespeare deliberately echoes Kyd, the association is apt. Isabella's repetitions carry a hint of her old irascibility, a hint reinforced by the immoderate judgments of line 30 ("You bid me seek redemption of the devil"), and line 91 ("this pernicious caitiff Deputy"). In *The Basilicon Doron*, King James cites a relevant and familiar Horatian tag while warning that personal anger and the administration of justice are incompatible: "forget not to digest ever your passion before ye determine upon anything, since *Ira furor brevis est*" (1:203). The conventional association of anger and madness is not lost upon Angelo, who attempts to save himself by attributing Isabella's actions to insanity (5.1.35). While literally untrue, this accusation and the Duke's subsequent repetition of it (5.1.92) serve to remind us that Isabella's plea for justice is tainted by irrational passion, the condition frequently symbolized by madness in medieval and Renaissance romance.[10]

[10] Cf. Harington's gloss on Orlando's recovery from madness, *Ludovico Ariosto's Orlando Furioso*, trans. Sir John Harington, ed. Robert McNulty (Oxford: Clarendon Press, 1972), p. 458.

Since Isabella's desire for justice is informed by desire for revenge, the Duke later tempts her sorely by urging that Angelo be put to death. In a speech that demands careful scrutiny, he asks merely that she acquiesce in her own former desire:

> For this new-married man approaching here,
> Whose salt imagination yet hath wrong'd
> Your well defended honour, you must pardon
> For Mariana's sake: but as he adjudg'd your brother,
> Being criminal in double violation
> Of sacred chastity and of promise-breach
> Thereon dependent, for your brother's life,
> The very mercy of the law cries out
> Most audible, even from his proper tongue:
> 'An Angelo for Claudio; death for death.
> Haste still pays haste, and leisure answers leisure;
> Like doth quit like, and Measure still for Measure.'
>
> [5.1.398-409]

The parallelisms of the last three lines deliberately recall typical and well known Old Law passages that require eye for eye, tooth for tooth, and, most important, life for life.[11] The final and climactic parallel alludes not merely to familiar injunctions of the Old Law, but to what is by now, perhaps, an excessively familiar passage of the Sermon on the Mount. In a context that encourages Isabella to take personal revenge through the legal mechanism of the Viennese court, the words "Measure for Measure" are violently misplaced. Originally, the words aimed to temper uncharitable judgments that lead to slander and may also precede violent revenge. They warn that slanderers and revengers will receive correspondingly merciless judgments from God and their fellowmen. The Duke's allusion to the Sermon on the Mount serves therefore to highlight the thematic implications of Isabella's position. It reminds

---

[11] Lever's note cites Gen. 9:6 and Lev. 24:17-20 as illustrations.

us of that compendium of Christian wisdom in which the charitable essence of the *lex talionis* was first made indisputably clear.

Like the themes of honor and slander, the theme of revenge receives repeated attention in the Sermon on the Mount. Picking up the Old Testament texts that Duke Vincentio paraphrases, Christ promulgates this attitude in Matt. 5:38-39. "Ye have heard that it hath been said, An eye for an eye, and a tooth for a tooth: . . . but whosoever shall smite thee on thy right cheek, turn to him the other also." Calvin once more draws out the meaning that Christians ordinarily find in this passage. The injunctions to recompense like with like were intended only for judges and magistrates, but with his usual perversity "every man under like pretence would revenge themselves. Therefore they thought they did not offend, so that they did not first provoke any: but being injured, did recompense like for like." Christ's exhortation to turn the other cheek is not, however, a precise rule for the government of Christian fisticuffs, but a concrete, metaphoric expression of the general doctrine that "everyone ought patiently to suffer the injuries done unto them."[12] Calvin's interpretation comprehends, in brief, the characteristic Christian attitude toward revenge as it is explained elsewhere in the Sermon on the Mount and the New Testament as a whole.

As other parts of the Gospels show, this doctrine in no way forbids punishments ordained and executed by Caesar and his ministers. But plaintiffs seeking through civil law to protect their rights or to gain redress of wrongs must preserve an attitude of charity toward their enemies. In view of the immense influence of the Bible on life in the sixteenth century, it is not surprising that Tudor legislation sometimes betrays the direct influence of the Sermon on the Mount. In Edward's and in Elizabeth's reigns, for example, it was ordained (on the authority of Matt. 5:23-

[12] *Harmonie*, sig. M2ᵛ.

26) that curates should refuse the sacrament to "any of their . . . flock who hath maliciously . . . contended with his neighbor, unless the same do first charitably reconcile himself again." Nonetheless, "their just titles and rights they may charitably prosecute, before any such as have authority to hear the same."[13]

Such charitable prosecution is the ideal that King James establishes also for the administration of justice: "do it only for the love of justice, and not for satisfying any particular passions of yours, under colour thereof: otherwise, how justly that ever the offender deserve it [i.e., capital punishment], ye are guilty of murder before God. For ye must consider, that God ever looketh to your inward intention in all your actions" (1:63). "Charitable prosecution" of justice also accords with the king's assertion that royal anger should conform to the traditional idea of good as opposed to sinful anger. Although evil anger is a temporary madness, utter your anger, he says, "according to the Apostle's rule, *Irascimini, sed ne peccetis*" [Eph. 4:26] (1:203; cf. 1:53). The meaning of Paul's exhortation and its source in Ps. 4:5 (Vulgate) is lucidly explained by Chaucer's Parson, who tells us that "good ire" is anger without bitterness, "nat wrooth agayns the man, but wrooth with the mysdede of the man" (*Parsons Tale* ll.538-40).[14] This charity in prosecution is the ideal that Angelo refuses in act 2:

> Condemn the fault, and not the actor of it?
> Why, every fault's condemn'd ere it be done:
> Mine were the very cipher of a function
> To fine the faults, whose fine stands in record,
> And let go by the actor.
>
> [2.2.37-41]

[13] *Tudor Royal Proclamations*, 1:400; 2:123.

[14] The conception of "good Ire" is also expressed by the Elizabethan homilist (*Certaine Sermons*, sig. Iiʳ). To show anger toward crimes rather than men is a commonplace ideal also advised by Erasmus (*Enchiridion*, sig. S6ᵛ), warranted elsewhere by Paul, and espoused by King James, who lists his subjects' vices, he says, "with the fatherly love that I owe to them all: only hating their vices" (1:95).

The king's Christian ideal of charitable prosecution foresees a middle way: condemning the fault and equitably punishing the offender rather than maliciously pursuing his life.

It is apparent, therefore, that the Duke's advice contradicts the laws of Christ and a conventional ideal of Christian societies. He not only forces into a foreign context words that encourage mercy; he also fosters an exaggerated view of Angelo's crimes. The exaggeration is underscored by the false distinction with which the Duke begins his temptation. One of Angelo's faults, his intended attack on Isabella's honor, must be pardoned, the Duke says, "for Mariana's sake" (5.1.400-401). But his other sins are less forgivable:

> but as he adjudg'd your brother,
> Being criminal in double violation
> Of sacred chastity and of promise-breach
> Thereon dependent, for your brother's life,
> The very mercy of the law cries out
> Most audible, even from his proper tongue:
> 'An Angelo for Claudio; death for death.'
>
> [5.1.401-7]

This distinction between forgivable and unforgivable sins is spurious. Angelo's criminal violation of sacred chastity and his promise-breach here have nothing whatever to do with his judgment of Claudio. If Vienna provides laws to punish his abuse of judicial power, or indeed for having intercourse with a "contracted" spouse, Angelo should be judged according to those laws. Yet the Duke argues that Angelo's judgment of Claudio is the act that merits death: "An Angelo for Claudio."

The argument is patently sophistical, and its purpose is to urge Isabella to acquiesce in private revenge, an acquiescence rendered likely by her former monkish adherence to a literal conception of the Law. This revenge is thinly disguised as justice, the disguise being the mere assertion that

Angelo has himself committed sins. One of those sins, "promise-breach," clearly cannot rank as a capital crime; the other, "violation of sacred chastity," can be a capital offense only if the Duke and Isabella enforce the outdated and merciless law that Angelo had revived and that we—and most characters in the play—consider tyrannous. We have learned from the Duke's original delegation of authority that they are free to adhere to the letter of the law or to relax it: "Your scope is as mine own, / So to enforce or qualify the laws / As to your soul seems good" (1.1.64-66).

On the other hand, as inquiries into Elizabethan marriage laws have suggested, even the harshest contemporary legalist might have been unable to find Angelo's liaison with Mariana culpable.[15] Since Claudio at one point suggests that a formal contract may have been undertaken between him and Juliet ("upon a true contract / I got possession of Julietta's bed," 1.2.134-35), scholars have argued that the pair are in fact married under a witnessed common-law contract of *sponsalia de praesenti*. But "contract" is mentioned only once, and since the word may mean a mere verbal agreement in the absence of all legal trappings or phrasing, Claudio is probably describing his and Juliet's firm mutual resolve—a marriage in intent but not in law.

By contrast, Angelo's previous relationship with Mariana is repeatedly described in legalistic terms. Whereas Claudio seems to rule out all legal ceremony ("she is fast my wife, / Save that we do the denunciation lack / Of outward order," 1.2.136-38), the first mention of Angelo's relationship with Mariana suggests the legal trappings often accompanying common-law betrothals, whether *sponsalia de praesenti* or *de futuro*: "She should this Angelo have married; was

[15] See especially Ernest Schanzer, "The Marriage-Contracts in *Measure for Measure*," *ShS* 13 (1960):81-89. Cf. S. Nagarajan, "*Measure for Measure* and Elizabethan Betrothals," *SQ* 14 (1963):115-19, and J. Birje-Patil, "Marriage Contracts in Shakespeare's *Measure for Measure*," *ShakS* 5 (1969):106-11.

affianced to her by oath" (3.1.213-14).[16] In similarly legalistic terms, the Duke rationalizes Mariana's nocturnal encounter with Angelo:

> He is your husband on a pre-contract: . . .
>   the justice of your title to him
> Doth flourish the deceit.
>
> [4.1.71-75]

Mariana emphasizes the ceremonial nature of their spousal when she accuses Angelo in act 5: "This is the hand which, with a vow'd contract, / Was fast belock'd in thine" (5.1.208-9). And Angelo confesses, shortly before the Duke's temptation of Isabella, that he was indeed "contracted" to Mariana (5.1.374). It may be, therefore, that Shakespeare's audience would indeed have recognized in Angelo's liaison with Mariana not a legally punishable act of fornication but a mere anticipation of the dues of marriage, an anticipation legitimized (but not made morally pristine) by their *de praesenti* contract—or one that rendered their *de futuro* agreement immediately valid and binding.[17]

Whether or not Angelo can thus be rescued from the draconian law he had himself revived, his faults remain a peripheral issue as the Duke pronounces sentence. The emphasis falls on Angelo's supposed execution of Claudio, and the sentence is a precise, literal manifestation of the dictum that "like doth quit like":

> We do condemn thee to the very block
> Where Claudio stoop'd to death, and with like haste.
>
> [5.1.412-13]

Such exact repayment of death for death, identical down to the very implements and the rash velocity of execution, is not unfamiliar in Renaissance revenge plays. One thinks,

---

[16] I have adopted the F2 reading. Lever follows F: "was affianced to her oath."

[17] Schanzer, "Marriage-Contracts," p. 86.

for example, of Hamlet's scrupulous weighing of the probabilities that Claudius will be damned as he presumes his
own father to be. The scrupulosity is identical, if more unquestionably mad, in Vendice's extravagant assassination
of the Duke in *The Revenger's Tragedy*:

> This very skull,
> Whose mistress the Duke poisoned with this drug,
> The mortal curse of the earth, shall be revenged
> In the like strain, and kiss his lips to death.
>
> [3.5.101-4]

The atmosphere of the revenge plays grows yet stronger as
the Duke claims that if Isabella joins Mariana in her plea
for Angelo's life, "Her brother's ghost his paved bed would
break, / And take her hence in horror" (5.1.433-34). And
immediately before Isabella speaks, the Duke again makes
clear that revenge, not Angelo's actual liabilities, is at issue:
"He dies for Claudio's death" (5.1.441).

The vengeful monks of medieval and Reformation
literature—and the wrathful Isabella of act 3 and the beginning of act 5—would accept the Duke's invitation without qualm. But Isabella has changed, and we have incon-
trovertible evidence of spiritual maturation in her refusal
to accept the proffered vengeance. Christians attest to the
validity of this evidence whenever they pray for forgiveness: "Forgive us our debts, as we forgive our debtors"
(Matt. 6:12). The petition is conventionally understood to
mean that "if the spirit of God doth reign in our hearts, all
. . . desire of revenge must cease. . . . here is simply set
down a note whereby the children of God may be discerned from strangers."[18]

Refusal of revenge is but one of the "notes" by which
Isabella dramatizes her regeneration. But because critics

---

[18] Calvin, *Harmonie*, sig. N3^r. In an interesting and amusing letter to
Thomas Smith, Lord Burghley makes the same point; see Thomas
Wright, ed., *Queen Elizabeth and Her Times* (London: Henry Colburn,
1838), 1:159-60.

often recognize that Isabella's argument on Angelo's behalf is itself legalistic, they sometimes conclude that her essential legalism continues intact and that she remains to the
end a repellent character.[19] Both Isabella's plea and its
immediate context consequently require very careful attention. The speeches immediately preceding her plea include
both the Duke's incitements to vengeance and Mariana's attempts to enlist Isabella's aid in seeking Angelo's pardon.
For a significant period of time, one of the play's most
dramatic and significant silences, Isabella stands uncer-
tainly between these opposing views.[20] The speech that
immediately precipitates Isabella's decision contains wisdom that her recent disillusionment has prepared her to
understand:

> They say best men are moulded out of faults,
> And, for the most, become much more the better
> For being a little bad. So may my husband.
> [5.1.437-39]

This is not mere folk wisdom calculated to play on Isabella's or the audience's sympathies. That even the best men
are composed of sins—"moulded out of faults"—is fundamental Reformed Christian doctrine. It is doctrine enforced by the play's scriptural text and once expressed by
Isabella with vigor and eloquence:

> How would you be
> If He, which is the top of judgement, should
> But judge you as you are?
> [2.2.75-77]

When joined with faith in the one who found out our remedy, this conviction of inherent sinfulness becomes the very
source of spiritual regeneration:

[19] See, for example, Harold Skulsky, "Pain, Law, and Conscience in
Measure for Measure," JHI 25 (1964): 165-68 and Schanzer, *Problem Plays,*
pp. 101-102.

[20] The time should not be exaggerated; the speeches of others that fill
part of this void extend for fourteen lines.

> O, think on that,
> And mercy then will breathe within your lips,
> Like man new made.
>
> [2.2.77-79]

As we have seen, refusal of vengeance, and mercy, are works that follow from such faith.

That most men "become much more the better / For being a little bad" is also solid, altogether familiar doctrine. Even the best men can, as Angelo says, "forget" their grace (4.4.31), and this possibility itself has the beneficial end that Mariana ascribes to it. As Calvin explains it in his *Institutes*, the freedom to fall into sin was ordained by providence for the benefit of the spiritually proud—the Angelos and Isabellas who incline to glory in their godliness: "But even while by the guiding of the Holy Ghost we walk in the ways of the Lord, lest yet we forgetting ourselves should wax proud, there are left certain remnants of imperfection, which may minister us matter of humility."[21]

Although we are not told what effect Mariana's speech has on Isabella, we recognize its aptness. Isabella has recently been brought to nothing in herself—shorn of that honor in which she had been inclined to glory, and deprived of all hope in her own powers and in human justice—and consequently imbued with a new, or newly conscious and thoroughgoing, faith in and dependence on divine providence. In her new state of humility and faith, she is prepared both to accept and to pattern her life upon the fundamental Christian ideas of which Mariana reminds her.

Only in a state of combined humility and faith, moreover, can men hope to obey the essential precepts of the Sermon on the Mount. Since those precepts can be epitomized in the word "charity," we may expect to find that Isabella's plea for Angelo is informed by the spirit of that virtue. This is suggested by the very fact that Isabella's

---

[21] *Institutes* 3.14.9; fol. 252ᵛ.

speech comes in direct response to Mariana's appeal. This act is undertaken, that is, directly on behalf of Isabella's "neighbor," and its tone is as significant as its content:

> Most bounteous sir:
> Look, if it please you, on this man condemn'd
> As if my brother liv'd. I partly think
> A due sincerity govern'd his deeds
> Till he did look on me. Since it is so,
> Let him not die. My brother had but justice,
> In that he did the thing for which he died:
> For Angelo,
> His act did not o'ertake his bad intent,
> And must be buried but as an intent
> That perish'd by the way. Thoughts are no subjects;
> Intents, but merely thoughts.
>
> [5.1.441-52]

We misconstrue the tone of this speech if we join those who condemn Isabella for pleading "with all the finesse of a seasoned attorney, on the most purely legalistic grounds for her would-be ravisher and the judicial murderer of her brother."[22] The argument shows little legal finesse, the whole being somewhat halting and awkward, expressive above all of confusion and diffidence. This is not the Isabella who, after initial reticence, could argue so cogently and confidently twice before Angelo and once before the Duke. This, the last of her four intercessions, is at once the briefest and the least accomplished, and it gains meaning from our recollections of her former confident assurance. We feel the lack of her old confidence most powerfully in the first four lines. The first request, "Look, if it please you, on this man condemned / As if my brother liv'd" (5.1.442-43) *is* a request, not a demand, and it asks a quite non-

[22] Schanzer, *Problem Plays*, p. 101. Cf. Sir Arthur Quiller-Couch, who dismisses this speech as "a string of palpable sophistry"; *Measure for Measure*, ed. Sir Arthur Quiller-Couch, The New Shakespeare (Cambridge: Cambridge University Press, 1922), p. xxxii.

legalistic act of imagination. The second part of the speech includes patently invalid reasoning—the argument takes an unproved supposition as if it were indisputable fact:

> I partly think
> A due sincerity govern'd his deeds
> Till he did look on me. Since it is so,
> Let him not die.
>
> [5.1.443-46]

Isabella's illogic is stressed by the rapid movement from uncertainty ("I partly think") to assertion ("since it is so").

The remaining seven lines are more assured, and they contain the legalistic argument that most offends Isabella's critics. But we should not exaggerate its legal expertise. That Claudio "did the thing for which he died" and that his deed violated an existing law no one in the play disputes. She is therefore correct to say that Claudio had "but justice," and in using that phrase Isabella is not guilty of treating her brother's death with callous nonchalance. "But justice" means "only," or "mere" justice—justice unmitigated by the mercy that transforms mere human justice into equity. Although she shows no narrowly judicial expertise, therefore, Isabella does reveal an important sensitivity to the limits of human justice. The court of Vienna is not the court of heaven, and as *The Basilicon Doron* reminded its readers, the scope of human law normally extends no further than the outward actions of men. Sins committed by a magistrate when he administers the law for his own malicious or selfish purposes are properly left to God, who alone "ever looketh to your inward intention in all your actions" (1:63).

In this the king, like Isabella, simply repeats a commonplace of legal theory. Since Angelo's is a case in which no overt action overtook his bad intent—his "execution" of Claudio being rigidly legal and his act of fornication being arguably "no sin" (and if a sin, irrelevant to the charge of judicial murder)—his faults, grave as they are, remain beyond the reach of the Duke's law: "Thoughts are no subjects; / Intents, but merely thoughts" (5.1.451-52). To recall the words of the Master of the Inner Temple, no punishment "can in this case be looked for from any other, saving only from Him who discerneth and judgeth the very secrets of all hearts,"[23] or from a Duke willing (and able) to bring other charges. Isabella's recognition that the powers of human judgment and human law ought to be confined to the external sphere provides another indication of spiritual rebirth. Had she recognized this principle earlier, she would have been less inclined to make rules of external observance the essence of her religion; she would have presumed less readily to judge Claudio's spiritual state; and she would have indulged less freely in exaggerated judgments of the state of Angelo's soul (3.1.91; 5.1.41-44, 61-62, 91).[24]

Isabella's earlier, repeated, and merciless judgments of Angelo help us to perceive the essential meaning of her

[23] See above, chap. 3. The idea that "intents are no subjects" of human law and, conversely, that the jurisdiction of such law extends only to external actions informs Calvin's commentary on the Sermon on the Mount, *Harmonie*, L6ʳ. This restriction of civil law to the sphere of external activity reappears frequently in contemporary discussions. See, for example, St. Germain, *Doctor and Student*, p. 9 ("the judgment of man may not be of inward things, but only of outward things"); the gloss on Rom. 1:17 in the Geneva Bible (where God's justice is contrasted to "man's justice, or the justice of works"); Erasmus's paraphrase of Matt. 5:28, *Paraphrase*, 1, fol. F1ᵛ; and *The Sermon of Salvation* ("the justice of man, that is to say, the justice of our works," *Certaine Sermons*, sig. B1ᵛ). See also Erasmus's general statement on Paul's use of the term "law" (*Paraphrase*, 2, fol. ✠ 4ʳ); Luther's assertion that "We leave to God the judgments that are his own, judgments that are hidden and to be feared" (*Monastic Vows*, in *Works* 44:302); and Tyndale's argument that "The King only ought to punish sin: I mean [sin] that is broken forth. The heart must remain to God" (*Doctrinal Treatises*, p. 240).

[24] This is not to say, of course, that Angelo is untainted by grave sins. Nonetheless, the proper attitude—especially for Christians nurtured on the doctrines of Wittenberg and Geneva—is exhibited by the Duke: "But that frailty hath examples for his falling, I should wonder at Angelo" (3.1.185-86).

plea on his behalf. We are guilty both of a most Angelolike literalism and of poor critical procedure if we judge Isabella solely on the basis of the literal terms of her argument rather than their intended meaning. In contrast to her phrases, her intent is both clear and coherent. She is struggling to fit arguments to her intention of refusing vengeance and of granting mercy. She has become charitable toward her enemy. Since charity arises from empathy, it is especially apparent that Isabella's first effort to understand Angelo occurs in this speech.

> I partly think
> A due sincerity govern'd his deeds
> Till he did look on me.
>
> [5.1.443-45]

Because it contrasts so strongly with her earlier consistently self-regarding and summary judgments, we recognize this as Isabella's first attempt to enter sympathetically into Angelo's passion-driven soul.

If charity is her intent, Isabella's legalism here is calculated to controvert the Duke's legalistic argument that Angelo should die "for Claudio's death." She illustrates, therefore, the proper application of "law" in all senses of the word, for Isabella's judgment here for the first time savors, as Erasmus put it in paraphrasing the "judge not" passage, of evangelical charity, "which doth expound every doubtful thing to the best, which doth gently . . . suffer many things, which desireth rather to heal than to punish, which considering her own infirmities and weakness, so judgeth other men's offences, as she would be judged offending her self."[25] In short, Isabella's action fulfills the very essence of the Law. Her argument reveals that she has at last attained—not without the struggle implied by her silence (5.1.428-41)—to its summary commandment, "Love your enemies" (Matt. 5:44).

[25] *Paraphrase*, 1, fol. G1^v-G2^r.

Isabella's new ability to obey this fundamental rule follows from the bitter satisfaction contrived by the Duke: "For he shall never satisfy this commandment, that banisheth not the love of himself, or rather deny himself, and so make much of those men, which God hath joined to him, that he goeth on to love even those, of whom he is hated."[26] The Duke's plot against Isabella resulted in the destruction of her proud self-love and so prepared her, first, to make much of Mariana, whom God (and the Duke) joined with her in the course of the play, and to proceed even to treat with charity the man who, at the prompting of his passions, had been her enemy.

Charitable actions like these are, in the view of human reason, highly improbable, and no one has been more aware of that improbability than the intellectual leaders of Christianity in all ages. The great Reformation commentators emphasized, for example, that all the particular precepts of the Sermon on the Mount, as of Christianity in general, sought essentially to subvert the dictates of man's common sense. In his general statement on the meaning of the sermon, Calvin grants "that this doctrine doth much disagree from common sense: but so it behooveth the disciples of Christ to be taught wisdom, that they might account their felicity to be out of this world, and beyond the understanding of the flesh. . . . Carnal reason will never allow that which Christ here teacheth."[27] In their unregenerate state, men are especially prone to follow the carnal letter of the law and to read the Old Law as an unqualified *lex talionis*. The Reformers were deeply aware of how difficult and unreasonable it seems, therefore, to demand that

[26] *Harmonie*, sig. M4ᵛ.

[27] *Harmonie*, sig. K7ʳ.Cf. sigs. K7ᵛ and M4ᵛ, and Erasmus, *Paraphrase*, 1, fol. E4ʳ, who writes with characteristic animation: "Blessed be the poor in spirit, for theirs is the kingdom of heaven: whose ears could have abidden so incredible a saying? . . . This kind of men is trod under feet everywhere. . . . But it is true, that Truth saieth."

men altogether abjure the natural impulse to repay like for like: "This is a very hard thing, and altogether against the nature of flesh, to recompense good for evil."[28]

Shakespeare's similar awareness of the difficulty and unreasonableness of Christian doctrine is not at all muted in his presentation of Isabella's charitable plea for Angelo. Picking up a word that has echoed significantly throughout the play, the Duke chides Mariana: "Against all sense you do importune her" (5.1.431). As William Empson has shown, Angelo earlier uses "sense" to mean both sensuality and common sense or rationality: "She speaks, and 'tis such sense / That my sense breeds with it" (2.2.142-43).[29] Employing the same ambiguity, Angelo expresses with powerful economy the inherent connection between the sensual, fleshly element in man and the impulse to revenge:

> He should have liv'd;
> Save that his riotous youth, with dangerous sense,
> Might in the times to come have ta'en revenge.
> [4.4.26-28]

By pointing out that in showing charity toward Angelo Isabella acts "against all sense," the Duke suggests that Isabella is acting in opposition to that part of herself that had dominated her character earlier in the play.

The same meaning is expressed in yet another way. On the completion of her intercession, the Duke echoes the economic imagery that had intruded itself at inopportune moments into Isabella's language: "Your suit's unprofitable." The words carry a dual meaning. Literally, the Duke is refusing to grant Isabella's suit. But his secondary, thematic meaning is something like "Your suit is foolish because you seek no profit of your own." By means of this ambiguity, the Duke reinforces our awareness that Isabel-

---

[28] Calvin, *Harmonie*, sig. M4ᵛ.

[29] *The Structure of Complex Words* (Norfolk, Conn.: New Directions, n.d.), pp. 270-88.

la's action, like all deeds of charity, works contrary to the egocentric emotions and rationality of sense. Shakespeare has clearly chosen to emphasize the improbability and irrationality of Isabella's action. He consequently implies, as Christ had done in the Sermon on the Mount, that all true wisdom and the actions that depend on wisdom at once suppress and transcend the motions of sense and of common sense.

The improbability of the plot in *Measure for Measure*, therefore, is not accidental: it gives evidence of the author's artful trade. We are made to feel the absurdity of Isabella's action and therefore to discover its "unreasonable" rationale. Although many modern critics are simply surprised and even repulsed by Isabella's improbable action, Shakespeare seems to have created an effect commonly sought in medieval and Renaissance symbolic art: the pleasurable surprise of being obliquely reminded of a familiar and respected truth.

A similar surprise arises from Isabella's final act, her decision to abandon the rule of St. Clare and marry the Duke. The full symbolic significance of this marriage will become clear only after we have considered more fully the Duke's character. Yet it is appropriate to point out here that Isabella's act of charity toward Angelo and her assent to the Duke's marriage proposal both confirm and symbolize the changes wrought by her penitential suffering. Although faith is by nature difficult to dramatize, Isabella's faith, like Desdemona's invisible fidelity, has been a central concern of the play. Her novice's robes and the meanings they imply keep this topic perpetually in the minds of the audience. Isabella's cruelty to Claudio and her pride have acted as indexes of the wrong-headed faith symbolized visually by her costume. Conversely, her charity toward Angelo manifests the accession of true faith that followed from the deep humiliation arranged by Duke Vincentio. For according to a familiar dictum included in the Sermon on the Mount and reflected in Shakespeare's persistent metaphor of "reading" external behavior, man's works constitute our only available index of his faith: "Ye shall know them by their fruits" (Matt. 7:16-20).[30]

If Isabella's changed behavior therefore represents a rectified faith, it is appropriate that she should abandon the prime symbol of her former error. As she gives the Duke her hand (5.1.490) and leaves the stage with him,[31] the audience receives a final indication that she has permanently abandoned the dead letter of the law, symbolized by her monastic rule, for a new obedience to the character who insists throughout the play on the law's living and merciful spirit. In short, Isabella tacitly renounces the sterile bondage of her rule and gains a liberty of love akin to that which the New Law offers all Christians. Isabella's final action confirms her departure from bondage to the elements of the world and her entry into a world governed by fruitful, married love. As often in the play, this implication is communicated deftly, as much by silence and action as by language.

Isabella's acceptance of the Duke therefore adds to our sense of exhilaration as the play ends. This effect does not appeal to the vacuous sentimentality that is likely to be pleased by any marriage contrived to finish off a recalcitrant narrative. Its appeal is primarily intellectual: appropriate emotional response is generated by the satisfying resolution of thematic structure in a rapid-fire series of dramatic unfoldings at the end of act 5—the destruction of

[30] The Duke paraphrases this commonplace at 3.2.140-41, "Let him be but testimonied in his own bringings-forth."

Following Christ's precedent, the twelfth article of Anglican faith applied this dictum directly to the crucial spiritual problem of discerning true faith: since good works "do spring out necessarily of a true and lively Faith . . . by them a lively faith may be as evidently known, as a tree discerned by the fruit." Cf. also *Certaine Sermons*, sig. Ss6ᵛ; Melanchthon, *Melanchthon and Bucer*, p. 112; Calvin, *Harmonie*, sig. O6ᵛ; Erasmus, *Enchiridion*, sig. K3ʳ. The commonplace is repeated twice in *The Basilicon Doron*, 1:15, 153.

[31] See Lever's explanation of the final stage direction.

Angelo's hypocritical mask, the uncasing of the Duke himself and of Claudio (5.1.487), the ending of Mariana's unwilling, celibate isolation at St. Luke's, and probably the removal of some part of Isabella's own monastic habit. These unfoldings join with the predominant mood of merciful judgment and of comedy to dissipate, finally, the claustrophobic atmosphere of imprisonment that permeates most of the play. We are made to feel deeply Isabella's exhilarating freedom from confining robes and the carnal law.

Just as the claustrophobia of imprisonment is relieved by Isabella's marriage, so the theme of honor reaches a tacit resolution. In marrying the Duke, Isabella ironically achieves a measure of true glory, for as Erasmus reminds us in his paraphrase of Matt. 6:1, "though praise be fled and shunned, yet it followeth virtue, of her own accord. And that surely is true praise, which doth chance without ambitious seeking for."[32] Now that she has ceased to overvalue worldly reputation, glory comes of its own accord as a reward of virtue. And because kings and dukes are petty earthly gods, the glory Isabella derives from her regal marriage reflects the true glory that consists in the good will of God. As Isabella leaves the stage, bearing with her the honor that follows a rectified faith and the charitable deeds that inevitably result from it, we may perceive, retrospectively, the accuracy of the Duke's promise "To make her heavenly comforts of despair." Her "comforts" have about them an aura of divinity, and they result, quite literally, from a purgative "despair."

[32] *Paraphrase*, 1, fol. F4ᵛ. Shakespeare dramatizes this conception in the honor that comes unsought (at least for its own sake) to Prince Hal in *Henry IV, Part 1*.

Chapter 6

Duke Vincentio: The Intermittent Immanence of Godhead

To the careful reader or auditor, the Duke's announced rationale for submitting Isabella to her trying series of factitious reversals is not simply an unconvincing excuse for further plotting, nor is it feckless hyperbole. His power to make "heavenly comforts" of "despair" "when they are least expected" provides the dominant and recurrent pattern of the denouement of *Measure for Measure*. Because our intellectual and emotional response to the play as a whole depends centrally on our understanding of Shakespeare's ubiquitous Duke of dark corners, and because his motives are shrouded in unrelieved obscurity, it will be profitable to seek in his ministrations to Angelo, Claudio, and some minor characters a tacit logic akin to that which explains his treatment of Isabella. Since Angelo is (after Isabella) the primary focus of the Duke's attentions throughout the play, I propose to concentrate first on the course of spiritual physic that the Duke imposes on him. And since Angelo's character coincides in many ways with Isabella's, we may expect to find that this cure includes a number of the same medicines.

A chief index of Angelo's character, as of Isabella's, is his relationship to law. While Isabella adheres to a set of man-made religious laws that tell us much about her nature, Angelo adopts an analogous attitude toward the civil laws he is enjoined to enforce. As the Duke explains it,

Angelo's discretionary power is enormous. The terms of the substitution suggest something of the godlike power of magistracy:

In our remove, be thou at full ourself.
Mortality and mercy in Vienna
Live in thy tongue, and heart.
[1.1.43-45]

This awesome power includes the ability "to enforce or qualify the laws / As to your soul seems good" (1.1.65-66). We must not overlook this statement. Although it has been assumed that the Duke's written commission enjoined strict enforcement of the laws, including the law against fornication,[1] we have no reason to doubt that Angelo could, if he wished, mitigate the terrible punishment that the law prescribes for Claudio. This is implicit in Escalus's intercession for Claudio (2.1.6 ff.) and in Angelo's evasion of Isabella's direct question: "but can you if you would?" (2.2.51). The "angry law" that threatens Claudio, therefore, has been resurrected by the mere will of the deputy and is as much the child of his will as it was of the original legislators'. It may in fact be more so, for it is an easy matter to guess—as the vagueness of the law encourages us to do—that the society that made "fornication" a capital offense intended to punish habitual sinners, not young men who are resolved to marry their partners.

As the Duke soon makes clear, the central statute in *Measure for Measure* provides small occasion for social protest. It is primarily a vehicle for dramatizing the disposition of Angelo's soul: "Hence shall we see / If power change purpose, what our seemers be" (1.3.53-54). Angelo's administration of the law is to be a touchstone of his virtue,

[1] G. Wilson Knight, "*Measure for Measure* and the Gospels," in *The Wheel of Fire* (London: Oxford University Press, 1930), p. 94. This may also underlie in part the frequent complaint that Duke Vincentio is responsible for the "mess" Vienna has fallen into both before and during the ministry of Angelo.

according to a principle as valid in the sixteenth century as in the twentieth: "promotions declare what men be: for even as vessels while they are empty, though they have some chink in them it can ill be perceived, but if they be filled with licour, they show by and by on what side the fault is, so corrupted and ill disposed minds seldom discover their vices, but when they are filled with authority."[2]

The violent lust eventually exposed by Angelo's accession to absolute power is patent; yet it is important to note that this vice follows logically from traits revealed very early in the play. From the conclusion of act 1, scene 3, we know that Angelo "scarce confesses / That his blood flows; or that his appetite / Is more to bread than stone" (1.3.51-53). We know further that Isabella and her fellow nuns likewise deny, or desire to deny, that natural affections have power to shake their frames. As the allusion indicates (see above, chap. 3), there is a hint of spiritual arrogance inherent in the effort to legislate into oblivion the universal condition of sexual frailty. Angelo shares this arrogance, and Lucio tells us—in a speech rendered emphatic by the setting of the convent itself—that Angelo is essentially a monk out of cloister:

> one who never feels
> The wanton stings and motions of the sense;
> But doth rebate and blunt his natural edge
> With profits of the mind, study and fast.
> [1.4.58-61]

Monkish in his private life, Angelo also parallels the monks in his enforcement of social law. He too revives "old" laws and both observes them himself and demands that others observe them without qualification and without reference to the essential burden of all legitimate law. As we learned in chapter 1, if he is to conform to their spirit, a

---

[2] *The Courtier*, in Milligan, *Three Renaissance Classics*, p. 562.

true administrator of positive laws must be, above all, a man "bound by [his] charity" (2.3.3). Both monks and magistrates ought to promote inner virtues above all; both often substitute the dead letter. Because of his affinities with the complex type idea of monasticism, therefore, we expect that Angelo might exhibit further features germane to that type. In particular, we expect prideful legalism based on ignorance of the limitations of civil law and of that law's human administrators.

Angelo's legalistic pride appears in the play's first debate on principles of legal administration. As we know, Escalus there reminds us of the law's ultimate origin, its true end, and its sources of validity, for he urges an act of charitable empathy based on the law's assurance that, by a law of nature, all men are frail, ready to fall the moment circumstances permit (2.1.8-16). We should notice, too, that the particular law under discussion in itself paraphrases or echoes a moral law of God, the seventh commandment, that forbids "all kind of filthy and wandering lust; and all uncleanness that riseth of such lust."[3] But although all men deserve spiritual death for inevitable transgressions, Moses' law against fornication prescribes an earthly punishment considerably more humane. Nonetheless, Angelo's reply to Escalus's doctrinally weighty argument resounds with confidence that he can himself fulfill the now symbolic law and that other men must do the same:

'Tis one thing to be tempted, Escalus,
Another thing to fall. . . .
You may not so extenuate his offence
For I have had such faults; but rather tell me,
When I that censure him do so offend,
Let mine own judgement pattern out my death,
And nothing come in partial. Sir, he must die.
                                        [2.1.17-31]

---

[3] Nowell, *Catechism*, p. 133.

Angelo's astounding arrogance is made apparent by this unwitting paraphrase of the play's scriptural text. He asks to be judged as he judges and to receive measure for measure, but he is blind to the central implication of the passage to which he unconsciously alludes—that none should judge harshly because all are "hypocrites" who violate ultimate laws not only when they fall, but also when they are tempted. Angelo's allusion exposes an arrogance predicted by the earlier announcement that he scarce confesses a preference for bread rather than stone (1.3.51-53). Angelo believes that his powers to fulfill the law's demands are equal to those of the unique man who had human passions which could not shake his frame (cf. chap. 3, above).

But long before Angelo succumbs to lust, we are reminded that no man who depends on his own powers can possibly remain chaste. Immediately after Angelo's debate with Escalus, Pompey delivers an opinion that has strong doctrinal authority:

Pom.   Does your worship mean to geld and splay all the youth of the city?
Esc.   No, Pompey.
Pom.   Truly, sir, in my poor opinion, they will to't then. If your worship will take order for the drabs and the knaves, you need not fear the bawds.[4]

[2.1.227-32]

Beneath its humor, Pompey's evasion alludes to the ineluctable law of postlapsarian human nature. Even those who, with Paul, fervently desire to do good fall victim to the lusts of the flesh—except, of course, when they are supported by grace: "For the good that I would I do not: but the evil which I would not, that I do" (Rom. 7:19).[5] After falling to lust, Angelo attests that his loss of grace has

---

[4] Cf. 3.2.97-99: "the vice is of a great kindred; it is well allied; but it is impossible to extirp it quite, friar, till eating and drinking be put down."

[5] Cf. the Geneva gloss on this text: "The flesh stayeth even the most perfect to run forward as the spirit wisheth."

subjected him to this interior warfare: "Alack, when once our grace we have forgot, / Nothing goes right; we would and we would not" (4.4.31-32). Unlike the tormented Angelo, Pompey and his friends represent the law of the members unrestrained even by the ineffectual will to do good:

> I thank your worship for your good counsel;
> [aside] but I shall follow it as the flesh and
> fortune shall better determine.
> > Whip me? No, no, let carman whip his jade;
> > The valiant heart's not whipt out of his trade.
> > > [2.1.249-53]

This willful determination to continue in sin makes non-sense of Angelo's subsequent assertion that strict legalistic justice will absolutely deter future crime:

> The law hath not been dead, though it hath slept:
> Those many had not dar'd to do that evil
> If the first that did th'edict infringe
> Had answer'd for his deed.
> > [2.2.91-94]

The symbolic amplitude of "the law," the generality of this statement, as well as the common belief that Adam's and Eve's original and comprehensive sin included fornication,[6] suggest that Angelo unconsciously alludes in this speech to the fall of man. For most of Shakespeare's original audience as for modern Christians, the pains of childbirth, the laboriousness of human life, and the inevitability of death argued feelingly that "the first that did th'edict infringe" and all their posterity had indeed "answered for his deed." As prophylactic against sin, the law whether of God or of man is inadequate. This point is aptly realized both in the comic arraignment of Pompey and

---

[6] See *Paradise Lost*, ed. Alastair Fowler, in *The Poems of John Milton* (London: Longmans, 1968), 9.1027-45, and note.

Master Froth—and in the assurance that some corruption
will inevitably evade the law:

Pom. All houses in the suburbs of Vienna must be plucked
    down.
Mis. O. And what shall become of those in the city?
Pom. They shall stand for seed: they had gone down too,
    but that a wise burgher put in for them.

[1.2.89-92]

The physical carnality of these stalwarts of the Viennese
underworld corresponds, as I suggested earlier, to the
spiritual carnality of Isabella, her monastic penchant to
take ceremonies for substance, flesh for spirit. Angelo's
conception of law betrays an identical adherence to the letter:

I not deny
The jury passing on the prisoner's life
May in the sworn twelve have a thief, or two,
Guiltier than him they try. What's open made to justice,
That justice seizes. What knows the laws
That thieves do pass on thieves? 'Tis very pregnant,
The jewel that we find, we stoop and take't,
Because we see it; but what we do not see,
We tread upon, and never think of it.

[2.1.18-26]

As a judicial principle, this corresponds to contemporary
theory. Sir Edward Coke maintains, for example, "What
appeareth not, is not, and in this case it appeareth not before process at law."[7] Although he has been accused of un-

---

[7] Quoted in Skulsky, "Pain, Law, and Conscience," p. 149. Swinburne
(*Treatise of Spousals*, sigs. M2ᵛ-M3ʳ) agrees and gives sound reasons for this
principle. In cases where young men falsely promise marriage in return
for sexual favors, their words only can be considered by the judge: "although (before God) they be not man or wife; for he which is the searcher
of the heart doth know their deceit and defect of mutual consent, without
the which, there can be no matrimony; and therefore, in his sight, they

principled tolerance (Lever, p., lxvi), Escalus in fact acts on this principle when he dismisses the case against Pompey and Master Froth: "Truly, officer, because he hath some offences in him that thou wouldst discover if thou couldst, let him continue in his courses till thou know'st what they are" (2.1.182-85). Nevertheless, the extreme harshness of Angelo's revived law against fornication in itself argues a failure of charity on the part of the judge. Since charity is the essence of all law, Angelo is plainly substituting the dead external manifestation of law for its living essence.

Furthermore, the deputy carries his self-righteousness with respect to secular law into the sphere of religion. As his very confidence suggests, he considers himself among the elect: "O cunning enemy," he exclaims after his first interview with Isabella, "that, to catch a saint, / With saints dost bait thy hook!" (2.2.180-81). This apparent confidence in his own election appears to rest entirely on obedience to the law; for charity, the fruit and the evidence of faith, is altogether foreign to Angelo's character.

This is manifest not only in his rigorous enforcement of the law against Claudio, but in the malice he exhibits both at the arraignment of Pompey (2.1.136) and in his treatment of Mariana. Between their contract of marriage and the planned ceremony, Angelo's espoused bride lost both her brother Frederick and her dowry. "There she lost a noble and renowned brother," the Duke reports, "in his love toward her ever most kind and natural; with him, the portion and sinew of her fortune, her marriage dowry; with both, her combinate husband, this well-seeming Angelo" (3.1.219-23). Frederick's "brotherly love" for his sister serves to stress that Angelo's subsequent action represents a terrible violation of charity: he "left her in her tears, and dried not one of them with his comfort: swal-

---

are not man and wife. But mortal man cannot otherwise judge of men's meanings, than by their sayings, for the tongue is the messenger of the heart: and although it sometimes delivers a false message, yet doth the law accept it for true, when as the contrary doth not otherwise appear."

lowed his vows whole, pretending in her discoveries of dishonour: in few, bestowed her on her own lamentation, which she yet wears for his sake; and he, a marble to her tears, is washed with them, but relents not" (3.1.225-30). Mariana's persistent love for Angelo, a love that is patently "against all sense," again recalls by contrast the virtue that Angelo's actions violate.[8] Mariana forthrightly loves her enemy.

As with the monks, Angelo's legalistic literalism leads to the pride of the Pharisees, and this pride is nowhere more evident than in his insistence, in debate with Isabella, that Claudio must die for fornication. Isabella's assessment of Angelo's disease is perfectly apt:[9] "So you must be the first that gives this sentence, / And he, that suffers" (2.2.107-8). Whatever the case may have been among those elusive originators of the Viennese law, this is certainly true with respect to the law of God: the Old Law itself punished fornication with enforced marriage and a fine. Angelo is more exacting than the Lord himself. Such presumption is decorously symbolized by the giant, traditional figure of pride:

> O, it is excellent
> To have a giant's strength, but it is tyrannous
> To use it like a giant.
>
> [2.2.108-10]

Like Isabella herself, Angelo has forgotten the glassy fragility of his nature:

> man, proud man,
> Dress'd in a little brief authority,

---

[8] Mariana's clearly passionate attachment to Angelo need not contradict this meaning. Cf. the reconciliation of passion and piety effected in Spenser's *Four Hymns*, in his *Epithalamion*, in their numerous Neo-Platonic progenitors, and in Lucio's speech on natural fertility.

[9] Though ironically applicable also, somewhat less apparently, to Isabella herself.

Most ignorant of what he's most assur'd—
His glassy essence—

[2.2.118-21]

In short, the deputy "scarce confesses / That his blood flows."

This self-ignorance is ironic in the extreme, for the symbolically rich "law" that Angelo administers has as its most comprehensive and fundamental purpose the revelation of human sinfulness. The Old Law was given, as Erasmus says, that men might know themselves, and self-knowledge in Christian literature means the conviction "that thou hast of thyself no strength, but to sin."[10] This is in part what Christ means when he warns "Think not that I am come to destroy the law, or the prophets: I am not come to destroy, but to fulfil" (Matt. 5:17); for even "the carnal and gross law was profitable to this intent, that men might acknowledge their sins."[11] In his *Catechism*, Thomas Becon urges the same lesson, pointing out that the idea originates with Paul (Rom. 3:20).[12] Not surprisingly, King James agrees. "The law," he says, "showeth our sin" (*BD*, 1:33; cf. 35).

To operate rightly on Lord Angelo, therefore, the law ought to breed a conviction of personal sinfulness—and that is exactly what the Duke brings about. Angelo's first step toward wisdom arises from a chain of events as providential as the death of Ragozine, "an accident that heaven provides" (4.3.76). Claudio, addicted to the pleasures of flesh, is a friend of Lucio, whose "lightness" includes sexual wantonness: "I am fain to dine and sup with water and bran: I dare not for my head fill my belly: one fruitful meal would set me to't" (4.3.151-54). Not only does he eagerly

---

[10] *Paraphrase*, 2, fol. ✚ ✚ 5ʳ.   [11] Ibid., 1, fol. E7ᵛ.
[12] Pp. 54-55. That the Law was given to convince man of his frail and glassy essence is a commonplace expressed also by Erasmus, *Enchiridion*, sig. S2ʳ-S3ᵛ; Fortescue, *Politique Laws of England*, sig. A7ʳ; Luther, *Libertie*, sig. C5ᵛ; Hooper, *Early Writings*, p. 282; Bullinger *Decades* 2.1; Parker Society, 7:206; Hooker, *Laws*, 2:415; and *Certaine Sermons*, sig. A4ʳ.

undertake Claudio's request for aid, but throughout
Angelo's first meeting with Isabella, this representative of
rampant natural warmth labors to ignite the natural affections of the chilly novice:

> You are too cold. If you should need a pin,
> You could not with more tame a tongue desire it.
> > [2.2.45-46]

> You are too cold.
> > [2.2.56]

The consequent accession of emotional warmth in Isabella
helps to thaw the deputy's own frozen affections, and as the
Duke had hinted, once having gained power to effect all his
purposes, Angelo begins to acknowledge his appetite for
"bread."[13] Shortly thereafter, his newly activated sexuality
explodes as Angelo's Platonic horses of passion subdue him
quite:

> > I have begun,
> And now I give my sensual race the rein:
> Fit thy consent to my sharp appetite;
> Lay by all nicety and prolixious blushes
> That banish what they sue for. Redeem thy brother
> By yielding up thy body to my will;
> Or else he must not only die the death,
> But thy unkindness shall his death draw out
> To ling'ring sufferance.
> > [2.4.158-66]

[13] This recognition appears in language saturated with imagery betraying Angelo's unnaturally repressed sexuality:
> Having waste ground enough,
> Shall we desire to raze the sanctuary
> And pitch our evils there?
> > [2.2.170-72]
("Pitch" means not only to set or place; it has a more kinetic sense: "to
thrust in," "fix in," "implant.")
> Heaven in my mouth. . . .

In this catastrophic capitulation to lust, Angelo both corresponds to and differs from his intended victim. He and Isabella each betray a form of carnality; hers issues frequently in the passion of wrath; his in explosive concupiscence.

The first link in the providential chain leading to Angelo's storm of passion is the Duke's deputation. By means of his own administration of the laws, Angelo is brought to know his own sin, and throughout much of act 5 he labors under the belief that he has violated the very law that had condemned Claudio. Meanwhile the Duke's odd behavior seems contrived to bring out the full depth of Angelo's villainy:

> Come, cousin Angelo,
> In this I'll be impartial: be you judge
> Of your own cause.
>
> [5.1.167-69]

As a result of this unusual scope, Angelo reaches the depths of hypocrisy, showing more eagerness than ever to hook both right and wrong to his appetite:

> I did but smile till now:
> Now, good my lord, give me the scope of justice.
> My patience here is touch'd.
>
> [5.1.232-34]

Like Isabella's shame, this exhibition of hypocrisy has been contrived to occur before a large and distinguished audience. Public shame is for Angelo, as for Isabella, a cure for Pharisaic pride, the weightiest beam in the deputy's hypocritical eye. By allowing and even encouraging this villainy to reach its extreme limit, the Duke renders Angelo's shame overwhelming. The deputy's confession betrays

---

And in my heart the strong and swelling evil
Of my conception.

[2.4.4-7]

both the intensity of his shame and a new awareness that,
according to his own strict interpretation of the law, he too
deserves to die:

> O my dread lord,
> I should be guiltier than my guiltiness
> To think I can be undiscernible,
> When I perceive your Grace, like power divine,
> Hath looked upon my passes. Then, good prince,
> No longer session hold upon my shame,
> But let my trial be mine own confession.
> Immediate sentence, then, and sequent death
> Is all the grace I beg.
>
> [5.1.364-72]

> I crave death more willingly than mercy;
> 'Tis my deserving, and I do entreat it.
>
> [5.1.474-75]

This excruciating conviction of sin and unflinching recognition that one fully deserves to die is precisely the lesson
that "the law" was intended to teach.[14]

But as commentators continually assert, "the law con-
cludeth all men under sin, not to damn them, but to save

[14] Cf. Ronald Berman, "Shakespeare and the Law," *SQ* 18 (1967):144.
Although Angelo seems dangerously close to despair in these scenes,
his state is a positive one. See Hooker's "Sermon of the Certainty and Per-
petuity of Faith in the Elect" (in *Laws*, 1:6-7): "Happier a great deal is that
man's case, whose soul by inward desolation is humbled, than he whose
heart is through abundance of spiritual delight lifted up and exalted
above measure. Better it is sometimes to go down into the pit with him,
who, beholding darkness, and bewailing the loss of inward joy and consolation, crieth from the bottom of the lowest hell, 'My God, my God, why
hast thou forsaken me?' than continually to walk arm in arm with angels,
to sit as it were in Abraham's bosom, and to have no thought, no cogita-
tion, but 'I thank my God it is not with me as it is with other men.' No, God
will have them that shall walk in light to feel now and then what it is to sit
in the shadow of death. A grieved spirit therefore is no argument of a
faithless mind." The utility of despair, and of near despair, is represented
in Redcrosse Knight's pangs in the House of Holinesse and in his struggle
with the ultimate dragon.

them,"[15] and Angelo's confession in itself contains hints of
a revivified faith. For Angelo, the Duke's disguised presence has borne a startling resemblance to divine omnipresence, and his apparent knowledge of Angelo's supposedly
secret actions (5.1.362-64) suggests divine omniscience.
This revelation is the catalyst that cures Angelo of the faithlessness apparent in his earlier concern primarily for the
eyes of men, a concern perceptibly narrow in the insistently
spiritual and ethical context of this play ("my gravity, /
Wherein—let no man hear me—I take pride," 2.4.9-10).
He here exhibits belief in the reality the Duke has
dramatized for him—no deed, good or ill, escapes the su-
preme witness: "your Grace, like power divine, / Hath
looked upon my passes." These words reveal renewed faith
in the commonplace stressed in Matthew 6 and in *The
Basilicon Doron*: "the deepest of our secrets, can not be hid
from that all-seeing eye, and penetrant light, piercing
through the bowels of very darkness itself" (1:12).

By interposing the Duke's treatment of Barnardine between Angelo's second confession of sinfulness (5.1.472-
75) and his sentence, Shakespeare provides a hyperbolic
and comic variant of Angelo's central failings and his cure:

> Sirrah, thou art said to have a stubborn soul
> That apprehends no further than this world,
> And squar'st thy life according. Thou'rt condemn'd;
> But, for those earthly faults, I quit them all,
> And pray thee take this mercy to provide
> For better times to come. Friar, advise him;
> I leave him to your hand.
>
> [5.1.478-84]

The Duke's action is not simply an irresponsible return to
the leniency that destroys social order (1.3.23-31). Although Barnardine's crimes are manifold, he is no habitual
murderer; his sins arise not from malice, but from uncom-

---

[15] The words are from John Hooper, *Early Writings*, p. 282.

promising carnality, a thoroughgoing submersion in the stupifying pleasures of this world.[16] He is above all "a man that apprehends death no more dreadfully but as a drunken sleep; careless, reckless, and fearless of what's past, present, or to come: insensible of mortality, and desperately mortal" (4.2.140-43). His greatest need is knowledge of things unseen. Accordingly, he does not receive unqualified liberty; he is consigned instead to the care of Friar Peter, a figure whose name and whose friendship with the Duke imply that he is well suited to a task that will require both uncommon charity and exemplary patience.

Nevertheless, the Duke's mercy is deliberately extravagant, and we are justified both in worrying that there is no clear provision for the charitable justice that protects society and in feeling that the Duke's grace toward Barnardine is entirely undeserved. The startling extravagance of this pardon suggests, as Angelo's words help us to recognize, that the Duke is once again imitating "power divine." The Lord himself ordinarily acts as extravagantly as does the Duke. Although all men deserve eternal damnation, their heavenly Father "ceaseth not . . . daily to fill heaven and earth with the rich treasures of most free and undeserved grace."[17] The Duke is imitating this divine extravagance, furthermore, in precisely the way that the Sermon on the Mount demands when it sets out God's gentleness toward the sinful as a pattern for all men to imitate in their charity. The relevant passage is Matt. 5:43-45; Erasmus clarifies its meaning: "If ye use this gentleness towards all men both good and evil, ye shall declare yourselves to be the kindly children of the heavenly father, who desiring all men to be saved, giveth so manifold benefits unto the worthy and the

---

[16] As I suggest in the Appendix, Barnardine's name, his literal blindness to things beyond this world, his unabashed self-indulgence, and his residence in a prison from which he has been given the chance to escape suggest that he represents an extravagant reductio ad absurdum of typical vices of monasticism.

[17] Hooker, *Laws*, 1:162-63.

unworthy. For he suffreth his sun indifferently to shine upon them that worship him . . . and upon them that despise him, and he suffreth his rain to profit both the just and the unjust, provoking the ill through his benefit to repent, and stirring the good to render thanks."[18] Duke Vincentio's exhortation that Barnardine take his mercy "to provide / For better times to come" imitates and paraphrases the august principle that "the goodness of God," expressed in his "forbearance and long suffering," "leadeth thee to repentance" (Rom. 2:4).[19] Barnardine's silent acquiescence in the Duke's sentence—a significant silence because it contrasts strongly with his earlier obstreperous desire to hear "not a word" (4.3.52-62)—suggests that he may be willing, like his yet-unborn kinsman Caliban, to "be wise hereafter, / And seek for grace" (*Tempest* 5.1.294-95). If this likelihood should prove wrong, then at least the Duke will have erred in the right direction. He has correctly weighed Barnardine's essential fault and applied the only remedy likely—so far as human judgment can ascertain— to succeed.

Angelo's more explicit, willing submission to the will of God's substitute, and thereby to God himself, makes the Duke's mercy to him still more clearly just. The deputy has abandoned his Barnardine-like principle of treading on things unseen, has acknowledged his depravity, and has felt the bitterness of true repentance:

> so deep sticks it in my penitent heart
> That I crave death more willingly than mercy;
> 'Tis my deserving, and I do entreat it.
>
> [5.1.473-75]

Although modern audiences often find such repentance perfunctory and therefore implausible, a Jacobean Christian—and moderns who have thought at all about historic

[18] *Paraphrase*, 1, fol. F4[r].
[19] Cf. Augustine *City of God* 1.8; and R. M. Frye, *Christian Doctrine*, p. 180.

conceptions of sin and its cures—might as readily consider it "realistic." For if evil is in essence a misdirection of the will,[20] then a mere interior change constitutes a complete repentance and receives God's immediate and unqualified pardon. To attempt to prove one's penitence or to "earn" forgiveness by some elaborate or histrionic external ritual would have appeared, in a play rife with anti-Catholic meanings, somewhat papistical.[21]

On seeing brief but unmistakable tokens of penitence in Angelo, therefore, the Duke once again plays the part of an admirable ruler. Hooker voices a relevant common ideal in admiring kings "if revenge hath slowly proceeded from them and mercy willingly offered itself, if so they have tempered rigour with lenity that neither extreme severity might utterly cut them off in whom there was manifest hope of amendment, nor yet the easiness of pardoning offences embolden offenders."[22] The Duke recognizes that severe public exposure of Angelo's depravity has reduced him to a condition that may profit from mercy. As one Shakespearean character says of an expression of penitence still more laconic than Angelo's,

> Who by repentance is not satisfied
> Is nor of heaven nor earth; for these are pleas'd;
> By penitence th'Eternal's wrath's appeas'd.
> [*Two Gentlemen of Verona* 5.4.79-81]

If we lean toward the opinion that the easiness of pardoning offenders might in this case embolden other offenders, we are aware once again that neither our judgment nor the Duke's can be absolutely sure. Our judgment, too, has its scope; we cannot see into Angelo's soul, and the Duke, like us and like the best of men, is on his own earlier admission "moulded out of faults." Yet the Duke has shown special acuteness in reading the behavior of others,

[20] Cf. Perkins, *Whole Treatise*, p. 11.
[21] See "An Homilie of Repentance," in *Certaine Sermons*, sig. Yy4[r].
[22] Hooker, *Laws*, 2:415.

and his words on remitting Angelo's sins hint that the deputy's penitence is indeed efficacious. For repentance, as we
know, has "two chief parts: the mortifying of the old man,
or the flesh; and the quickening of the new man or the
spirit."[23] In the penitential context that momentarily dominates the play, to "quicken" means to endow with new life,
the life of the spirit rather than the life of the flesh.[24] The
Duke claims therefore to perceive in Angelo more than
mere relief at the prospect of escaping execution:

> By this Lord Angelo perceives he's safe;
> Methinks I see a quickening in his eye.
>   [5.1.492-93]

Because Angelo's lust most powerfully dramatized his
bondage to the old man of the flesh, the Duke reminds us
that he has mercifully provided a God-given remedy for
lust, a remedy not perfect, yet more promising and fruitful
than the deputy's self-imposed austerities (1.4.58-61):
"Look that you love your wife: her worth, worth yours"
(5.1.495). The Duke's words, too, recall the play's persistent concern with human "worth." His repetition of the
word suggests that Angelo's love ought not only offer
legitimate release for natural human potency. It should
also become an earthly reflection of the divinely ordained
law of love: "her worth, worth yours."

Shakespeare's earlier audiences would probably have
had little difficulty recognizing the conventional idea that
Angelo's marriage represents an imperfect yet positive
antidote for fornication. For, as King James illustrates, earlier ages exhibit a healthy frankness about the practical
ends of marriage, an institution God ordained, among
other things, "for staying of lust." "Defer not then," the
king advises, "to marry till your age: for it is ordained for
quenching the lust of your youth" (*BD*, 1:127). Every Anglican who married heard the priest declare that marriage

---

[23] Nowell, *Catechism*, p. 177.   [24] Cf. *Certaine Sermons*, sig. Ss3^r.

was intended, among other things, as "a remedy against sin, and to avoid fornication, that such persons as have not the gift of continency might marry, and keep themselves undefiled members of Christ's body."[25] Angelo's enforced marriage to Mariana, therefore, promises to mitigate his lust by providing a legitimate release for potency unnaturally contained. Once again, an apparent punishment administered by the Duke becomes a physic that, at least potentially, is bitter to sweet end.[26]

This, I might add, applies also to Lucio, whose sexual lightness may be mitigated by the acquisition of a wife. Furthermore, his relationship with one of Mistress Overdone's harlots allows us to perceive that Viennese law administered by the Duke himself—unlike Angelo's—coincided with the law of God:

Lucio. I was once before him for getting a wench with child.
Duke. Did you such a thing?
Lucio. Yes, marry, did I; but I was fain to forswear it; they would else have married me to the rotten medlar.

[4.3.167-72]

The Duke's law reflects the very law of Moses: "And if a man entice a maid that is not betrothed, and lie with her, he shall surely endow her to be his wife" (Exod. 22:16).[27]

---

[25] *The Book of Common Prayer*, *1559*, pp. 290-91. See also Bullinger *Decades* 2.10; Parker Society, 7:400; Calvin *Institutes* 4.13.17; fol. 421ʳ; Swinburne, *Treatise of Spousals*, sig. G4ᵛ; Erasmus, "The Young Man and the Harlot," in *Colloquies*, trans. Craig R. Thompson (Chicago: University of Chicago Press, 1965), p. 157; *Certaine Sermons*, sig. Vv6ʳ; and Archbishop Parker's broadside *Admonition To all Such as shall intende hereafter to enter the state of Matrimony Godly, and agreably to the Lawes*.

[26] For some acute remarks on the topic of marriage, see R. J. Kaufmann, "Bond Slaves and Counterfeits: Shakespeare's *Measure for Measure*," *ShakS* 3 (1968):96.

[27] Deut. 22:29 adds a provision allowing for further penalties: "the man . . . shall give unto the damsel's father fifty shekels of silver, and she shall be his wife."

We may well feel qualms about the personal effects such rough justice would have if the resulting marriages involved real people. Could Mariana have a satisfactory relationship with *that* man? Will Kate Keepdown be able to maintain a grip on her slippery mate? Perhaps not—in either case. Yet a sound marriage is not altogether out of the question for Mariana. The lady is notoriously willing to suffer and to forgive, and, despite his pride and his intended crimes, Angelo is normally governed by due sincerity. His traumatic humiliation and new self-knowledge may produce a humane and loving husband, especially for a woman who once had proved attractive even after completing, under Angelo's exacting eye, the customary tests of courtship (her dowry alone falling short of expectation). Critics given to shrill assertions that there is nothing amiable in Angelo fail to recognize that his frailties are as likely to be their own. Only the self-ignorant can say with assurance that, given the power, he would not fall to an offered temptation and the subsequent desire to hide his fall.[28] Angelo may be tainted with pride, lust, and treachery, but he is for that reason our image and similitude. Because of his bald amorality, Lucio, on the other hand, is less clearly our *semblable* and *frère* and likely also to be a less tractable spouse than Angelo. Yet even if he remains impervious to the potential goods residing in marriage, that state will at least bind Lucio to provide for the prostitute whose poverty or wantonness he had exploited and for the child he had begotten.

Whatever we decide about these matters, the intrinsic genre of *Measure for Measure* renders them peripheral, if not illegitimate, matters of concern. We are not normally invited to ask probing questions about the psychological compatibility of partners who marry at the end of romantic

[28] Crimes like Angelo's are commonplace among modern administrators and bureaucrats. For those of us who might naively think otherwise, Miles, *Problem of "Measure for Measure,"* Appendix C, has provided evidence to the contrary.

and symbolic narratives. Nor does Shakespeare ask us to do so here. We are conditioned instead to respond primarily to the fulfillment of narrative and thematic patterns. Mariana completes the quest and satisfies the desire that is the very substance of her character. Lucio, his bride to be, and Angelo receive charitable justice—retribution that promises future good.

After Angelo and Lucio, Claudio is the play's most prominent adherent of the flesh. Although the nature of his relationship with Juliet serves to make his an obvious case for judicial mercy, it does not acquit him of sin:

> Thus stands it with me: upon a true contract
> I got possession of Julietta's bed.
> You know the lady; she is fast my wife,
> Save that we do the denunciation lack
> Of outward order. This we came not to
> Only for propagation of a dower
> Remaining in the coffer of her friends,
> From whom we thought it meet to hide our love
> Till time had made them for us.
>
> [1.2.134-42]

As I suggested in chapter 5, we must avoid jumping to conclusions about the nature of Claudio's "contract." To contract marriage, he and Juliet need merely have agreed that they "are" man and wife. In law, this would constitute *sponsalia de praesenti*, as scholars have often said, but it has not been emphasized that such a contract, even without witnesses, was also considered binding.[29] This follows from the contemporary conception that defined marriage as a disposition of the will. Like virtue and sin, marriage is essentially a condition of the inner rather than the outer man: "it is the consent alone of the parties whereby this

[29] Swinburne, *Treatise of Spousals*, sig. C1ᵛ, calls the unwitnessed spousals "private" ones.

knot is tied, and whereby this *Desponsation or Affiance* is sufficiently wrought, being the very substance (and as it were the life and soul) of this contract."[30] Therefore, "spousals *de praesenti* are *improperly* called *spousals*, being in nature and substance, rather matrimony than spousals,"[31] and that is why both "the Sacred Scriptures . . . [and] the civil and ecclesiastical laws, do usually give to women betrothed only, or affianced, the name and title of a wife, because in truth the man and woman, thus perfectly assured, by words of *present time*, are husband and wife before God and his Church."[32] As marriage is indissoluble for life (except for adultery) so too is betrothal that signifies present intent: "she is fast my wife."[33]

Consequently, in treating Angelo's betrothal to Mariana as marriage—

> He is your husband on a pre-contract:
> To bring you thus together 'tis no sin,
> Sith that the justice of your title to him
> Doth flourish the deceit.
>
> [4.1.72-75]

—the Duke may tacitly depend, quite literally, on the law of England. His assumption conforms to the law of God, for Moses too treats betrothal as marriage (cf. Deut. 22:23-24). It follows also that Angelo betrays his characteristic, carnal attachment to the external manifestations of things in treating Claudio's sin as outright fornication. He is *more* legalistic than the Old Law. He does not see and therefore treads upon the substance of their relationship. That it was there to see, we who have seen better can testify.

[30] Ibid., sig. B3^{v}.

[31] Ibid., sig. C1^{r}. Cf. sigs. J4^{r}, L2^{r}, Cc3^{r}.

[32] Ibid., sig. C3^{v}.

[33] Though binding "before God and his Church," such betrothals lacked some of the material consequences of matrimony solemnized by the church, "whether we respect the legitimation of their children, or the property which the husband hath in the wife's goods, or the dower which she is to have in his lands." Swinburne, *Treatise of Spousals*, sig. P2^{v}.

Still, Claudio has sinned. In a generally religious age when weighty material rights and obligations accompanied espousal and wedlock, secret marriages were forbidden as threats both to personal virtue and to public order. The second injunction of Archbishop Parker's *Admonition* on marriage orders, therefore, "That they [who intend marriage] make no secret contracts without consent and counsel of their Parents or Elders, under whose authority they be: contr[ar]y to God's laws and man's ordinances." The "discommodities" that may result from secret contracts such as Romeo's with Juliet, Hermia's with Lysander, and Claudio's with Juliet are set out by Swinburne: "hereby it cometh to pass oftentimes, that the parties secretly contracting, are otherwise formally affianced, or so near in blood that they cannot be married; or being free from those impediments, yet do they alter their purposes, denying and breaking their promises, whence perjuries, adulteries, and bastardies, with many more intolerable mischiefs do succeed."[34] To avoid such disorder, both parental consent and public ceremony were repeatedly urged as necessary prerequisites to sound marriage.[35]

Claudio is culpable, therefore, both for hiding his marriage from Juliet's guardians and for lacking "the denunciation . . . of outward order." Here his situation contributes to the theme of ceremony, which as an especially public extension of the theme of honor, pervades the play. For just as political ceremony is important to the government of a city or a nation, religious ceremony is essential to the government of the little polity of man. The point is aptly made in Chapman's continuation of *Hero and Leander*, where "the Godesse Ceremonie" "appeard, and sharply did reprove /

[34] *Treatise of Spousals*, sig. Cc1^{r-v}.

[35] See Becon, *Catechism*, pp. 355, 358, 371, 372; Bullinger *Decades* 2.10; Parker Society, 7:403; Rabelais *Gargantua* 3.46; and Paul A. Olson, "*A Midsummer Night's Dream* and the Meaning of Court Marriage," *ELH* 24 (1957):101.

Leanders bluntnes in his violent love" (ll.145-46).[36] This downright surrealistic figure embodies and represents the universal order in its social, political, religious, and planetary manifestations. Through her combination of auditory and visual didacticism, she leads men to imitate that order on earth:

> The Goddesse Ceremonie, with a Crowne
> Of all the stars, and heaven with her descended.
> Her flaming haire to her bright feete extended,
> By which hung all the bench of Deities;
> And in a chaine, compact of eares and eies,
> She led Religion: . . .
> Devotion, Order, State, and Reverence
> Her shadows were; Societie, Memorie;
> All which her sight made live, her absence die.
> [ll.112-22][37]

In its blunt disregard for social decorum, Leander's relationship with Hero corresponds to Claudio's with Juliet. Chapman's radical imagery indicates that man's natural inclinations, unrestrained by visual and aural reminders that public order depends on social and cosmic hierarchy, threaten to unleash barbarism, cupidity, and heaven-defying pride:

> From her bright eyes Confusion burnes to death,
> And all estates of men distinguisheth.
> By it Morallitie and Comelinesse
> Themselves in all their sightly figures dresse.
> Her other hand a lawrell rod applies,
> To beate backe Barbarisme, and Avarice,

[36] I quote *Hero and Leander* from Elizabeth Story Donno, ed., *Elizabethan Minor Epics* (New York: Columbia University Press, 1963).

[37] M. C. Bradbrook, "Authority, Truth, and Justice in *Measure for Measure*," *RES* 17 (1941):390, adduces Chapman's Goddess as evidence of "what immense stress was laid on the public nature of the marriage contract."

That followd, eating earth and excrement
And human lims; and would make proud ascent
To seates of Gods, were Ceremonie slaine.

[ll.132-41]³⁸

Although Claudio's possession of Juliet's bed ought not
to be considered simple fornication then, it nonetheless
represents an error that, if unchecked by legal restraints,
can have serious consequences. And it indicates still more
clearly that his flesh has gotten the better of his spirit. He is
a less violent and much less culpable Angelo who has
"given his sensual race the rein." The personal consequences could be dire—as Prospero warns:

If thou dost break her virgin-knot before
All sanctimonious ceremonies may
With full and holy rite be minist'red
No sweet aspersion shall the heavens let fall
To make this contract grow; but barren hate,
Sour-ey'd disdain, and discord shall bestrew
The union of your bed with weeds so loathly
That you shall hate it both.

[*Tempest* 4.1.15-22]

In the familiar passage discussed earlier, Claudio himself
recognizes the predominance of his flesh over his spirit:

Our natures do pursue,
Like rats that ravin down their proper bane,
A thirsty evil; and when we drink, we die.

[1.2.120-22]

It is the nature of man—of "natural man"—to pursue
goods of the sensible world. To cling to the flesh is to die,
and Claudio's use of the word "die" signifies more than
physical death. He alludes also to the death of the spirit
wrought when one abandons himself to unrelieved natural

³⁸ Cf. Chapman's conception of ceremony with the view expressed by
Hooker in his defense of the rites of Anglican worship; *Laws*, 1:361-63.

impulse. Probably without intending it, Claudio recalls, that is, the common Christian inversion of the meanings of both "life" and "death."

Claudio's current life is the death that Christianity historically defines as a heedless immersion in this life. Although Claudio's carnal adherence to the world is most apparent in the nature of his crime, it also appears in his motive for eschewing "the denunciation . . . of outward order"—"only for the propagation of a dower" (1.2.138-39). As we have seen, "propagation" is certainly one of the three causes for which matrimony was ordained, but what is to be propagated is not ordinarily money.[39] Echoing central petitions of the marriage service, Spenser indicates in the beautiful prayer that concludes his *Epithalamion* that the ultimate end of matrimony is to swell the heavenly choir:

> Poure out your blessing on us plentiously,
> And happy influence upon us raine,
> That we may raise a large posterity,
> Which from the earth, which they may long possesse,
> With lasting happinesse,
> Up to your haughty pallaces may mount,
> And for the guerdon of theyr glorious merit
> May heavenly tabernacles there inherit,
> Of blessed Saints for to increase the count.
> [ll.415-23][40]

Instead of swelling heavenly choirs, Claudio will, as his metaphor implies, "breed . . . barren metal."[41] Biological

---

[39] Natural procreation is a private, a public, and a religious act, for the "begetting of children alone is very profitable both to every private or particular house, and also to the commonweal: for . . . the honor and glory of God is very greatly augmented, if children be not only begotten, but also brought up in the fear of God and knowledge of his word" (Bullinger *Decades* 2.10; Parker Society, 7:408).

[40] Cf. *The Book of Common Prayer, 1559*, pp. 290 and 296.

[41] See *The Merchant of Venice* 1.3.66-129 and E. C. Pettet, "*The Merchant of Venice* and the Problem of Usury," in *Shakespeare: The Merchant of Venice*, ed. John Wilders (London: Macmillan, 1969), p. 108.

and economic overtones clash sharply in this passage from *The Merchant of Venice*, and they do so with identical effect in *Measure for Measure*. As we have seen (chap. 3), a similar discord occurs when Lucio describes Claudio's intercourse with Juliet: "as blossoming time / That from the seedness the bare fallow brings" (1.4.41-42). Because such seasonal change manifests the perfect orderliness of divine wisdom, this passage contrasts powerfully with Claudio's unceremonious desire both for sexual intercourse and for Juliet's dower. Such desires represent the stormy "flaws of . . . youth" (2.3.11).

In short, Claudio's primary offense is "an excessive attachment to life," and Shakespeare's age well knew that "nothing can more effectively withdraw the human soul from the wretched affections of the body than a sincere remembrance of death."[42] This idea is central to the venerable and, in Shakespeare's age, the flourishing genre of the *ars moriendi*. It is well represented, for example, by Becon's extremely popular *Sick Man's Salve*: "There is not a stronger bit to bridle our carnal affects, nor a better school-master to keep us in an order, than the remembrance of our latter end."[43] Appropriately, this is the remembrance that Falstaff refuses: "peace, good Doll! Do not speak like a death's-head. Do not bid me remember mine end" (*Henry IV, Part 2* 2.4.209-10), and it is precisely the memory Claudio needs in order to recover his spiritual health.

Consequently, Angelo's rigorous insistence on the death penalty—in itself an evil—becomes the source of Claudio's good. Once again, the providence that brings about this happy coincidence is effected through the play's demi-

---

[42] S. Nagarajan, ed., *Measure for Measure*, Signet Shakespeare (New York: New American Library, 1964), p. xxvi.

[43] In *Prayers and Other Pieces*, ed. Rev. John Ayre, Parker Society (Cambridge: Cambridge University Press, 1844), p. 90. Cf. Miles Coverdale, *A most frutefull piththye and learned treatyse, how a christen man oughte to behave hymselfe in the daynger of death*, in *Remains of Miles Coverdale*, ed. Rev. George Pearson, Parker Society (Cambridge: Cambridge University Press, 1846), pp. 60-61.

providence, Duke Vincentio. As he awaits death, Claudio receives a visit from the Duke in his disguise. Our memories of his prior meeting with Juliet prompt us to expect that he will minister to this afflicted spirit according to the nature of his crime (2.3.5-8). We are not disappointed, for the ministration begins when Claudio affirms that he is hoping for a pardon from Angelo: "I have hope to live, and am prepar'd to die" (3.1.4). He hopes, clearly, for worldly life. Since his sin consists in an excessive attachment to this world, the Duke paraphrases for him those elements of conventional *artes moriendi* that are precisely concerned with this malady.[44] The youth's excessive attachment to the flesh is to be moderated by an accurate sense of life's value, and this is to be accomplished by reference to those portions of the *artes* that aim to instill the conventional Christian view that death "is not to be abhorred nor feared . . . it is rather most fervently to be desired, seeing by that we pass hence unto eternal joys."[45] To attain this attitude, says Lupset, another prominent professor of the art, "the learning to die well requireth a necessary lesson, how much the goodness of this world be worthy to be regarded." This most necessary lesson is taught, Lupset continues, in the Sermon on the Mount, which urges that

[44] The general relevance of the *ars moriendi* to the Duke's speech has been recognized by J. W. Lever (pp. lxxxvii and xciii), but he believes that this speech and Claudio's subsequent speech on the fear of death are subtle distortions: "The Duke's description of the human condition eliminates its spiritual aspect and is essentially materialist and pagan." This idea and J. W. Bennett's similar view (*"Measure for Measure" as Royal Entertainment* [New York: Columbia University Press, 1966], p. 50) derive primarily from failure to respond to the Duke's rhetorical aim.

[45] Becon, *Catechism*, p. 575. The same view is taken by the original *Speculum, artis bene moriendi* itself (see Nancy Lee Beaty, *The Craft of Dying: A Study in the Literary Tradition of the Ars Moriendi in England*, Yale Studies in English, no. 175 [New Haven: Yale University Press, 1970], p. 8); by Coverdale, *Remains*, p. 60; by Becon, *The Sick Man's Salve*, in *Prayers and Other Pieces*, p. 121; by Thomas Lupset, *A Compendious and a Very Fruteful Treatyse teachynge the waye of Dyenge well . . .* , in John Archer Gee, *The Life and Works of Thomas Lupset* (New Haven: Yale University Press, 1928), pp. 271-72; and by the Tudor homilists in *Certaine Sermons*, sig. F4^{r-v}.

in this life, all things (other than the kingdom of heaven) are to be valued only as "instruments and tools" to be used in "the pilgrimage and passage of this strange country." "If your treasure be once couched in heaven, straight your heart shall also be there: and so shall you take no pleasure of tarrying in this life."[46]

The *artes moriendi* endeavor to destroy one's pleasure of tarrying by using arguments strikingly similar to those Duke Vincentio voices in *Measure for Measure* (3.1.6-41). Coverdale is typically comprehensive:

> a short, transitory and shifting life ought not to make us sorry. Though this life had nothing else but pleasure, what is yet shorter and more in decay than the life of man? Half the time we do sleep out; childhood is not perceived; youth flieth away so, that a man doth little consider it; age creepeth on unawares, before it is looked for. . . . Among all things most undurable and most frail is man's life, which innumerable ways may be destroyed. . . . A man in his time is as the grass, and flourisheth as a flower of the field; for as soon as the wind goeth over it, it is gone. . . . There be more kinds of diseases than the best learned physicians do know: among the same some are so horrible and painful, that if one do but hear them named, it maketh him afraid; as the falling sickness, the gout, frenzy, the sudden stroke, and such like. . . . The whole childhood, what is it else but a continual weeping and wailing? . . . When he is come to man's stature, all that he suffereth in his youth doth he count but a small travail, in comparison of it that he now from henceforth must endure. The old man thinketh that he carrieth an heavy burden or mountain upon his neck. Therefore weigh well the miserable body and the miry sack of thy flesh. . . . And be not so sore afraid of death, that easeth thee of this wretched carcass.[47]

[46] *Works of Lupset*, pp. 285-87.
[47] Coverdale, *Remains*, pp. 56-57. Cf. pp. 58-59 and Becon, *Prayers and Other Pieces*, p. 151.

The burden of this passage is identical with that of the Duke's speech. The positive side of the overall consolation is not altogether omitted, however, for the Duke reverts to scriptural wordplay on "life" and "death":

> What's yet in this
> That bears the name of life? Yet in this life
> Lie hid moe thousand deaths; yet death we fear
> That makes these odds all even.
>
> [3.1.38-41]

In one of the play's most important and significant elliptical remarks, Claudio proves that he has received the positive and comforting point of the Duke's reasoning on life:

> I humbly thank you.
> To sue to live, I find I seek to die,
> And seeking death, find life.
>
> [3.1.41-43]

Although this is not, as many have asserted, an outright allusion to Matt. 16:25, it does allude to a commonplace founded on that and similar texts. Claudio means that in order to find true life, whether in this world or in the next, one must (as Lupset urged) seek willingly to die. In seeking death, one finds the life of the spirit because he attempts to die to the world and to mortify the members of sin. This psychological effort leads to an enrichment of life even in this world: "either death or life / Shall thereby be the sweeter,"[48] and once again we join the Duke in recognizing typical though silent continuations of Claudio's explicit language.

But Claudio's resolution is weak, and his confrontation with death becomes an excruciating exercise in terror (3.1.117-31). As Lupset explains in a passage that accurately describes Claudio, such fear, not surprisingly, is one of the major obstacles to willing death: "The glad desire of

[48] A similar point is made by Kirsch, "Integrity of *Measure for Measure*," p. 98.

dying is letted chiefly by two things: one by the fear of death, the other by the love of this life. The one of these followeth the other. . . . For he that loveth this life, feareth to / die: and he that feareth to die, loveth this life."[49] Likewise, the arts of dying discuss the sensations Claudio feels as he fearfully considers in minute detail the physical consequences of death. Although when we are healthy it is a vivifying exercise to "picture to ourselves the effect of death on each several part of our bodily frame"[50] as Claudio begins to do (3.1.118-20), we ought at the moment of death to consider only the death that has prepared a ready and easy way for our life:

> in sickness, and when we must die, that is, when the horrible image of death would make us afraid, we must not unquiet ourselves with heavy remembrance of death. We should not behold or consider death in itself, nor in our own nature, neither in them that are slain through the wrath of God; but principally in Christ Jesu, and then in his saints, which through him overcame death, and died in the grace of God. . . .
>
> When we now behold death and the pangs of death in itself with our own feeble reason . . . then hath death his whole power and strength in our feeble nature . . . so that we forget God, and are lost forever.[51]

The second paragraph describes Claudio's despairing and "faithless" (3.1.136) vision, one prompted, as his own words testify, by "fear of death" (3.1.131).

Once again providence, seconded by the Duke, brings good out of evil. Angelo's perverse rigor, Isabella's hysterical anger, and the Duke's (partly mendacious) persuasion reduce Claudio once again to the resolution his state requires. "Therefore prepare yourself to death," the Duke

[49] *Works of Lupset*, p. 272.

[50] Petrarch, *Secret*, trans. William H. Draper (London: Chatto and Windus, 1911), p. 32.

[51] Coverdale, *Remains*, pp. 80-81.

urges, "Do not satisfy your resolution with hopes that are
fallible; tomorrow you must die; go to your knees, and
make ready" (3.1.166-69). Crushed by harsh treatment,
Claudio submits, abjures his former love of temporal life,
and adopts the position urged by the *artes moriendi* and by
the Duke's selective use of them—he seeks willingly to die:
"Let me ask my sister pardon; I am so out of love with life
that I will sue to be rid of it" (3.1.170-71). His desire for
pardon demonstrates that Claudio recognizes the baseness
of his fear and of his request—a fact that in no way justifies
Isabella's merciless tirade. Isabella's desire to preserve her
honor, although it be a goal of limited value and sought in
pride, ought to have taken precedence over such a base
though "natural" affection. Because he no longer loves it,
Claudio is prepared for life in this world, a life rendered
less susceptible to lust by his readiness for death and by the
warmer consolations of the God-given gift of matrimony:
"She, Claudio, that you wrong'd, look you restore"
(5.1.522).

The Duke's ministrations to Claudio—like those to
Juliet, Lucio, Barnardine, Angelo, and Isabella—are
adapted precisely to the nature of his crime and aim to restore his spiritual health. The old fantastical Duke of dark
corners, therefore, spends the entire play laboring for the
good of his subjects. By definition, such labor is charity. As
we saw in chapter 4, the Duke's effort to know himself resulted in his recognition of personal frailty and his confession of responsibility for the corruptions rife in Vienna
(1.3.19-39). His self-knowledge and his confession represent traits for which the Duke is to be admired: rulers are
truly admirable if they eschew pride and if "the true
knowledge of themselves hath humbled them in God's
sight no less than God in the eyes of men hath raised them
up."[52]

Yet the nature of his own crime—excessive leniency in

[52] Hooker, *Laws*, 2:415.

the administration of justice—is not unrelated to the chief crimes of both Angelo and Isabella. As King James argues in *The Basilicon Doron*, all extremes "although they seem contrary, yet growing to the height, runs ever both in one . . . what difference is betwixt extreme tyranny delighting to destroy all mankind; and extreme slackness of punishment, permitting every man to tyrannize over his companion?" (1:141). In allowing Liberty to pluck Justice by the nose, the baby to beat the nurse, and decorum to perish, the Duke's sin becomes identical in its effects with Angelo's. Both, moreover, offend directly against the essence of all law:

> The one office of charity is, to cherish good and harmless men. . . . The other office of charity is, to rebuke, correct, and punish vice. . . . So that both offices should be diligently executed, to fight against the kingdom of the Devil, the Preacher with the word, and the Governor with the sword. Else they neither love God, nor them whom they govern, if (for lack of correction) they wilfully suffer God to be offended, and them whom they govern, to perish. For as every loving father correcteth his natural son when he doeth amiss else he loveth him not [Heb. 12]: so all governors of Realms, Countries, Towns, and Houses, should lovingly correct them which be offendors.[53]

In failing to punish, Duke Vincentio dramatizes the moral frailty common to *all* men, even to God's earthly substitutes.

Having recognized his error, the Duke sets about to correct it and to gain the worldly and spiritual salvation of his

---

[53] *Certaine Sermons*, sig. D4ᵛ. Owen Chadwick, *The Reformation*, p. 399, paraphrases Beza's argument that "the truest charity [is] to protect a flock of sheep from a marauding wolf, not to leave them defenceless." Cf. Hooper, *Early Writings*, p. 282; R. M. Frye, *Christian Doctrine*, pp. 210-11, and Ernst T. Sehrt, *Vergebung und Gnade bei Shakespeare* (Stuttgart: Koehler, 1952), pp. 164-65.

subjects. In his friar's robes, he embodies the Erastian role often assigned, in Reformation Europe, to the prince.[54] "Your office is likewise mixed," King James asserts, "betwixt the Ecclesiastical and civil estate. For a King is not *mere laicus*" (*BD*, 1:173).[55] Unlike the Pharisaic Angelo, Duke Vincentio refuses to tread upon what he does not see and therefore undertakes the restoration both of outward and of inward order by acting on both the spirit and the letter of law. In this, he parallels the exemplar presented in the Sermon on the Mount, who came not to destroy but to fulfill the law by actualizing its true spirit. In contrast to Isabella's, therefore, his monastic garb sometimes very clearly represents the total dedication to Christ and his charity that it had meant to true monks and nuns: "*Cucullus non facit monachum.*"

If the Duke appears at times to imitate Christ's *caritas*, he elsewhere displays other prominent attributes of the Deity whose image appears in earthly kings. In an extension of the providential speculations we explored earlier, Roger Hutchinson cites Psalms 146 and 147 to prove that "as the body liveth through the life of the soul, even so the world continueth through God's governance . . . without whom it perisheth in the twinkling of an eye."[56] This omnipresent immanence is aptly termed "god," Hutchinson declares in what may strike us as a quaint exercise in etymology, "for he is called in Latin *Deus* . . . which word signifieth to *run*; because he hasteth unto every place, to govern and order all creatures."[57] This may constitute a description somewhat undignified for the Aristotelian unmoved mover, the static emanating Platonic One, or the awesome Judeo-Christian Yahweh; yet it may pass as a homely definition of his busiest attribute. The Duke has moments every bit as busy, and potentially comic, as this. His seeming ubiquity

---

[54] Lever, p. lxxxi.   [55] See also Hooker, *Laws*, 1:xi-xii.
[56] *The Works of Roger Hutchinson*, ed. John Bruce, Parker Society (Cambridge: Cambridge University Press, 1842), p. 69.
[57] Ibid., p. 89.

on stage, his provision of an elaborate scenario for several of the principal actors in the long final act, and the consequent bustle by which he hasteneth unto every place, to govern and order all his creatures, are among the most apparent traits that associate him with contemporary conceptions of providence.

Of course, he is not providence, but an earthly and therefore imperfect and intermittent simulacrum of it. As the Duke himself acknowledges (4.3.76), Ragozine's convenient head marks the direct intervention of providence itself: it is an "accident," according to ordinary human perception; yet it is provided and guided by "heaven." The Duke in this instance is supplying the means by which providence works its eternally predetermined ends: for "as God's providence doth proceed in a certain order by middle means, so that it is his [man's] part to apply himself to means in the fear of God, and by all assays to do his best for his own defence."[58] The death of Ragozine accords with other events like the Duke's false expectations (4.2.99-112) to reaffirm his humanity and prevent us from viewing him as an embodiment of the incarnate Lord.[59] It is worth recalling with regard to such rigid allegorical interpretations that Protestant doctrine considered representations of God in art to be blasphemous, and to represent a faultless man in literature would have seemed as foolish then as it would in our own skeptical age. As Hooker points out, not even the "admirable patterns of virtue" who appear in Scripture are without some "stain of human frailty even for this cause, lest we should esteem of any man above that which behooveth."[60] The Duke is certainly stained by human frailty, and he is afflicted by human impotency—as my account of his ministrations to Claudio, Angelo, and Isabella suggested, the Duke uniformly acts to reinforce patterns of

---

[58] Bullinger *Decades* 4.4; Parker Society, 9:182.
[59] See Lever, p. lviii.
[60] *Laws*, 1:114; Cf. Nowell, *Catechism*, p. 123.

events only partly of his own conceiving, events directed ultimately by a higher power.

Nonetheless, as he does so, in another way he suggests a salient characteristic of that power, its facility in bringing good out of evil. As Bullinger says, "oftentimes he [God] of his goodness turneth our evil purposes unto good ends."[61] This is implied throughout *Measure for Measure* by the good that comes of error. It is also an idea implicit in the central event of Christian history. Having heard the story of man's distant but certain redemption, Milton's Adam "replete with joy and wonder" expresses the characteristic view:

> O goodness infinite, goodness immense!
> That all this good of evil shall produce,
> And evil turn to good; more wonderful
> Than that which by creation first brought forth
> Light out of darkness! Full of doubt I stand,
> Whether I should repent me now of sin
> By me done and occasioned, or rejoice
> Much more, that much more good thereof shall spring.
>
> [*Paradise Lost* 12.469-75]

The typical divine modus operandi, unceasingly bringing good out of evil, also characterizes the Duke's ministrations throughout *Measure for Measure*. As I have indicated in surveying his treatment of Claudio and of Angelo, the Duke cooperates with providence to ensure that good results from his subjects' respective evils. He ensures that Angelo's legalism and Isabella's proud and merciless treatment of Claudio provide the latter a corrected attitude toward life. He arranges that Angelo's explosive lust for Isabella be used, first, to humble the deputy's pride by public revelation and shame, then to induce him to marry and thereby to mitigate appetites natural to the flesh. The Duke further arranges that Isabella's own rigid and prideful defense of her honor results not in Claudio's

---

[61] Bullinger *Decades* 4.4; Parker Society, 9:184.

death but in her own public humiliation and consequent willingness to live the religion she had formerly parodied. Lucio's voluble lightness—manifested partly in frivolous chatter that betrays his own fatherhood—at the Duke's instigation becomes the means to ballast, through the honest endeavors of Kate Keepdown, his sexual lightness. It is, unquestionably I think, better to marry than to burn, and we can assume that Lucio henceforth may eat fruitful meals without exaggerated fear of the magistrate. And even Pompey, "an unlawful bawd time out of mind" (4.2.14-15), consents, at the urging of the Duke's faithful minister, to become "a lawful hangman" (4.2.15-16). All these goods, some weighty, others comic, and all undoubtedly imperfect, arise from a mixture of interacting evils. The catalyst of this beneficial reaction among human elements is a Duke who, like God's providence, "hasteth unto every place, to govern and order all creatures." Because of his sometimes comic busyness, their individual, self-involved passions bear the good fruit of social harmony and personal reformation.[62]

It should also be noticed that the Duke avoids constraining his subjects to fulfill his ends—each remains as God created him, sufficient to stand though free also to fall. At no point do they "behave like animated puppets in furtherance of the Duke's designs" (Lever, p. xcv). On the contrary, the freedom of his subjects is often stressed. This is apparent when Angelo and Escalus (1.1.81-84), the Provost (4.2.191-201), and Isabella and Mariana (4.6.1-8) ponder written instructions left by the Duke—and when Isabella refuses the Duke's expressed wishes (5.1.442-46). Because of his other associations with deity, the very

---

[62] In *The Basilicon Doron*, King James perceives such providential action in the disorders that wracked Scotland during its Reformation. All, he says, "was extraordinarily wrought by God, wherein many things were inordinately done by popular tumult and rebellion, of such as were blindly doing the work of God, but clogged with their own passions and particular respects" (1:75).

number of the stage properties that bear his instructions again suggests that the Duke is acting in imitation of his divine prototype, leaving in his absence written laws for all to follow or to disregard as the spirit moves them. This freedom is made especially evident in the actions of the Provost (4.2.191-209). The Duke could easily reveal himself, but he asks instead for faith based on a written document. The Provost performs well, "I am thy free dependent" (4.3.90).

Freedom is stressed above all in the elaborate machinations by which the Duke treats Isabella in act 5, for once he had revealed his identity, he might have persuaded her to be merciful to Angelo. Instead, he allows her freedom of choice and even tests her newly won virtue by pressing for revenge. Although the Duke is constrained to force Angelo to confess, the deputy afterward totally submits and freely requests punishment. In the closing moments of the play, Claudio and Barnardine obey silently, and even Lucio, after a parting comic complaint, lapses into silence. All are "tamed and subdued with troubles" and so "commit themselves unto his custody." They therefore approach with varying degrees of perfection the poverty of spirit enjoined by the Sermon on the Mount.[63] Their general change from the unwilling pursuit of general good through particular evils to willing obedience imitates the free dependence which is the Christian's ultimate law—to be "bound" by uncoerced "charity."

The Duke's providential transmutations of evil into good relate to another theme implicit in numerous intriguing parallels that occur throughout *Measure for Measure*. This theme is stated explicitly when the Duke says of Mariana's music " 'Tis good; though music oft hath such a charm / To make bad good, and good provoke to harm" (4.1.14-15). As Hooker puts it, "good things do lose the grace of their goodness, when in good sort they are not performed."[64] The opposite is also true; things ordinarily evil can in cer-

---

[63] Calvin, *Harmonie*, sig. K7^v.   [64] Hooker, *Laws*, 1:231.

tain circumstances be good. This is one of the less apparent implications of the Sermon on the Mount, which, as we have often seen, teaches above all that God demands not merely good deeds but charity of heart. It follows that things outward are to be judged tolerantly, as King James urges especially with respect to the ceremonies, the adiaphora, of religion (*BD*, 1:16-17). This point of view resulted, in the period during which *Measure for Measure* was being written, in an unwonted leniency toward Catholics and an attempt to mitigate religious controversy.[65] In general, James showed an attitude similar to that of Hooker, who urged that "suspense of judgment and exercise of charity were safer and seemlier for Christian men than the hot pursuit of these controversies, wherein they that are most fervent to dispute be not always the most able to determine."[66]

With respect to religious discipline, therefore, both James and Hooker expressed conformity to the ideal of charitable judgment enjoined by the Sermon on the Mount. A similar attitude informs a series of parallels that throughout *Measure for Measure* urge suspense of judgment on the ground that virtue and sin are matters of will rather than of act and that visible things are imperfect gauges of the state of the will. Hence, for example, both good and evil are represented by the habits of the regular clergy. Although the play clearly recognizes that fornication is evil, Isabella's proposed fornication with Angelo need not necessarily be sinful: "grace, being the soul of your complexion, shall keep the body of it ever fair" (3.1.181-83). Similarly, the act that most appalls modern audiences, the substitution of Mariana for Isabella, may in direct opposition to our normal expectations represent virtue, not sin.

[65] See D. Harris Willson, *King James VI and I* (New York: Henry Holt, 1956), pp. 218-23, and Manfred Ebert, *Jakob I von England als Kirchenpolitiker und Theologe* (Hildesheim: Verlag Dr. H. A. Gerstenberg, 1972), pp. 90-94.

[66] *Laws*, 1:427.

Mariana's action may be sinless, first, because Angelo had previously made her his bride by "contract," and therefore in fact, before God and the law; second, because her love's durable fervor and its relation to charity—which is always directed, "against all sense," toward one's enemies—indicate that despite her frankly sexual desire for Angelo, she supplies Isabella's place for no simply sensual gain.[67] Likewise, although in arranging Mariana's liaison with Angelo, the Duke and Isabella perform outwardly the acts of bawds—a fact forced on our attention by the entrance of Elbow and Pompey at act 3, scene 2—their deeds may be hallowed by their aims.[68] This may also be true, moreover, of the Duke's frequent deceptions and half-truths, all of which promote the good of his subjects. When it convinces Angelo that he deserves to die, the very law itself, so powerful a source of sin for Angelo and Isabella, shows its legitimate and positive uses. Mercy, which can become a warrant for sin (1.3.37-39), is so mingled with bitter suffering in act 5 that it promises, as it ought, to bring forth only good. And, as we saw in chapter 4, the honor that is abused by both Isabella and Angelo is employed by the Duke in important and beneficial ways, especially in the play's concluding moments.

If we observe with care the respects that make foul fair and fair foul throughout *Measure for Measure*, we are likely to join with the king and endeavor to obey the precept "Judge not." Only occasionally, after scrupulous observation and inquiry, and then imperfectly can human eyes discern the intent behind the act and therefore the goodness or the evil concealed within it. This was perceived as we now know (see chap. 4, n. 43), from Augustine's age onward, to be a major implication of the scriptural text that informs central ideas as well as key phrases of *Measure for*

[67] Cf. James Black, "The Unfolding of *Measure for Measure*," *ShS* 26 (1973):119-28, who views Mariana's substitution as an illustration of Christian selflessness.

[68] Cf. Perkins, *Whole Treatise*, p. 516.

Measure. As Augustine had seen, Christ intended that actions capable of favorable construction deserve such construction because we cannot know perfectly all the attendant circumstances. This venerable wisdom was badly
needed in the sphere of religious politics in Shakespeare's
age, and its essence, that charity should be obeyed above
all, is unquestionably a message for all times. In accord
with this central implication of the play, we as critics are
constrained not only to temper our frequently angry
judgments of Isabella and Angelo, but also to concede that
we simply do not know whether Duke Vincentio, in his as-
sorted subterfuges and mendacities, can be convicted of
downright sinfulness. We do know, or should recognize,
that his intentions appear consistently positive. Beyond
that, on the moral level of interpretation, we cannot go.
Our judgments too have a determined scope.

Yet, having observed both the vagueness of his motiva-
tions and how frequently and apparently the Duke acts as a
little image of God, we are prepared to perceive in the final
scene certain nearly unavoidable cosmic overtones, a touch
of allegory properly so-called. The very comprehensiveness of the judgments meted out by a newly returned
monarch to every significant member of the little world of
Vienna suggests the return of the divine justice whose perfect knowledge will bring an end to the need for suspense
of judgment. It is worth noting that that apocalyptic event
is described by Paul in a passage that echoes Matt. 7:1 *and* is
cross-referenced with Matt. 7:1 in the Geneva Bible (as well
as in the Vulgate). "Therefore judge nothing before the
time, until the Lord come, who both will bring to light the
hidden things of darkness, and will make manifest the
counsels of the hearts: and then shall every man have
praise of God" (1 Cor. 4:5). Despite Lucio's confidence that
"the Duke yet would have dark deeds darkly answered: he
would never bring them to light" (3.2.170-72), he has performed a thorough earthly imitation of Paul's description
of the Judgment, a description echoed by Lucio. Not only

has he made manifest the counsels of every heart, but he has awarded true praise where it is due.

This is the case with Escalus and the Provost (5.1.525-28), but it is most clearly true of Isabella, who because of her previous sinfulness can represent in this scene common erring humanity.[69] Coghill was only a short distance at sea when he spoke of Isabella as the "Bride of Christ."[70] His statement cannot be discredited simply by observing that she has her faults. She has manifestly sinned, but she has also changed radically and become a "free dependant" of the play's chief imitator of Christ. Like us, she is both faulty and well meaning—and she will undoubtedly fall again. But in the apocalyptic context of this scene, she may become momentarily our surrogate. Her marriage to God's imperfect earthly simulacrum symbolizes the marriage that awaits every flawed but endeavoring soul, all of whom expect one day to become brides of the Lamb. And, as I argued earlier, Isabella's marriage also confirms her rejection of monastic bondage and the puerile good intentions that had led her into it. In every way, then, this wedding is a fitting conclusion for a plot that endeavors throughout to lead its principal actors from private and public contentions bred of the flesh and the letter to the tranquil joy that follows love's true essence.

[69] The "common erring humanity" of the main plot and of the comic scenes presents no "obstinate challenge to doctrinal rigidity," as Lever (p. lviii), among others, contends. Rather, it confirms the doctrine that humanity will commonly err—and obstinately too.

Appendix

The tracing of direct sources is unnecessary and, in the main, irrelevant to my interpretation of Isabella's character and of *Measure for Measure* as a whole. Like any other, that reading must stand entirely on its power to make sense of the varied details of the text. Nonetheless, knowledge of the genesis of Shakespeare's works is never without independent interest. And in this case such knowledge may strengthen the reader's conviction that I have correctly identified the play's most important ideological parent genre. My point is that two early documents concerning monasticism may have directly influenced the creation of *Measure for Measure*.

Kenneth Muir first suggested that an Erasmian colloquy, "The Funeral," should be counted among the probable sources of the play because Shakespeare had consulted it for "background information about friars and nuns." Citing the 1571 edition of the *Colloquies*, Muir notes that a dying man's son is dedicated, by his father's will, to the order of St. Francis. A daughter is simultaneously bequeathed to the service of St. Clare. This might have suggested the name Shakespeare gave to his nun, Francisca, and to her order. And "on the page next to the one which contains the reference to St. Clare," Muir continues, "Erasmus speaks of *Barnardino tantundem Vincentio*. Here the misprint for Bernardino and the case in which Vincentio appears seems to have suggested the names Barnardine and Vincentio."[1]

Muir's list of details is suggestive. But to say that Shakespeare sought in "The Funeral" "background information" about the religious orders implies a misconstruction of the

[1] *Shakespeare's Sources* (London: Methuen, 1957), p. 108, n. 3. For evidence that Shakespeare knew Erasmus's *Colloquies*, see T. W. Baldwin, *William Shakespere's Small Latine & Lesse Greeke* (Urbana, Ill.: University of Illinois Press, 1944), passim, and especially 1:735-37, 738-39, 742-44.

colloquy. It is, in fact, an unusually well known and brilliantly comprehensive attack on the vices of contemporary monasticism.[2] We may therefore be unwise to assume that Shakespeare's use of "The Funeral" extended only to details like a misprint of Bernardine or the dative case of Vincentius. Unlike modern readers, he probably recognized the representative quality of those names. As scholars have pointed out, "Vincentius" alludes to one of Erasmus's severest critics, Vincent Theodorici, a professor at the Sorbonne and, after 1517, at the University of Louvain.[3] But Erasmus's point, I suggest, transcends personal animosities. As the colloquy develops, we begin to understand that Vincentius represents what was, to Erasmus, the traditional but unholy alliance between the religious orders and the conservative Scholasticism of the universities. Vincentius clearly displays the spiritual and academic arrogance and the facile, slanderous tongue conventionally attributed to friars in antifraternal satire.

Rather more to the point here is Bernardine's name. Scholars have not as yet pointed out that his name makes him also, and more obviously, representative. Although the individual character is a Franciscan, his name ought to remind us of one of the most prominent orders of monks. Erasmus uses "Barnardine" elsewhere in antimonastic satire when he argues that the regulars believe "a great part of their felicity to consist in the names of their orders. For some of them rejoice to be called Gray Friars, some White,

---

[2] But cf. "The Usefulness of the Colloquies" (in *Colloquies*), pp. 623-37, where Erasmus avers that in "The Funeral" he has "attacked no order, unless perchance one who has uttered a warning against corrupt Christian morals impugns all Christianity!" (p. 632). He attacks, that is, the morals of the members rather than the institutions themselves. But the substance of the satire is nearly indistinguishable from that produced by frankly Protestant Reformers. The colloquy helps us to understand why even Erasmus's friends among the Catholics sometimes suspected him of being a closet Lutheran. See Roland H. Bainton, *Erasmus of Christendom*, chap. 7.

[3] See *Colloquies*, p. 358.

these Colletes, they Minors, other Observants, other
Crossed, some Benedictines, some Bernardines."[4] Although there was after 1577 a branch of the Feuillants
popularly known as Bernardines, Erasmus is obviously referring, by allusion to their most famous member, to the
Cistercians. When he briefly outlines the origin of monasticism, Erasmus refers to St. Bernard as one of the two great
founders of monastic devotion. In the sixteenth-century
English translation, the name is often spelled "Barnarde."[5]
We may safely conclude, I believe, that either "Bernardine" or "Barnardine" was a familiar name for a prominent
monastic order—one that had owned some of England's
most prosperous religious houses (e.g., Rievaulx, Foun-
tains). In accordance with Renaissance orthographic nonchalance, moreover, the spelling of the name varied at the
mutable whim of writer, scribe, or compositor.[6]

Although it employs them, Erasmus's satire does not depend heavily on the use of these type names. The author is
best at dramatizing the monastic abuses that are his primary objects of attack. For instance, if Shakespeare did in
fact use Erasmus's "Funeral," he would have found the
characteristic Protestant association of monasteries with
prisons vividly rendered in the discussion of the dying
man's will. That document, as I have mentioned, bestows a
son and a daughter on the Franciscans and the Poor
Clares. These children are too young to resist, but the
stubborn resistance of an older son and of their mother
(also generously intended for other monastic orders)
makes painfully clear that none of his survivors embraces
eagerly the role of currency in the dying man's effort to
purchase a place within St. Peter's gates. For them, the devoted life will be an unmitigated servitude to the "elements

---

[4] *Folie*, sig. N1ᵛ.   [5] *Enchiridion*, sig. C5ʳ.
[6] To the above examples, we may add the homilist's reference to "St.
Barnards verses," *Certaine Sermons*, sig. D1ᵛ, and Arthur Dent's marginal
notation referring to St. "Barnard," *Plaine Mans Path-way To Heaven*, sig.
N1ᵛ.

of the world"—the bondage that Paul had taught Protestants and reforming Catholics to see in the ceremonial provisions of the Old Law and its medieval reincarnations.

Besides dramatizing the monks' (and their dupes') coerciveness, Erasmus stresses the greed that leads members from all the orders to attend assiduously at the deathbeds of the wealthy and to engage in vociferous and slanderous skirmishes with each other. Meanwhile, their victim, George Balearicus, exhibits the varied superstitions engendered by the friars' eager pursuit of legacies. As George's life ebbs away, his counselors read a papal bull "in the which was granted remission of all his sins . . . and all the fear of Purgatory was taken away."[7] George thereupon places his trust not in Christ, but in the pope's bull. But George's brother-in-law, a lawyer, notices an error in the bull and tactlessly suggests that it has been forged. Understandably, "the sick man was so troubled with this matter, that he was not far off from desperation [i.e., despair]. And there Father Bachelor Vincent played the man. He commanded George to be of a quiet mind, he said that he had authority . . . to correct anything which was false in the bulls." "But if the bull deceive thee," he adds, "even very now I put my soul for thine / that thine may come to heaven" (pp. 36-37). It would be difficult to imagine an impudence more brazen. In this exchange of souls, Vincent takes upon himself the office unique to Christ.

Substitution of men for God is a recurrent motif in "The Funeral." Another striking example appears at the last moment of George's life: "Barnardine [*sic*] stood hard by him on the right hand, and Vincent on the left side . . . the one showed the picture of St. Francis, the other of St. Dominic . . . Vincent on the other side said, be nothing adread George / thou hast St. Francis and St. Dominic thy defenders, care nothing at all. Remember what a great sort

---

[7] *The Dyalogue called Funus*, p. 36. Further references appear in my text.

of merits, what a strong Bull. Briefly, remember that my soul is pledged for thine" (p. 38). Unquestionably, Erasmus's readers were expected to agree with the interlocutor's comment on George's "great sort of merits": "I would be afraid lest I should be thrust down to the bottom of Hell, if I should bear such an unprofitable burden" (p. 37).

Having noticed its salient features, we may readily perceive the generic affinities between Erasmus's "Funeral" and prominent portions of *Measure for Measure*. Isabella's well-meaning desire to substitute her soul for Angelo's can now be recognized as a sympathetic version of the friars' more cynical folly. And by naming a character "Barnardine" in a play rife with monastic figures and themes, Shakespeare invites us to speculate that his engaging and highly particularized rogue might have been conceived as an extravagant reductio ad absurdum of typical monastic vices. This suggestion is not unalloyed fantasy, for Barnardine's chief characteristics are those of the satirized monks. Besides spending years in paradoxically self-imposed imprisonment (4.2.129-47), Barnardine reveals his unremitting attachment to the letter in a spiritual myopia "that apprehends no further than this world" (5.1.479) and consequently "apprehends death no more dreadfully but as a drunken sleep" (4.2.140-41). Like Spenser's monk, Idleness, Barnardine is inclined to perpetual sleep, and like all the hypocritical regulars, he serves his belly above all (4.2.147-48; 4.3.42-62).

The possibility that Shakespeare created Barnardine from raw materials he found in an Erasmian antimonastic satire provides interesting matter for speculation. It cannot, of course, prove anything about his function in the text. There he exists as an extreme and comic version of degradations to which Isabella's and Angelo's spiritual astigmatism can sometimes lead. His chronic vices and the monastic aura created by his name compel us to see that

Barnardine too, is close spiritual kin to Isabella, to Angelo, and through them, to all men.[8]

In addition to "The Funeral," Shakespeare clearly had access to other sources concerning the monastic orders. In particular, there are some intriguing hints that he did find somewhere, though not in "The Funeral," what can rightly be described as background information about monks and nuns. The name "Francisca," for instance, is unlikely to be a gratuitous detail or one snatched at random from Erasmus. The Poor Clares were founded by St. Francis, and they remained under the tutelage and protection of the Franciscan Order. Francisca's name, therefore, seems strikingly apt. As G. K. Hunter has observed, moreover, a convent of Minoresses, the ascetic branch of the Poor Clares, stood (until 1539) just outside Aldgate on the street now called the Minories. The Minoresses followed a version of the rule of St. Clare that had been prepared by the Blessed Isabella, sister to Louis IX. This version was popularly known as the "Isabella Rule."[9] I doubt that Shakespeare's heroine received so appropriate a name by accident. My suspicion gains some support from the fact, unnoted by Hunter, that the details of the Isabella Rule might easily have been known to members of Shakespeare's theatrical world. The manuscript of the rule that had belonged to the London Minoresses passed sometime after the dissolution into the library of Charles Howard, earl of Nottingham and long-time patron of the Admiral's Company.[10]

This rule shows intriguing similarities to the details of the one Shakespeare creates for Francisca. Its very title, for

[8] Cf. my discussion of Barnardine in chap. 6.

[9] G. K. Hunter, "Six Notes on *Measure for Measure*," *SQ* 15 (1964):168-69.

[10] On the peregrinations of the manuscript, see *The Rewle of the Sustris Menouresses Enclosid*, in *A Fifteenth Century Courtesy Book and Two Franciscan Rules*, ed. R. W. Chambers and Walter W. Seton, *EETS* (London: Kegan Paul, 1914), pp. 75-76. Subsequent citations of the rule itself appear in my text.

an audience imbued with the basic principles of Protestant dogma, sounds the theme of claustrophobic enclosure—*The Rewle of the Sustris Menouresses Enclosid*. The first paragraph reasserts this theme. Each sister is to dwell, it says, "all days of her life enclosed as a treasure kept to the sovereign king" (p. 82). The intended self-abnegation and total dedication to God warrant admiration from readers of religious sympathies, but a very slight change of tone could infuse such constricting manifestations of devotion with the pungent savor of satire.

Such tonal transmutation is still more imminent in those places where the text, rather like Francisca, lavishes detail on the means by which sisters can avoid all contact with the outside world—the revolving gate, for instance, designed to admit supplies without allowing carriers to glimpse receivers (p. 99). The abbey's keys—stage properties of considerable significance in *Measure for Measure*—become rather a preoccupation of the rule (pp. 89 and 91). And in both play and rule, special attention is given to the relationships that may be established between nuns and visitors. The nuns were to veil their faces even when there were no outsiders present, and "in none other manner be they not so hardy for to appear before strangers" (p. 84). Furthermore, "when anybody to any of the sisters shall speak, first shall the Abbess be warned thereof or the president, and if she grant, then shall the sister speak with the stranger so that she have two other sisters at the least with her, that they may see and hear all what they do or speak" (p. 88). And, of course, the sisters were to "take good keep that with all diligence they eschew that none of them . . . speak to no man . . . but in the manner . . . aforesaid."[11]

Even to a reader sympathetic to monastic aspirations, this seems somewhat hysterical and oppressive. To Christians concerned that God's charity be imitated in the world, the rule must appear downright repugnant. To leave the

---

[11] The last two passages are quoted by Hunter, "Six Notes," p. 168.

abbey on emergencies like Isabella's would have been extremely difficult, departure being allowed only "by leave of the minister general" of the Franciscans or by permission of his provincial or of the pope (p. 82). On the other hand, the rule does provide that novices be given a detailed foretaste of the austerities they would suffer after submitting to their vows (p. 83). As Hunter points out, a detail like this might have suggested Isabella's dialogue when she first appears on stage with Francisca. The important point, however, is that even if Shakespeare knew nothing of the London Minoresses' Isabella Rule, his nun Francisca imitates with considerable accuracy its actual tone.

Bibliography

PRIMARY SOURCES

Ariosto, Ludovico. *Ludovico Ariosto's Orlando Furioso*. Trans. Sir John Harington. Ed. Robert McNulty. Oxford: Clarendon Press, 1972.

Augustine, St. *Commentary on the Lord's Sermon on the Mount with Seventeen Related Sermons*. Trans. Denis J. Kavanagh. New York: Fathers of the Church, 1951.

Becon, Thomas. *The Catechism*. Ed. Rev. John Ayre, Parker Society. Cambridge: Cambridge University Press, 1844.

————. *Prayers and Other Pieces*. Ed. Rev. John Ayre, Parker Society. Cambridge: Cambridge University Press, 1844.

Blackstone, Sir William. *The Sovereignty of the Law: Selections from Blackstone's "Commentaries on the Laws of England."* Ed. Gareth Jones. Toronto: University of Toronto Press, 1973.

The Book of Common Prayer, 1559. Ed. John E. Booty. Charlottesville: University Press of Virginia, 1976.

Bullinger, Henry. *Decades*. Ed. Rev. Thomas Harding, Parker Society. Cambridge: Cambridge University Press, 1849.

Calvin, John. *A Harmonie upon the Three Evangelists*. Trans. E[usebius] P[aget]. London: George Bishop, 1584.

————. *The Institution of Christian Religion*. Trans. Thomas Norton. London: Richard Harrison, 1562.

Castiglione, Baldassare. *The Courtier*. Trans. Sir Thomas Hoby. In *Three Renaissance Classics*, ed. Burton A. Milligan. New York: Scribner's, 1953.

Certaine Sermons or Homilies. Ed. Mary Ellen Rickey and Thomas B. Stroup. 2 vols. in 1. 1623; rpt. in facsimile. Gainesville, Fla.: Scholars' Facsimiles and Reprints, 1968.

Chaucer, Geoffrey. *The Works of Geoffrey Chaucer*. Ed. F. N. Robinson. 2d ed. Boston: Houghton Mifflin, 1957.

Coverdale, Miles. *Remains of Miles Coverdale*. Ed. Rev. George Pearson, Parker Society. Cambridge: Cambridge University Press, 1846.

Dent, Arthur. *The Plaine Mans Path-way To Heaven*. 1601; rpt. in facsimile. Amsterdam: Theatrum Orbis Terrarum, 1974.

Downame, John. *The Christian Warfare*. 1604; rpt. in facsimile. Amsterdam: Theatrum Orbis Terrarum, 1974.

Elyot, Sir Thomas. *The Boke Named the Governour*. London: n.p., 1544.

Erasmus, Desiderius. *A booke called in latyn Enchiridion militis christiani and in englysshe the manuell of a christian knyght*. . . . London: W. de Worde, 1533.

————. *Colloquies*. Trans. Craig R. Thompson. Chicago: University of Chicago Press, 1965.

————. *De copia rerum ac verbum*. Trans. D. B. King and H. D. Rix. Milwaukee: University of Wisconsin Press, 1963.

————. *The Dyalogue called Funus*. Ed. Robert R. Allen. Chicago: Newberry Library, 1969.

————. *The Education of a Christian Prince*. Trans. Lester K. Born. New York: Columbia University Press, 1936.

————. *The First [second] tome or volume of the Paraphrase of Erasmus upon the Newe Testamente*. 2 vols. London: E. Whitchurche, 1548-49.

————. *The praise of Folie*. Trans. Sir Thomas Chaloner. London: Thomas Berthelet, 1549.

A Fifteenth Century Courtesy Book and Two Franciscan Rules. Ed. R. W. Chambers and Walter W. Seton, *EETS*. London: Kegan Paul, 1914.

Fortescue, Sir John. *A learned commendation of the politique lawes of England*. Trans. Robert Mulcaster. London: Richard Tottel, 1573.

Fulke, William. *Stapleton's Fortress Overthrown*. Ed. Richard

Gibbings, Parker Society. Cambridge: Cambridge University Press, 1848.

Hooker, Richard. *Of the Laws of Ecclesiastical Polity*. Intro. Christopher Morris. New York: Dutton, 1907.

Hooper, John. *Early Writings of John Hooper*. Ed. Rev. Samuel Carr, Parker Society. Cambridge: Cambridge University Press, 1843.

Hutchinson, Roger. *The Works of Roger Hutchinson*. Ed. John Bruce, Parker Society. Cambridge: Cambridge University Press, 1842.

James I. *The Basilicon Doron*. Ed. James Craigie. Edinburgh: William Blackwood and Sons, 1944.

Jewel, John. *An Apologie; or, Aunswer in defence of the Church of England, concerning the state of Religion used in the same*. London: Reginald Wolfe, 1562.

Latimer, Hugh. *Sermons*. Ed. George Elwes Corrie, Parker Society. 2 vols. Cambridge: Cambridge University Press, 1844.

Luther, Martin. *Luther's Works*. Ed. Jaroslav Pelikan and Helmut T. Lehmann. 55 vols. Philadelphia: Fortress Press, 1955-73.

———. *A Treatise, Touching the Libertie of a Christian*. Trans. James Bell. London: Ralph Newbery and H. Bynneman, 1579.

Machiavelli, Niccolò. *The Prince*. Trans. Edward Dacres. In *Three Renaissance Classics*, ed. Burton A. Milligan. New York: Scribner's, 1953.

Marlowe, Christopher. *Hero and Leander*. In *Elizabethan Minor Epics*, ed. Elizabeth Story Donno. New York: Columbia University Press, 1963.

Melanchthon, Philip. *Melanchthon and Bucer*. Ed. Wilhelm Pauck. Philadelphia: Westminster Press, 1969.

Milligan, Burton A., ed. *Three Renaissance Classics*. New York: Scribner's, 1953.

Milton, John. *The Poems of John Milton*. Ed. Alastair Fowler. London: Longmans, 1968.

Montaigne, Michel. *The Essays of Montaigne*. Trans. John
    Florio. New York: Modern Library, 1933.
More, Sir Thomas. *Utopia*. Trans. Ralph Robynson (1551).
    In *Three Renaissance Classics*, ed. Burton A. Milligan.
    New York: Scribner's, 1953.
Nowell, Alexander. *A Catechism*. Ed. George Elwes Corrie,
    Parker Society. Cambridge: Cambridge University
    Press, 1853.
Parker, Matthew. *Admonition To all Such as shall intende
    hereafter to enter the state of Matrimony Godly, and agreably
    to the Lawes*.
Perkins, William. *The Whole Treatise of the Cases of Conscience*.
    1606; rpt. in facsimile, New York: Da Capo Press,
    1972.
————. *The Workes of that Famous and Worthie Minister of
    Christ . . . M. William Perkins*. 2 vols. Cambridge: John
    Legat, 1609.
Petrarca, Francesco. *Petrarch's Secret*. Trans. William H.
    Draper. London: Chatto and Windus, 1911.
Philpot, John. *The Examinations and Writings of John Philpot*.
    Ed. Rev. Robert Eden, Parker Society. Cambridge:
    Cambridge University Press, 1842.
St. Germain, Christopher. *The Doctor and Student*. Ed. Wil-
    liam Muchall. Cincinnati: Robert Clarke, 1874.
Shakespeare, William. *The Complete Works of Shakespeare*.
    Ed. Irving Ribner and George Lyman Kittredge.
    Waltham, Mass.: Xerox College Publishing, 1971.
————. *Measure for Measure*. Ed. J. W. Lever. The Arden
    Shakespeare. London: Methuen, 1965.
Swinburne, Henry. *Treatise of Spousals*. London: S. Roy-
    croft for Robert Clavell, 1686.
The Thirty-nine Articles of the Church of England. Ed. William
    Wilson. Oxford: Abrams, 1840.
Tudor Royal Proclamations. Ed. Paul L. Hughes and James F.
    Larkin. 3 vols. New Haven: Yale University Press,
    1969.
Tyndale, William. *Doctrinal Treatises*. Ed. Henry Walter,

Parker Society. Cambridge: Cambridge University Press, 1848.

―――. *Expositions and Notes on Sundry Portions of the Holy Scriptures*. Ed. Henry Walter, Parker Society. Cambridge: Cambridge University Press, 1849

SECONDARY SOURCES

Auerbach, Eric. *Mimesis: The Representation of Reality in Western Literature*. Trans. Willard Trask. 1953; rpt. Garden City, N.Y.: Doubleday, 1957.

Bainton, Roland H. *Erasmus of Christendom*. New York: Scribner's, 1969.

―――. *Here I Stand: A Life of Martin Luther*. New York: New American Library, 1950.

Baldwin, T. W. *William Shakespere's Small Latine & Lesse Greeke*. Urbana, Ill.: University of Illinois Press, 1944.

Barth, Gerhard. "Matthew's Understanding of the Law." In *Tradition and Interpretation in Matthew*, ed. Günther Bornkamm. Philadelphia: Westminster Press, 1963.

Battestin, Martin C. *The Providence of Wit*. Oxford: Clarendon Press, 1974.

Beaty, Nancy Lee. *The Craft of Dying: A Study in the Literary Tradition of the Ars Moriendi in England*. Yale Studies in English, no. 175. New Haven: Yale University Press, 1970.

Beckerman, Bernard. *Shakespeare at the Globe*. London: Collier, 1962.

Bennett, Josephine W. *"Measure for Measure" as Royal Entertainment*. New York: Columbia University Press, 1966.

Berman, Ronald. "Shakespeare and the Law." *SQ* 18 (1967): 141-50.

Birje-Patil, J. "Marriage Contracts in Shakespeare's *Measure for Measure*." *ShakS* 5 (1969): 106-11.

Black, James. "The Unfolding of *Measure for Measure*." *ShS* 26 (1973): 119-28.

Booth, Wayne C. *A Rhetoric of Irony*. Chicago: University of Chicago Press, 1974.

Bradbrook, M. C. "Authority, Truth, and Justice in *Measure for Measure*." *RES* 17 (1941): 385-99.

Chadwick, Owen. *The Reformation*. Harmondsworth: Penguin, 1964.

Colie, Rosalie. *The Resources of Kind: Genre Theory in the Renaissance*. Berkeley: University of California Press, 1973.

Council, Norman. *When Honour's at the Stake*. London: George Allen and Unwin, 1973.

Davies, Horton. *Worship and Theology in England from Cranmer to Hooker, 1534-1603*. Princeton: Princeton University Press, 1970.

De Man, Paul. "The Rhetoric of Temporality." In *Interpretation: Theory and Practice*, ed. Charles S. Singleton. Baltimore: Johns Hopkins University Press, 1969.

Ebert, Manfred. *Jakob I von England als Kirchenpolitiker und Theologe*. Hildesheim: Verlag Dr. H. A. Gerstenberg, 1972.

Ellis, John. *The Theory of Literary Criticism: A Logical Analysis*. Berkeley: University of California Press, 1974.

Empson, William. *The Structure of Complex Words*. Norfolk, Conn.: New Directions, n.d.

Fenton, J. C. *Saint Matthew*. Harmondsworth: Penguin, 1963.

Finberg, H.P.R. *Tavistock Abbey*. Cambridge: Cambridge University Press, 1951.

Fleming, John. *The "Roman de la Rose": A Study in Allegory and Iconography*. Princeton: Princeton University Press, 1969.

Fletcher, Angus. *Allegory: Theory of a Symbolic Mode*. Ithaca: Cornell University Press, 1964.

Frye, Northrop. *Anatomy of Criticism*. 1957; rpt. New York: Atheneum, 1965.

Frye, Roland Mushat. *Shakespeare and Christian Doctrine*. Princeton: Princeton University Press, 1963.

Gee, John Archer. *The Life and Works of Thomas Lupset.* New Haven: Yale University Press, 1928.

Goldman, Michael. *Shakespeare and the Energies of the Drama.* Princeton, Princeton University Press, 1972.

Hawkins, Harriet. *Likenesses of Truth in Elizabethan and Restoration Drama.* Oxford: Clarendon Press, 1972.

Hay, Douglas. *Albion's Fatal Tree: Crime and Society in Eighteenth-century England.* New York: Pantheon, 1975.

Heath, Peter. *The English Parish Clergy on the Eve of the Reformation.* Toronto: University of Toronto Press, 1969.

Hill, Christopher. *Society and Puritanism in Pre-Revolutionary England.* London: Secker and Warburg, 1964.

Hill, David, ed. *The Gospel of St. Matthew.* New Century Bible. London: Oliphants, 1972.

Hirsch, E. D. *The Aims of Interpretation.* Chicago: University of Chicago Press, 1976.

——. *Validity in Interpretation.* New Haven: Yale University Press, 1967.

Hunter, G. K. "Six Notes on *Measure for Measure.*" *SQ* 15 (1964): 167-72.

Hunter, Robert Grams. *Shakespeare and the Comedy of Forgiveness.* New York: Columbia University Press, 1965.

Jauss, Hans Robert. "Literary History as a Challenge to Literary Theory." In *New Directions in Literary History*, ed. Ralph Cohen. Baltimore: Johns Hopkins University Press, 1974.

Jones, Emrys. *Scenic Form in Shakespeare.* Oxford: Clarendon Press, 1971.

Kaufmann, R. J. "Bond Slaves and Counterfeits: Shakespeare's *Measure for Measure.*" *ShakS* 3 (1968): 85-97.

Keeton, G. W. *Shakespeare's Legal and Political Background.* New York: Barnes and Noble, 1968.

Kirsch, Arthur. "The Integrity of *Measure for Measure.*" *ShS* 28 (1975): 89-105.

Knight, G. Wilson. *The Wheel of Fire.* London: Oxford University Press, 1930.

Knowles, Dom David. *The Religious Orders in England*. 3 vols. Cambridge: Cambridge University Press, 1959.

Koonce, B. *Chaucer and the Tradition of Fame: Symbolism in "The House of Fame."* Princeton: Princeton University Press, 1966.

Lascelles, Mary. *Shakespeare's "Measure for Measure."* London: Athlone Press, 1953.

Leavis, F. R. *The Common Pursuit*. London: Chatto and Windus, 1952.

MacLure, Millar. *The Paul's Cross Sermons, 1534-1642*. Toronto: University of Toronto Press, 1958.

Miles, Rosalind. *The Problem of "Measure for Measure."* New York: Barnes and Noble, 1976.

Mincoff, Marco. *"Measure for Measure*: A Question of Approach." *ShakS* 2 (1966): 141-52.

Muir, Kenneth. *Shakespeare's Sources*. London: Methuen, 1957.

Murrin, Michael. *The Veil of Allegory: Some Notes toward a Theory of Allegorical Rhetoric in the English Renaissance*. Chicago: University of Chicago Press, 1969.

Nagarajan, S., ed. *Measure for Measure*. Signet Shakespeare. New York: Signet, 1964.

————. *"Measure for Measure* and Elizabethan Betrothals." *SQ* 14 (1963): 115-19.

Neale, J. E. *Elizabeth I and Her Parliaments 1559-1581*. London: Jonathan Cape, 1953.

Noble, Richmond. *Shakespeare's Biblical Knowledge*. London: Society for Promoting Christian Knowledge, 1935.

Nohrnberg, James. *The Analogy of "The Faerie Queene."* Princeton: Princeton University Press, 1976.

Olson, Paul A. *"A Midsummer Night's Dream* and the Meaning of Court Marriage." *ELH* 24 (1957): 95-119.

Orgel, Stephen. *The Illusion of Power*. Berkeley: University of California Press, 1975.

Pettet, E. C. *"The Merchant of Venice* and the Problem of Usury." In *Shakespeare: The Merchant of Venice*, ed. John Wilders. London: Macmillan, 1969.

Pope, Elizabeth M. "The Elizabethan Background of *Measure for Measure*." *ShS* 2 (1949): 66-82.

Quiller-Couch, Sir Arthur, ed. *Measure for Measure*. The New Shakespeare. Cambridge: Cambridge University Press, 1922.

Robertson, D. W., Jr. "The Idea of Fame in Chrétien's *Cliges*." *SP* 69 (1972): 414-33.

———. *A Preface to Chaucer*. Princeton: Princeton University Press, 1962.

Roche, Thomas P., Jr. *The Kindly Flame: A Study of the Third and Fourth Books of Spenser's "Faerie Queene."* Princeton: Princeton University Press, 1964.

Rossiter, A. P. *Angel with Horns and Other Shakespeare Lectures*. Ed. Graham Storey. London: Longmans, 1961.

Schanzer, Ernest. "The Marriage-Contracts in *Measure for Measure*." *ShS* 13 (1960): 81-89.

———. *The Problem Plays of Shakespeare*. London: Routledge and Kegan Paul, 1963.

Sehrt, Ernst T. *Vergebung und Gnade bei Shakespeare*. Stuttgart: Koehler, 1952.

Shalvi, Alice. *The Relationship of Renaissance Concepts of Honour to Shakespeare's Problem Plays*. Salzburg: Institut für Englische Sprache und Literatur Universität Salzburg, 1972.

Skulsky, Harold. "Pain, Law, and Conscience in *Measure for Measure*." *JHI* 25 (1964): 165-68.

Stevenson, David L. *The Achievement of Shakespeare's "Measure for Measure."* Ithaca: Cornell University Press, 1966.

———. "Design and Structure in *Measure for Measure*." *ELH* 23 (1956): 256-78.

Thomas, Keith. *Religion and the Decline of Magic*. New York: Scribner's, 1971.

Tillyard, E.M.W. *Shakespeare's Problem Plays*. Toronto: University of Toronto Press, 1949.

Tuve, Rosemond. *Allegorical Imagery: Some Mediaeval Books*

and Their Posterity. Princeton: Princeton University Press, 1966.

Watson, Curtis Brown. *Shakespeare and the Renaissance Concept of Honor*. Princeton: Princeton University Press, 1960.

Williams, Arnold. "Chaucer and the Friars." *Speculum* 28 (1953): 499-513.

Willson, D. Harris. *King James VI and I*. New York: Henry Holt, 1956.

Wright, Thomas, ed. *Queen Elizabeth and Her Times*. London: Henry Colburn, 1838.

Index

LIBRARY OF CONGRESS CATALOGING IN PUBLICATION DATA

Gless, Darryl J.   1945-
Measure for measure, the law, and the convent.

Bibliography: p.
Includes index.
1. Shakespeare, William, 1564-1616.   Measure for
measure.   I.   Title.
PR2824.G5   822.3'3   79-83990
ISBN 0-691-06403-2